Engagements with Shakespearean Drama

Rather than treating the plays as *objects* to be studied, described and interpreted, *Engagements with Shakespearean Drama* examines precisely what about Shakespeare's plays is so special – why they continue to be discussed and performed all around the world. This book highlights the importance of our experience as readers and audiences and argues that what makes the plays great is that they cause a wide range of intense, pleasurable and valuable experiences. This highly personal and emotive approach allows students to engage with the plays on a new level, taking their own responses seriously as grounds for assessing the plays' success and quality. The book also engages with the essential criticism of the plays from Shakespeare's time to our own, equipping students to engage in contemporary debates about the nature and achievement of Shakespearean drama.

William Walker is Associate Professor in the School of the Arts and Media at the University of New South Wales, Sydney.

Routledge Engagements with Literature
Series Editor: Daniel Robinson

This series presents engagement as discovery. It aims to encourage ways to read seriously and to help readers hone and develop new habits of thinking critically and creatively about what they read—before, during, and after doing it. Each book in the series actively involves its readers by encouraging them to find their own insights, to develop their own judgments, and to inspire them to enter ongoing debates. Moreover, each *Engagements* volume:

- Provides essential information about its topic as well as alternative views and approaches;
- Covers the classic scholarship on its topic as well as the newest approaches and suggests new directions for study and research;
- Includes innovative "Engagements" sections that demonstrate practices for engaging with literature or that provide suggestions for further independent engagement;
- Provides an array of fresh, stimulating, and effective catalysts to reading, thinking, writing, and research.

Above all, *Engagements with Literature* shows that actively engaging with literature rewards the effort and that any reader can make new discoveries. My hope is the books in this series will help readers discover new, better, and more exciting and enjoyable ways of doing what we do when we read.

Available in this series:

Engagements with Close Reading
Annette Federico

Engagements with Narrative
Janine Utell

Engagements with Shakespearean Drama
William Walker

For more information about this series, please visit: https://www.routledge.com/Routledge-Engagements-with-Literature/book-series/EWL

Engagements with Shakespearean Drama

William Walker

LONDON AND NEW YORK

First published 2019
by Routledge
2 Park Square, Milton Park, Abingdon, Oxon OX14 4RN

and by Routledge
52 Vanderbilt Avenue, New York, NY 10017

Routledge is an imprint of the Taylor & Francis Group, an informa business

© 2019 William Walker

The right of William Walker to be identified as author of this work has been asserted by him in accordance with sections 77 and 78 of the Copyright, Designs and Patents Act 1988.

All rights reserved. No part of this book may be reprinted or reproduced or utilised in any form or by any electronic, mechanical, or other means, now known or hereafter invented, including photocopying and recording, or in any information storage or retrieval system, without permission in writing from the publishers.

Trademark notice: Product or corporate names may be trademarks or registered trademarks, and are used only for identification and explanation without intent to infringe.

British Library Cataloguing-in-Publication Data
A catalogue record for this book is available from the British Library

Library of Congress Cataloging-in-Publication Data
Names: Walker, William, 1958- author.
Title: Engagements with Shakespearean drama / William Walker.
Description: Abingdon, Oxon ; New York, NY : Routledge, 2019. |
Series: Routledge engagements with literature | Includes bibliographical references and index.
Identifiers: LCCN 2018048112| ISBN 9780815392736 (hardback : alk. paper) | ISBN 9780815392743 (paperback : alk. paper) | ISBN 9781351190190 (ebook)
Subjects: LCSH: Shakespeare, William, 1564-1616--Appreciation.
Classification: LCC PR2976 .W27 2019 | DDC 822.3/3--dc23
LC record available at https://lccn.loc.gov/2018048112

ISBN: 978-0-8153-9273-6 (hbk)
ISBN: 978-0-8153-9274-3 (pbk)
ISBN: 978-1-351-19019-0 (ebk)

Typeset in Sabon
by Taylor & Francis Books

Contents

List of figures vi
Note on the text vii
Acknowledgements viii

Introduction 1

1 Emotion 24

2 Laughter and delight 62

3 Wisdom and moral instruction 98

4 Sublimity 132

Conclusion 167

Index 170

Figures

1.1	"Willow, willow," from *Othello*	54
1.2	"Bonny sweet Robin," from *Hamlet*	56
1.3	"Come away, come away, death," from *Twelfth Night*	57
2.1	"Flout 'em and Cout 'em," from *The Tempest*	94
2.2	"The Woosel Cock," from *A Midsummer Night's Dream*	95
2.3	"Full Fathom Five," from *The Tempest*. From John Playford's collection of music to *The Tempest* [manuscript] (ca. 1650–67)	96
3.1	"O mistress mine," from *Twelfth Night*	129
3.2	"Blow, blow, thou winter wind," from *As You Like It*	129
4.1	"Where the bee sucks," from *The Tempest*. From John Playford's collection of music to *The Tempest* [manuscript] (ca. 1650–67)	165

Note on the text

All references to the text of Shakespeare's plays are to the version of it that appears in *William Shakespeare: Complete Works*, edited by Jonathan Bate and Eric Rasmussen (Palgrave Macmillan, 2007). For references to other works I have followed a streamlined version of the Harvard system: where the context provides enough information to identify the source in the list of works cited, I provide only author name and/or page number. The works listed at the ends of chapters are also intended as suggestions for further reading.

I have placed technical terms in italics and provided definitions of them along the way.

Acknowledgements

For helpful discussions and responses to chapter drafts, I'd like to thank Kirk Dodd, Beverley Sherry, and Gordon Spence. A special thanks to Adam Potkay, long-time friend and colleague, for his enthusiastic and learned support all along the way. I'm also grateful to Daniel Robinson for supporting this project and including it in the *Engagements with Literature* series. I thank the Digital Image Collection at the Folger Shakespeare Library for permission to reproduce images of "Full fathom five" and "Where the bee sucks." And I'm grateful to Ross Duffin and Norton for allowing me to print reproductions of seven songs from *Shakespeare's Songbook* (Norton, 2004).

Introduction

At schools and universities we usually treat Shakespeare's plays as objects to be studied, analyzed, and interpreted. Approaching them this way, I think we often lose touch with what is special about them and why we are studying them in the first place. I want to get back in touch with what is special about them and understand what accounts for it. I propose to do this, first, by remembering how men and women responded to and discussed them before they achieved the status of monumental objects in our modern educational institutions. Remembering this discussion, and its roots in ancient Graeco-Roman writings about the purposes of literature and drama, we can see that over the last four hundred years, one of the main reasons people have said the plays are special is that they cause us to have experiences of a certain kind. What kind of experiences?

Pity, fear, and sadness

Emotional experiences: pity, compassion, sympathy, sadness, fear, horror. There is, first of all, considerable evidence that in Shakespeare's day, however rowdy and diverse they may have been, theatre audiences expected to have and did have intense emotional experiences at performances of his plays. Probably describing a performance of Shakespeare's early history play, *Henry VI, part 1*, for example, one of Shakespeare's contemporaries, Thomas Nashe, observes the following about Talbot (a character in this play):

> [H]ow would it have joyed brave Talbot (the terror of the French) to thinke that after he had lyne two hundred yeares in his Tombe, hee should triumphe againe on the Stage, and have his bones newe embalmed with the teares of ten thousand spectators at least, (at severall times) who, in the Tragedian that represents his person, imagine they behold him fresh bleeding?
> (Chambers: 188)

Modern scholars who have studied Renaissance audiences and theories of emotion confirm that, while different audience members responded in different ways to the plays, they often shared an emotional response, such as the one Nashe describes (Gurr, Levin, Steggle, Rowe, Whitney). And the western European critical heritage suggests that, especially in connection with the tragedies, this emotional response persisted in both theatre-goers and readers. In one of her private letters from 1664, for example, the poet, fiction writer, and playwright, Margaret Cavendish, observes that

> in his Tragick Vein, he [Shakespeare] Presents Passions so Naturally, and Misfortunes so Probably, as he Pierces the Souls of his Readers with such a True Sense and Feeling thereof, that it Forces Tears through their Eyes, and almost Perswades them, they are Really Actors or at least Present at those Tragedies.
>
> (13)

In the preface to the edition of Shakespeare's plays that he published in the early eighteenth century, Alexander Pope, too, observes that

> The *Power* over our *Passions* was never possess'd in a more eminent degree or display'd in so different instances.... But the heart swells, and the tears burst out, just at the proper places: ... the passions directly opposite to these, Laughter and Spleen, are no less at his command!
>
> (65–6)

Later in the century, in his *Preface to Shakespeare* (1765), Samuel Johnson speaks of "the power to move, which constitutes the perfection of dramatick poetry." He then observes,

> *Shakespeare* has united the powers of exciting laughter and sorrow not only in one mind, but in one composition. Almost all his plays are divided between serious and ludicrous characters, and, in the successive evolutions of the design, sometimes produce seriousness and sorrow, and sometimes levity and laughter.
>
> (67)

Later eighteenth-century theatre-goers went to Shakespearean tragedy for an experience of sympathy, pity, sadness, and weeping—and they got it (Marsden).

Romantic and Victorian readers, theatre-goers, and reviewers, too, often praise Shakespeare because of the emotional experience the plays afford. Speaking of "the emotion excited by Shakespeare," the French/Swiss woman of letters, Madame de Staël (1766–1817), observes that he "excelled in exciting pity," but also that "he makes us feel that dreadful emotion which chills the blood of him who in the full enjoyment of life and health learns that death awaits him" (Bate 1992: 79–80). In his *Lectures on Dramatic Art and Literature* (1809–11), the translator of Shakespeare into German, A. W. Schlegel, observed that Shakespeare was "always sure of his power to excite ... powerful emotions." He was a "tragical Titan" who, "more terrible than Aeschylus, makes our hair to stand on end, and congeals our blood with horror" in plays such as *Macbeth*, but he also exhausts "the science of compassion" in plays such as *Lear* (365, 368, 411). In *Characters of*

Shakespear's Plays (1817), the Romantic essayist William Hazlitt shares Schlegel's great enthusiasm for the histories and tragedies because the main characters' passions and suffering command our pity, sympathy, fear, and dread. And in her comprehensive discussion and celebration of Shakespeare's female characters, *Shakespeare's Heroines* (1832), Anna Jameson frequently comments on how they move us: Juliet commands "our unreproved sympathy"; "it is the helplessness of Ophelia, arising merely from her innocence, and pictured without any indication of weakness, which melts us with such profound pity"; we acknowledge the supreme refinement and elevation of Miranda in *The Tempest* through "the emotions of sympathy she feels and inspires" (99, 137, 155). Finally, in his lectures on Shakespeare's tragedies that he published in the early twentieth century, A. C. Bradley describes "the full tragic effect" in terms of "tragic feelings" that include pity, sympathy, and terror (19, 14).

In making these claims about how Shakespeare's plays—especially the tragedies—evoke pity, sorrow, compassion, sympathy, horror, and fear in the audience, many of these men and women are recalling an ancient Greek commentary on plays that Aeschylus, Sophocles, and Euripedes wrote for performance in fifth-century BC Greece: Aristotle's *Poetics*. In this work the philosopher provides a definition of tragedy that has resounded through the centuries:

> tragedy is a representation of a serious, complete action which has magnitude, in embellished speech, with each of its elements [used] separately in the [various] parts [of the play]; [represented] by people acting and not by narration; accomplishing by means of pity and terror the catharsis of such emotions.
>
> (7)

Later in this work Aristotle makes more clear that this kind of drama has what he calls a particular *ergon* or *telos*. These terms are usually translated as "function," "job," "purpose," or "end." The function of tragedy is to cause the audience to experience "the pleasure [arising] from pity and terror" (9, 16, 17–18). Aristotle also describes this experience as a "purgation" (*catharsis*) of emotion—though there has been great debate over exactly what he means by describing it in this way. He then identifies the kind of plot, character, thought, language, song, and spectacle a play must have in order to fulfill this function and qualify as this kind of drama. In so doing, he sets an enormously powerful precedent in western society for thinking of tragedy not as art for art's sake but as art for *our* sake. Tragedy has a particular function to perform, and that function is to make *us*—the audience—experience pity and fear. Thinking about tragedy in this way, he also sets a precedent for a way of assessing the quality of any given play that claims to be a play of this kind: any given play is a *good* tragedy insofar as it fully performs this function.

Observing that some of Shakespeare's plays cause the audience to experience pity, fear, and sorrow, then, European men and women over the centuries have claimed that these plays perform the function that, at least for Aristotle, goes to define tragedy. And because many of these people also share Aristotle's view that a good tragedy is one that fully performs this function, they think that Shakespeare's tragedies are special and good.

Laughter, delight, and joy

If you have read Umberto Eco's wonderful novel, *The Name of the Rose* (1980), or seen the movie (starring Sean Connery and Christian Slater), you'll know that scholars think that Aristotle's *Poetics* consisted of two books, the second of which treated comedy and is now lost. But fragments of it survive, as does a medieval Greek manuscript—the *Tractatus Coislinianus*—which appears to be a summary of this lost book on comedy. On the basis of these texts, and the *Poetics* itself, it is reasonable to conclude that Aristotle understood the main function of comedy to be that of causing the audience to laugh. And there is a vast testament to the power of Shakespeare's comedies—but also the comic scenes in the histories, romances, and tragedies—to fulfill this function.

The surviving accounts of late sixteenth and seventeenth-century audience responses to Shakespeare's comedies and histories indicate, first of all, that the popularity of these plays depended in part on their success in providing the pleasures of mirth and laughter (Levin, Gurr, Steggle). As we have seen, both Pope and Johnson in the eighteenth century comment on Shakespeare's "powers of exciting laughter," and they find them not just in the comedies but in the tragedies as well. And why does Hazlitt think that "Shakespeare was the most universal genius that ever lived"? In part because he has "the same absolute command over our laughter and our tears" (238). That command is apparent in accounts of performances of Shakespeare's plays in Victorian newspapers and periodicals, such as *The Era*, *The Theatrical Journal*, and *Theatrical Examiner*. If you browse through these accounts, you can see that reviewers and audiences responded in many different ways to ever-changing styles of performance, but it is also clear that many performances of Shakespearean comedy during the Victorian period succeeded in doing one of the things comedy was supposed to do: appeal to the play-goers' sense of humor and make them laugh (Adler, Prince, Poole). We should note, too, the association between Shakespearean comedy and laughter in Victorian comic theory. In his *Essay on Comedy* (1877), for example, the poet and novelist George Meredith claims that "the test of true comedy is that it shall awaken thoughtful laughter." Since Shakespeare's characters are "saturated with the comic spirit" and Shakespeare himself overflows with it, his plays pass this test, and Meredith sees him, along with the ancient Greek, Aristophanes, and the seventeenth-century Frenchman, Molière, as great comic playwrights (11, 38, 47, 49). And there is plenty of evidence that the comedies have continued to affect modern audiences in this way. If, for example, you watch any video recording of recent performances of Shakespearean comedy at the Globe theatre in London, England, you can see that Shakespeare's comedies are still making London audiences laugh. That observation is also central to the work of a wide range of modern scholars, critics, actors, and directors (Richman).

But some of Shakespeare's contemporaries felt that comedy should do more than make us laugh. This is because, like the ancient Graeco-Roman and Renaissance theorists of rhetoric, they strongly associated laughter with feelings of scorn and superiority, and this did not sit well with their commitment to more charitable and positive attitudes towards other people and life in general (Skinner: 198–211). The Elizabethan poet and courtier, Sir Philip Sidney, is perhaps the most accomplished author who felt that comedy ought to do more than make us laugh. He probably wrote *An Apology for Poetry* in the early 1580s, and it seems to have been circulating in manuscript before it was published in 1595. In this landmark work of English Renaissance literary criticism, which Shakespeare may have known, Sidney observes that "the whole tract of a comedy should be full of delight." He then explains that "delight hath a joy in it, either permanent or present. Laughter hath only a scornful tickling ... . All the end of the comical part [should] be not upon such scornful matters as stirreth laughter only, but, mixed with it, that delightful teaching which is the end of Poesy" (103–4).

For some, the comical parts of Shakespearean drama have indeed succeeded in making us not only laugh *at* others but also laugh *with* them, and feel joy and delight. In his *Preface*, for example, Samuel Johnson observed that these parts produce not just laughter but also "levity" and "merriment" (67, 68); speaking of the two *Henry IV* plays in which Falstaff appears, he observes that "perhaps no author has ever in two plays afforded so much delight" (522). Hazlitt observes that Falstaff in these plays "is represented as a liar, a braggart, a coward, a glutton, etc. and yet we are not offended but delighted with him" (279). Jameson often notes the "charming" effect Shakespeare's heroines have on the audience. In the case of Beatrice in *Much Ado About Nothing*, she observes, "we are not only inclined to forgive Beatrice all her scornful airs, all her biting jests, all her assumption of superiority; but they amuse and delight us the more" when we see her fall for Benedick (67). We also note that Meredith emphasizes that the laughter evoked by Shakespearean comedy is not "derisive laughter" but "thoughtful laughter" that provides us with a sense of "high fellowship" (47–9).

The great nineteenth-century German philosopher, Hegel, also observes that Shakespeare provides us with an experience that differs from mere laughter, or at least the more common kinds of laughter that arise out of feelings of scorn and superiority. For Hegel observes that Shakespeare presents us with many characters who are light-hearted, self-assured, happy, and not deadly serious in the pursuit of their aims. Because they are like this, they can maintain their joviality even when they fail to achieve their aims, and even in the face of socio-political situations that are corrupt. They can, in addition, *along with the audience*, laugh at themselves. The laughter provoked by this kind of comedy is thus not the laughter of scorn, despair, or superiority; it is the laughter that arises out of joviality, good humor, delight, gaiety, and a cheerful heart. And since Shakespearean comedy is an occasion for the audience to share in the good cheer and gaiety of the characters, it is on par with what in Hegel's view is the greatest comedy in western European tradition—the Old Comedy of Aristophanes (1192–1236). In twentieth-century criticism this evaluation may be found in C. L. Barber's classic, *Shakespeare's Festive Comedy* (1957). Barber observes the many ways in which Shakespearean comedy draws on English popular traditions of celebration, holidaying, sporting, acting, clowning, and feasting. On the basis of this observation, he claimed that Shakespeare's comedy is a festive comedy in the spirit of Aristophanes. Though in Shakespeare's festive comedy there is occasional satire and some characters, such as Malvolio, are the butts of laughter, there is always a "communion embracing the merrymakers in the play and the audience, who have gone on holiday in going to a comedy" (3–9; see also Berry).

Moral instruction and wisdom

Though Aristotle thinks of the function of tragedy mainly in terms of the causation of emotional experience, he suggests that great tragedy also provides the pleasures of learning and acquiring certain kinds of knowledge. After establishing in the opening of the *Poetics* that tragedy is a representation of human actions, he claims that humans learn their first lessons through representation and that "everyone delights in representations." This is in part because "learning is most pleasant" and we sometimes learn things when we look at representations. If we have seen that which any given representation represents, for example, we learn or recognise that that representation is a representation of that thing, and we enjoy the recognition. But in a famous passage later in the work, Aristotle suggests that poetry in general affords another kind of learning:

> it is the function of a poet to relate not things that have happened, but things that may happen, i.e. that are possible in accordance with probability or necessity. For the historian and the poet do not differ according to whether they write in verse or without verse—the writings of Herodotus could be put into verse, but they would be no less a sort of history in verse than they are without verses. But the difference is that the former related things that have happened, the latter things that may happen. For this reason poetry is a more philosophical and more serious thing than history; poetry tends to speak of universals, history of particulars. A universal is the sort of thing that a certain kind of person may well say or do in accordance with probability or necessity—this is what poetry aims at.
>
> (12)

Distinguishing between history and poetry in this way, Aristotle claims that one of the other functions or aims of poetry—which for Aristotle includes epic, tragedy, and comedy—is to speak of or represent human behavior in general. And he implies that poetry affords the pleasures of learning about humans, achieving insight into how different kinds of people behave, and recognizing representations as accurate representations of what we are.

Horace was an ancient Roman who admired the ancient Greeks but was animated by a very different sensibility. Writing in the first century BC under the first Roman emperor, Augustus, he elaborates upon and revises Greek ideas about literature in a letter that we now refer to as *The Art of Poetry*. Horace here makes good on his claim to "teach function and duty" to authors, especially dramatists, when he claims that "poets aim either to do good or to give pleasure—or, thirdly to say things which are both pleasing and serviceable for life." "The man who combines pleasure with usefulness," Horace observes, "wins every suffrage, delighting the reader and also giving him advice" (106–7). These assertions by the Roman, read by every grammar-school boy in the Renaissance, helped to establish the idea that one of the other main things that makes any play good is that it serves as an occasion for the moral edification, instruction, and enlightenment of the audience.

Observing that good drama did this was one of the main ways of defending it against charges of immorality that were often brought against it in Shakespeare's day. As we have seen, Sidney associates good comedy with not just laughter, joy, and delight, but also teaching and moral improvement. In his wonderful account of the origins and nature of English poetry, *The Art of English Poesy* (1589), George Puttenham, too, observes that the earliest comedy "tended altogether to the good amendment of man by discipline and example. It was also much for the solace and recreation of the common people, by reason of the pageants and shows." This "Old Comedy" produced by Aristophanes and others, however, was still rather too "bitter" and was therefore replaced by the "New Comedy," which was "more civil and pleasant a great deal and not touching any man by name, but in a certain generality glancing at every abuse" (121–2).

In connection with tragedy, Sidney highlights the didactic function of

> the high and excellent Tragedy, that openeth the greatest wounds, and showeth forth the ulcers that are covered with tissue; that maketh kings fear to be tyrants, and tyrants manifest their tyrannical humors; that, with stirring the affects of admiration and commiseration, teacheth the uncertainty of this world, and upon how weak foundations gilden roofs are builded.
>
> (94)

Sidney also discusses what is generally regarded as the first English tragedy in blank verse, *Gorbuduc*, written by Thomas Sackville and Thomas Norton, and first performed in 1561. This play, he observes, "is full of stately speeches and well-sounding phrases, climbing to the height of Seneca's style, and as full of notable morality, which it doth most delightfully teach, and so obtain the very end of Poesy" (102). Puttenham, too, observes that in ancient times, some poets "set forth the doleful falls of unfortunate and afflicted princes, and were called poets tragical. Such were Euripedes and Sophocles with the Greeks, Seneca among the Latins" (115). Puttenham then classifies this kind of poetry as one of the "three kinds of poems reprehensive." This kind of reprehensive poetry dealt in particular with "*the evil and outrageous behaviors of princes.*" Ancient tragedy showed this kind of behavior "to the intent that such exemplifying (as it were) of their [the princes'] blame and adversities, being now dead, might work for a secret reprehension to others that were alive, living in the same or like abuses" (115–24).

Many over the centuries have praised Shakespeare on grounds that the plays do indeed provide us with not just the pleasures of learning about ourselves and seeing accurate representations of what we are, but also moral instruction and wisdom. But there are wildly varying accounts of what that wisdom and instruction is. Indeed, we could well discriminate between not just different aesthetic and socio-political movements in western Europe over the last four hundred years but also different schools or theories of contemporary criticism by differentiating between these accounts of the wisdom and instruction afforded by Shakespearean drama. The surviving accounts of late sixteenth and seventeenth-century audience responses to Shakespeare's tragedies indicate that many people felt these plays taught them about the destructive consequences of extreme passion and immoral conduct—in particular, extreme love, extreme jealousy, and adultery. But many Renaissance readers also regarded these plays as a storehouse of wisdom because they included so many sayings and proverbs about a wide range of ethical and political issues. Those sayings and proverbs were thought to be useful in dealing effectively with many specific situations encountered in life (Roberts, Whitney).

One of the major eighteenth-century assertions of the pleasure Shakespearean drama in general provides by way of accurate representation of what we are comes in Johnson's *Preface*:

> Nothing can please many, and please long, but just representations of general nature. ... Shakespeare is above all writers, at least above all modern writers, the poet of nature; the poet that holds up to his readers a faithful mirrour of manners and of life. His characters are not modified by the customs of particular places, unpractised by the rest of the world; by the peculiarities of studies or professions, which can operate but upon small numbers; or by the accidents of transient fashions or temporary opinions: they are the genuine progeny of common humanity, such as the world will always supply, and observation will always find. His persons act and speak by the influence of those general passions and principles by which all minds are agitated, and the whole system of life is continued in motion. In the writings of other poets a character is too often an individual; in those of Shakespeare it is commonly a species.
>
> (59–60)

So Johnson celebrates Shakespeare for giving us the pleasures that we experience when we observe what we take to be accurate representations of what we are. And like Renaissance audiences, he also thinks some moral instruction and wisdom may be "collected" from the axioms and precepts in the plays. However, reiterating the Horatian tenet that "the end of writing is to instruct; the end of poetry is to instruct by pleasing," he finds fault with Shakespeare for seeming "to write without any moral purpose" (61–71).

In her *Essay on the Writings and Genius of Shakespeare* (1769), Elizabeth Montagu defends Shakespeare from this charge by arguing that Shakespeare was "one of the greatest moral philosophers that ever lived." For giving us characters who are true-to-life, he excites our interest and sympathy in them with the result that what they say and do amounts to an authoritative instruction:

> Shakespeare's dramatis personae are men, frail by constitution, hurt by ill habits, faulty and unequal. But they speak with human voices, are actuated by human passions, and are engaged in the common affairs of human life. We are interested in what they do, or say, by feeling every moment, that they are of the same nature as ourselves. Their precepts therefore are an instruction, their fates and fortunes an experience, their testimony an authority, and their misfortunes a warning.
>
> (31)

In the nineteenth century, Hazlitt, in his discussion of *Othello*, summarizes some of the traditional views of the powers of tragedy to provide moral instruction, and he praises this play in particular for doing it all. But the instruction he finds here is neither counsel to tyrants and evil men nor collections of precepts and axioms. It is more in line with the transformation of our moral and emotional sensibility of which Montagu speaks:

> It has been said that tragedy purifies the affections by terror and pity. That is, it substitutes imaginary sympathy for mere selfishness. It gives us a high and permanent interest, beyond ourselves, in humanity as such. It raises the great, the remote, and the possible to an equality with the real, the little and the near. It makes man a partaker with his kind. It subdues and softens the stubbornness of his will. It teaches him that there are and have been others like himself, by showing him as in a glass what they have felt, thought, and done. It opens the chambers of the human heart. It leaves nothing indifferent to us that can affect our common nature. It excites our sensibility by exhibiting the passions wound up to the utmost pitch by the power of imagination or the temptation of circumstances; and corrects their fatal excesses in ourselves by pointing to the greater extent of sufferings and of crimes to which they have led others. Tragedy creates a balance of the affections. It makes us thoughtful spectators in the lists of life. It is the refiner of the species; a discipline of humanity.—*Othello* furnishes an illustration of these remarks.
>
> (200)

A little later in the nineteenth century, Jameson finds that Shakespeare's women across all genres are "complete individuals" who are true to "the feminine character," and who display "the manner in which the affections would naturally display themselves in women—whether combined with high intellect, regulated by reflection, and elevated by imagination, or existing with perverted dispositions, or purified by the moral sentiments" (10, 13, 26). Jameson leaves it to the reader "to deduce the moral themselves," but she makes clear that by providing these "images and examples" of *real* women (8), Shakespeare achieves many important things: he enlightens western society about the nature and capacities of women; he helps to reform an educational and system that diminished and stultified them; and he promotes a way of life that is consistent with "the mild and serious spirit of Christianity" (6). Mary Cowden Clarke, who published her massive *Complete Concordance to Shakespeare* in 1845 and her edition of Shakespeare's works in 1860, also praises Shakespeare for being "our great poet-teacher." For by providing so many accurate representations of women, he "has vindicated their truest rights and celebrated their best virtues." Indeed,

> to the young girl, emerging from childhood and taking her first step into the more active and self-dependent career of woman-life, Shakespeare's vital precepts and models render him essentially a helping friend. To her he comes instructively and aidingly; in his page she may find warning, guidance, kindliest monition, and wisest counsel. Through his feminine portraits she may see, as in a faithful glass, vivid pictures of what she has to evitate [avoid], or what she has to imitate, in order to become a worthy and admirable woman.
> (101)

The nineteenth-century Germans also found moral instruction in Shakespeare. Georg Gottfried Gervinus, for example, forcefully affirmed in his *Shakespeare Commentaries* (1849–52) that Shakespeare was "a teacher of indisputable authority" (830). "It is true," Gervinus observed, that

> Shakespeare never aims at preaching morals by express and direct precept. He does it [and only in the tragedies] for the most part indirectly by the mouth of the least prejudiced, by the spectators rather than by the actors in his plays ... by living, acting impulses, by illustration and example.
> (889)

This teaching is essentially that "the taming of the passions is the aim of human civilization," that by controlling and moderating our impulses and passions by reason we "maintain the freedom of determining for ourselves as we will" and enable ourselves to live an active life of moral perfection (889, 893). In his dazzling discussion of ancient Greek tragedy, *The Birth of Tragedy* (1872), the German philosopher, Friedrich Nietzsche, scorns those who think that what makes tragedy great is that it provides moral instruction. Nevertheless, he too finds instruction in tragedy, but of a late nineteenth-century kind. For him, great tragedy provides insight into "the terror and horror of existence," but also "the fundamental knowledge of the oneness of everything existent" (42, 60, 74). It is this special kind of insight and knowledge which is afforded by great tragedy that Nietzsche calls "tragic insight," "Dionysian wisdom," and "Dionysian knowledge" (98, 103, 104). And it is because he feels that "the lesson of Hamlet" includes this kind of insight and knowledge that Nietzsche celebrates this play.

In the twentieth century, when Shakespeare criticism reached industrial proportions, we find a staggering array of descriptions of the bard's teachings, some of which ground positive evaluations of the plays. I won't pretend to identify them all, but will just note that in *The Elizabethan World Picture* (1944), E. M. W. Tillyard claimed that Shakespeare's plays espouse a moral and political outlook grounded in the view that Elizabethan England was consistent with a just, rational, hierarchical world order overseen by the God of Christianity. Many since then have produced refined accounts of Shakespeare's "conservative" moral and political outlook. But some have also challenged this view by observing Shakespeare's praise of disobedience and the way he seems, at least in some plays, to grant priority to the life of grandiose passion, the body, and sensual pleasure over the rational, temperate life (Strier). A third option is the "elusive" Shakespeare who, in dramatizing arguments on both sides of major moral and political questions, reveals and fosters an essentially skeptical and cynical political outlook (Armitage).

I want also to note that although some modern feminist critics think of Shakespeare as a "patriarchal bard" (McLuskie), others argue in the spirit of Montagu, Jameson, and Cowden Clark that the plays ultimately promote the wellbeing and advancement of women in western liberal democratic societies. Juliet Dusinberre, for example, claims that Shakespearean drama is feminist in sympathy in that it represents women as self-sufficient, independent, intelligent individuals. That kind of representation shows that "Shakespeare saw men and women as equal in a world which declared them unequal" (308). Germaine Greer aligns Shakespeare with figures such as Bacon and Montaigne who "sought to open the mind to all kinds of protean possibility rather than to mechanize its operations in the development of a system." While not directly instructing us in any ethical system, Shakespeare thus "displays the mentality that made possible the development of the pluralism and tolerance that came, after a period of agony, to characterize English political thought and institutions" (85–6; 125). And while noting Shakespeare's "occasional indifference to ethics," Peter Holbrook argues that the plays are driven by a commitment "to fundamentally modern values: freedom, individuality, self-realization, authenticity"; his works have therefore "helped legitimate the liberal civilization of our epoch," and he is "an author for a liberal culture of self-realization" (12–13, 35, 41, 234; see also Fernie).

Finally, Harold Bloom, one of Shakespeare's ardent modern devotees, locates the grounds of Shakespeare's merit in his freedom from moral and religious commitments. But he, too, claims that Shakespeare is in the game of teaching and instructing us, and he praises him for it. Bloom sees Falstaff, for example, as a sage who "teaches us *not to moralize.*" More generally, Bloom observes that

> Shakespeare teaches us how and what to perceive, and he also instructs us how and what to sense and then to experience as sensation. Seeking as he did to enlarge us, not as citizens or as Christians but as consciousnesses, Shakespeare outdid all his preceptors as an entertainment.... The ultimate use of Shakespeare is to let him teach you to think too well, to whatever truth you can sustain without perishing.
>
> (9–10, 295–7)

Sublimity

The ancient Graeco-Roman world provided a precedent for yet another major dimension of readers' and playgoers' accounts of what makes Shakespeare so special. In *On Sublimity*, the author (traditionally referred to as "Longinus") observes that

> sublimity is a kind of eminence or excellence of discourse. It is the source of the distinction of the very greatest poets and prose writers and the means by which they have given eternal life to their own fame. For grandeur produces ecstasy rather than persuasion in the hearer; and the combination of wonder and astonishment always proves superior to the merely persuasive and pleasant. This is because persuasion is on the whole something we can control, whereas amazement and wonder exert invincible power and force and get the better of every hearer.
>
> (143)

Longinus goes on to observe that sublime works cause the audience to feel "elevated and exalted," fill them "with joy and pride," dispose their minds to greatness, and make them feel "emotion and excitement" (148, 159, 172). And he uses the term "sublime" to refer to not just works of a certain kind but also the *feelings* that these works cause us to have. Longinus agrees with Aristotle that great tragedies—such as those by Aeschylus, Sophocles, and Euripedes—command the emotions of the audience. But he also claims that they cause the audience to experience *other* emotions (such as pride and joy), as well as sensations of elevation, grandeur, wonder, ecstasy, awe, amazement, and astonishment (but let's remember that Aristotle, too, mentions in passing that producing "amazement" and "astonishment" in the audience is also part of the function of tragedy [13, 25]). Given Longinus' account of it throughout the work, it seems that while the sublime experience can include emotion, it also involves states of mind and states of consciousness. And he does not think that it is the function of only *one* genre or kind of discourse to cause this special kind of experience. Rather, he thinks of it as a function that is proper to a wide range of discourses that includes epic, oratory, tragedy, lyric, scripture, history, and philosophy. In so doing, Longinus establishes another strong precedent in western tradition for thinking of drama (especially tragedy) in terms of how it affects us, and for assessing the merit of any given play in a particular way: any given play is great insofar as it causes us to experience the states of being, heart, and mind that Longinus comprehends under the term "sublime."

Shakespeare may have known of Longinus' treatise, since the original Greek text and Latin translations of it were published on the continent during the sixteenth century. A few sixteenth-century French and Italian humanists discussed it, and the great French essayist whom Shakespeare read, Montaigne, may also have known of it (Logan). But the first English translation of this treatise was published in England in 1652, and the treatise was not widely known in England until the late seventeenth-century, after Boileau had published his translation of it into French in 1674. Since then, however, many have indeed claimed that it is this power to provoke in us these feelings of ecstasy, elevation, joy, pride, exhilaration, awe, nobility, and wonder that qualify Shakespeare's plays (especially the tragedies) as great plays—and many have used the term "sublime" to describe this effect of the tragedies, as well as the plays themselves and their author.

In England, for example, the great Restoration playwright, John Dryden, cites Aristotle, Horace, and Longinus as his authorities and affirms Shakespeare's sublimity—though he also thinks Shakespeare sometimes overdoes it (244–7). Samuel Johnson, too, speaks of how "the mind" is "exhilarated" in the face of the "seriousness" of Shakespearean tragedy (68). Indeed, a host of eighteenth-century figures, including Edmund Burke, who wrote a treatise on the beautiful and the sublime, praise Shakespeare as the dramatist who provides his readers and audience with the pleasures of the sublime (Hopkins, Cheney). Once the great eighteenth-century German philosopher, Immanuel Kant, had presented his account of the sublime in the *Critique of Judgment* (1790), many German scholars also used the term *das Erhabene*—usually translated into English as "the sublime"—in order to describe their experience of these plays. The nineteenth-century German philosopher, Arthur Schopenhauer, for example, saw tragedy "as the summit of poetic art, both as regards the greatness of the effect and the difficulty of the achievement" (I: 252), and he describes this effect in terms of the "feeling of the sublime." But for Schopenhauer, this feeling is a "frame of mind" which consists in the "rising above all the aims and good things of life, this turning away from life and its temptations, and the turning, already to be found here, to an existence of a different kind, although wholly inconceivable to us." What makes any given tragedy great is its power to invoke in us "this resigned exaltation of the mind," this "exalted pleasure" we experience as we "turn away from the will-to-live itself" and enter a state of "resignation." And it is because Shakespeare's tragedies provide him with this experience that Schopenhauer claims they are great—superior even to those of the ancient Greeks (II: 433–5).

Nietzsche, too, observes, though only in passing, that Shakespearean tragedy is great because it affects us as only great, authentic tragedy can. But in his study of "the sublime and celebrated art of *Attic tragedy*" (47), his account of this effect is very different from Schopenhauer's. Here are a couple great passages from *The Birth of Tragedy* in which Nietzsche discusses "the effect of tragedy" (84):

> This is the most immediate effect of the Dionysian tragedy, that the state and society and, quite generally, the gulfs between man and man give way to an overwhelming feeling of unity leading back to the very heart of nature. The metaphysical comfort—with which, I am suggesting even now, every true tragedy leaves us—that life is at the bottom of things, despite all the changes of appearances, indestructibly powerful and pleasurable—this comfort appears in incarnate clarity in the chorus of satyrs [in ancient Greek tragedy].
>
> (59)

> We are really for a brief moment primordial being itself, feeling its raging desire for existence and joy in existence; the struggle, the pain, the destruction of phenomena, now appear necessary to us, in view of the excess of countless forms of existence which force and push one another into life, in view of the exuberant fertility of the universal will. We are pierced by the maddening sting of these pains just when we have become, as it were, one with the infinite primordial joy in existence, and when we anticipate, in Dionysian ecstasy, the indestructibility and eternity of this joy. In spite of fear and pity, we are the happy living beings, not as individuals, but as the *one* living being, with whose creative joy we are united.
>
> (104–5)

Nietzsche's brief but celebrated comments on Hamlet as Dionysian man indicate that he thinks this tragedy is of the highest quality because it provides us with the special kind of experience that all "true tragedy" provides: the feeling of joy, rapture, ecstasy, exhilaration, oneness with the life-force, and metaphysical comfort on the basis of which we affirm life even in the face of the destruction of the hero and the horrors of existence at large. Not that everyone who sees authentic tragedies, such as *Hamlet*, have such experiences; countless people do not, Nietzsche claims. His point is rather that the value of great tragedy lies in its powers to provide this kind of experience to those who have an aesthetic nature, those who are "more nobly and delicately endowed by nature" (132–4).

So by the twentieth century, the sublime Shakespeare was firmly established, and many over the last century have continued to praise and value his tragedies on grounds of their sublimity and their power to make the audience feel elation, wonder, awe, ecstasy. In his study of Shakespeare's tragedies, for example, Bradley says of *Macbeth* that "the whole tragedy is sublime" (277), and he observes how it, along with the other tragedies, causes the audience to experience not just pity and fear, but also admiration, awe, and wonder. Reaffirming much of what Bradley says, and claiming allegiance with Longinus, Bloom has recently gone further and claimed that

> Shakespeare's sublimity is the richest and most varied in all literary history. Surely its heights-of-heights are the great personalities: Falstaff, Hamlet, Rosalind, Othello, Iago, Lear, Cleopatra. They are sublime because they

expand our consciousness without distorting it. To meditate upon them is to apprehend greatness—negative and positive—and so share in the potential for greatness in ourselves.

(Hobby: xv)

Note that Bloom includes some of the main characters from the histories and comedies—Falstaff and Rosalind—in his list of sublime personalities. This is in keeping with many others who have observed in recent times that Shakespeare is in the business of making us feel *wonder* across all genres (Berry, Richman, Cohen).

Shakespeare and us

What is so special about Shakespeare's plays? One of the main answers that European men and women over the last four hundred years have given to this question takes the form of a claim about how these plays affect us: the plays are special because, when we read them or see them performed, we often have intense, pleasurable emotional experiences; we laugh; we feel delight and joy; we experience the pleasure of seeing accurate representations of what humans are; we have the impression of acquiring knowledge and wisdom about ourselves and our world; we feel sublime. Another way of putting this, and a way in which many *have* put it, is that what makes the plays special is their *power*: the plays are special because of the tremendous *power* they have to make us have such a wide range of experiences.

This is not to say that everyone has these experiences, that you have them, that you ought to have them, or that people continue to have them—though I think there is plenty of evidence that many people do continue to have them. It is not to deny that different people have different responses to any given play or performance and have a wide range of experiences other than those I have identified here. Some scholars have recently argued that emotional experience during the Renaissance differed in important ways from modern emotional experience (Kern Paster). And we may well want to be skeptical concerning those who have claimed to have had the experiences that are repeatedly identified in commentary on the plays. As Bradley wisely observes, "many a man will declare that he feels in reading a tragedy what he never really felt, while he fails to recognize what he actually did feel" (17). Still, when we attend to some of the great Shakespeare criticism over the centuries, records of audience response, and modern audience experiences, we can see that one of the main things that makes Shakespeare's plays special is that they make people *feel* certain things, that they have a *power* to cause people to have particular experiences.

This way of thinking about the merit, value, and success of Shakespeare is in line with what I think is Shakespeare's own way of thinking about his work. For there are several indications that, like other Renaissance authors, he himself evaluated (and would have approved of those who evaluated) the achievement of his plays at least in part on grounds of how they affected his audience. First of all, as we see in the film, *Shakespeare in Love*, Shakespeare himself acted in some of the plays, invested in the theatre companies that performed his plays, and depended for his income on how they fared at court and in the London theatre venues. Deeply invested in what might fairly be called "the entertainment business" of Elizabethan and Jacobean London, Shakespeare was writing plays for a theatre audience—though it seems that he also had in mind readers of his scripts (Erne). And he measured the plays' success and achievement at least in part on grounds of their success in providing an experience for which people were willing to pay. This is not to say that he did not have other aims and ambitions, but that the aim to entertain his audiences and readers, and to provide the experiences that he understood were appropriate to different kinds (and combinations of kinds) of plays was one of his aims, possibly the main one.

That Shakespeare wanted his plays to fulfill some of the functions that, in accordance with the ancient Greeks and Romans he studied at grammar school, were thought of as being appropriate to different genres of drama is also suggested by the plays themselves. For many characters in the plays identify, claim to experience, and encourage others to experience particular emotions and states of mind. At the end of *Richard II*, for example, Bullingbrook brings proceedings to a close by chastising and banishing Exton for having murdered Richard, confessing to his lords that his soul is "full of woe," and invoking them to join him in mourning and lamenting (5.6.38–52). The Prologue to the late history play, *The Life of King Henry the Eighth* (on which Shakespeare collaborated with Fletcher), is even more explicit on this point:

> things now
> That bear a weighty and a serious brow,
> Sad, high, and working, full of state and woe:
> Such noble scenes as draw the eye to flow
> We now present. Those that can pity here
> May, if they think it well, let fall a tear:
> The subject will deserve it.
>
> (1–7)

This kind of thing is also common in the tragedies. At the opening of *Romeo and Juliet*, for example, the chorus claims that it is the lovers' "piteous overthrows" that will put an end to their parents' strife, and that the play will represent "the fearful passage of their death-marked love"—the audience, it would seem, is meant to feel pity and fear in the face of the destruction of the young lovers they are about to witness. At the end of the play, the Prince observes the "sorrow" of the sun, "these sad things," and the story of "woe" (5.3.316–19). At the end of *Lear*, Albany tells everyone that "our present business / Is general woe," while Edgar asserts that "we" must obey "the weight of this sad time" (5.3.338–44). In *Antony and Cleopatra*, Octavius Caesar weeps on receiving news of the death of Antony. Shortly before her death, Cleopatra observes that because "we, the greatest" are often judged on the basis of the merits and qualities of those around us, "when we fall" we are "to be pitied"

(5.2.207–10). Presiding over both of the dead lovers at the very end, Octavius Caesar observes that "their story is / No less in pity than his glory which / Brought them to be lamented" (5.2.412–14). And in *Coriolanus*, after observing the conspirators kill the protagonist, one of the Volscian lords commands everyone, "mourn you for him" (5.6.166–8). Aufidius then shares his feelings: "my rage is gone, / And I am struck with sorrow" (5.6.166–73). Pity, fear, sorrow, grief, woe—these are some of the emotions that the characters in the histories and tragedies themselves explicitly claim they experience, that they express, and that they encourage others—including the audience, it seems—to experience.

Throughout the comedies and romances, the characters are of course laughing and being merry, and these plays often conclude with a call for laugher, joy, mirth, merriment, and delight—a call that in many live performances is addressed to both characters onstage and the audience. In the final hilarious scene of *A Midsummer Night's Dream*, for example, Theseus greets the two pairs of lovers with "here come the lovers, full of joy and mirth. / Joy, gentle friends! Joy and fresh days of love / Accompany your hearts!" (5.1.28–30). Wondering what masques, dances, mirth, revels, and music are at hand, and what "delight" they shall have between dinner and bedtime, he then rejects a proposed "satire, keen and critical," since that is "not sorting with a nuptial ceremony" (5.1.43–57). He chooses instead the Pyramus and Thisbe play that Bottom and the other mechanicals have prepared. As Quince haltingly observes in the Prologue to their performance, "Our true intent is. All for your delight" (5.1.28–118). In *Twelfth Night*, Fabian explains to Olivia the joke they have played on Malvolio and expresses his "hope" that it will all "pluck on laughter [rather] than revenge" (5.1.351). At the end of *As You Like It*, Duke Senior invites Sir Rowland de Bois' son to "fall into our rustic revelry," calls for music, and commands "brides and bridegrooms all, / With measure heaped in joy, to th'measures fall" (5.4.151–53). Though Jaques declines to join in on the "pleasures" and "dancing measures," the Duke brings the action to a close by saying, "We'll begin these rites, / As we do trust they'll end, in true delights" (5.4.171–2). And at the end of *The Tempest*, as Gonzalo sees the happy ending unfold, he exclaims, "O, rejoice / Beyond a common joy" (5.1.233).

Shakespeare's plays do not conclude with the author coming forward and saying something like, "and from all of this, the reader/audience should learn that ... ." But they do include countless scenes in which some characters claim to learn something about "us," gain wisdom, teach something, and tell others to pay attention. Such moments, moreover, are often the most intense and moving scenes of the plays in which they occur. Consider, for example, the end of *Hamlet*. Hamlet recounts to his friend Horatio how, on board the ship that was taking him to England, he "rashly" got out of bed, procured the packet that was carried by his false friends, Rosencrantz and Guildenstern, and opened the king's commission that ordered the English to put Hamlet to death. Since this rash, indiscrete act enabled him to escape this fate, Hamlet observes to his friend,

>   let us know
> Our indiscretion sometimes serves us well,
> When our dear plots do pall, and that should teach us
> There's a divinity that shapes our ends,
> Rough-hew them how we will.

As if to confirm Hamlet's claim about what this incident should teach not just him but "us," Horatio replies, "That is most certain" (5.2.4–12).

Or look at the famous scene in *King Lear* when the old king is out on the heath during a storm. He imagines how the poor will suffer in the storm and expresses his profound compassion and regret for not having taken better care of them. After that, he commands "pomp" (the rich and powerful) to pay attention:

> Poor naked wretches, whereso'er you are,
> That bide the pelting of this pitiless storm,
> How shall your houseless heads and unfed sides,
> Your lopped and windowed raggedness, defend you
> From seasons such as these? O, I have ta'en
> Too little care of this! Take physic, pomp,
> Expose thyself to feel what wretches feel,
> That thou mayst *shake the superflux* to them   [distribute the excess]
> And show the heavens more just.
>
> (3.4.35–9)

The rich and powerful people of Lear's world of course cannot hear him as he teaches what he himself has learned the hard way out on the heath—but we can. So, too, can we hear Gloucester repeat the lesson when, in the wake of *his* terrible suffering, he hopes the heavens make the rich and powerful suffer, "so distribution should undo excess, / And each man have enough" (4.1.72–3).

Though in the comedies we do not get such grave moments of learning and instruction grounded in profound suffering, we do get many moments where characters assert general claims about life in light of all the fun and games they have been having. At the end of *A Midsummer Night's Dream*, for example, Theseus reflects on all that has passed during the night, and his broader experience, and he gives Hippolyta something of a lesson on the lunatic, the lover, and the poet—one that she does not entirely accept. He then overrides her objections to seeing the mechanicals' play on grounds of his understanding of eloquence, duty, modesty, and love in general:

>   Trust me, sweet,
> Out of this silence yet I picked a welcome,
> And in the modesty of fearful duty
> I read as much as from the rattling tongue

Of saucy and audacious eloquence.
Love, therefore, and tongue-tied simplicity
In least speak most, to my capacity.
(5.1.103–9)

The point here is not that Shakespeare propounds any doctrine or view in particular—though many have said that he does. I want to say just that his plays often show people formulating and changing their beliefs and attitudes in light of their own experience. They often show people arriving at what *they*, at least, take to be wisdom, a wisdom they often attempt to pass on to others. Shakespeare thereby provides the audience with an occasion for considering those beliefs and attitudes as wisdom. Even if we do not take on what these people take to be their wisdom, or accept the lessons on offer, their *activity* of reflecting on their own experience and thinking about life sets an example for us to follow, especially when they speak of "us" and what "we" think and feel.

In the final scenes of the tragedies, no one uses the word "sublime" to describe what they are feeling—I don't think that word ever occurs in Shakespearean drama. But we will see that many of the protagonists do assert that they feel transported, elevated, exalted, noble. And though the prevailing feeling of the other characters in the final scenes of the plays might be one of sympathy, fear, and sorrow, many of them display impulses to raise, to respect, to elevate the noble dead, and they speak of "high" events and "solemnity." At the end of *Romeo and Juliet*, for example, Montague and Capulet resolve to "raise" statues to the dead lovers. At the end of *Hamlet*, Horatio orders that the bodies of Hamlet and the others "high on a stage be placed to the view" (5.2.330). At the end of *Antony and Cleopatra*, Caesar claims that "high events as these / Strike those that make them," orders that his entire army will "in solemn show" attend Cleopatra's funeral, and commands Dolabella to "see / High order in this great solemnity" (5.2.411–17). And at the end of *Julius Caesar*, Antony commands that Brutus be used "with all respect and rites of burial" and resolves that within his own tent will his bones "lie, / Most like a soldier, ordered honourably" (5.5.82–4). These witnesses of devastation display strong and deep impulses to elevate not just the noble dead but also themselves—in many cases, to rise above the enmity and violence that have driven the action of the play and resulted in that devastation. They express this impulse and often command others to feel it too, in order to make everybody behave honorably, respectfully, in a dignified way that is in keeping with their participation in the solemn funerary ritual which they feel is demanded by the occasion.

And many characters in the final scenes of the romances, comedies, and tragedies speak of their wonder. In the final scene of *The Winter's Tale*, for example, Paulina likes the silence of Leontes for showing off his "wonder" as he beholds what he thinks is the statue of Hermione (5.3.24–25); telling him to prepare for more "amazement," she commands the statue to descend and "strike all that look upon with marvel" (5.3.25, 105, 122). In the final scene of *The Tempest*, several characters (including Miranda, whose name in Latin means wonder) speak of their "amazement," "admiration," and "wonder." At the end of *Much Ado About Nothing*, several characters learn that Hero is not dead as they had thought, but is there with them, ready to marry her true love, Claudio. Observing how Claudio and others respond to this revelation, Friar Francis observes,

> All this amazement can I qualify,
> When after that the holy rites are ended,
> I'll tell you largely of fair Hero's death.
> Meantime let wonder seem familiar.
> (5.4.68–71)

Amazement will be qualified, and wonder may fade, but for the moment that is what at least some of the characters are feeling. Similarly, in the final scenes of *Twelfth Night*, Sebastian observes that "'tis wonder that enwraps me" (4.3.3), while Olivia exclaims, "most wonderful!" as she along with everyone else on stage beholds the marvelous spectacle of Viola (dressed as Cesario) and her twin brother, Sebastian. Fabian then observes that he has "wondered at" what for all except Malvolio are the happy and surprising proceedings. (5.1.210, 343). And at the end of *A Midsummer Night's Dream*, Hippolyta observes that the events of the night strike her as being "strange and admirable" (5.1.27)—"admirable" in Shakespeare's day strongly connoted wondrous, marvelous.

Some of the survivors in the tragedies also feel wonder. At the end of *Hamlet*, the dying hero seems to encourage those around him—including the audience—to feel fear when he directly addresses "You that look pale and tremble at this chance, / That are but mutes or audience to this act" (5.2.280–1). But after the Ambassador from England observes that "the sight" of the dead Danish nobility "is dismal," Horatio tells Fortinbras to cease searching if he would see "aught of woe or wonder" (5.2.313), as though wonder is also an appropriate response to that dismal scene. And at the end of *Lear*, the broken-hearted Kent observes, "the wonder is he [Lear] hath endured so long" (5.3.330–6).

In the plays themselves, then, the characters often speak of their responses to what is going on, and in a variety of ways they encourage, request, and even command other characters to respond in this way as well. Many have observed that, in so doing, they give readers and members of the audience a cue to what they, too, are to feel, think, and do (Howard, Honigman, Richman, Steggle, Cohen). That cue may have been especially strong in the Renaissance theatre, where the stage was seen to be continuous with the world of the audience (Whitney). But I think it can be strong in any performance that breaks down the fourth wall separating the audience from the stage. Giving this cue, Shakespeare's characters attest to his deep and abiding ambition to entertain us and shape our engagement with the text and the performance. This way of thinking about Shakespeare's achievement departs from the construction of the plays as an object that in and of itself is great and demands our study and reverence, regardless of how it makes people feel. It also departs from the common view that the main function of literary criticism is simply to describe or interpret the literary text, which is conceived essentially as some kind of code or puzzle. Understanding that the plays have a purpose that involves us, the audience, and that the success and quality of the plays depend to an important extent on how they affect us, helps us see the importance of our own engagement with the plays in relation to the project of understanding why they are good. It leads us to study not just the plays, but our own engagement with them, and to take that engagement seriously as an index to their quality and success. Taking this approach to the plays will, I hope, make studying and teaching them less of an act of reverence to a strange old thing foisted upon us, and more of a vital and significant engagement with theatre and ourselves.

If we answer the question of what is special about the plays in this way, you might then well ask the following question: what allowed *the man*, Shakespeare, to produce plays that could affect us in these ways? Many over the centuries have posed this question and provided rich, complex answers to it in the form of accounts of his education and "genius" (Bate 1997). Another question you might well ask is the following: what is it about *us*, the audience, that accounts for what we experience when we attend Shakespearean tragedy? What kind of education, intelligence, memory, erotic sensibility, moral sensibility, knowledge of Renaissance English, cultural conditioning, and attention span must people have in order to experience these things? And, again, there is a comprehensive answer to this question about Shakespeare's readers and audiences in the scholarship devoted to him. I will address these questions in passing, but the question I propose to answer directly is the following: what is it about *the plays* that enable them to affect us in these ways and to fulfill Shakespeare's ambition to entertain us? In the next four chapters I propose to answer this question by observing how specific aspects of the plays' plots, characters, thought, language, song, and spectacle link up to specific pleasures and responses. In so doing, I hope to enhance your knowledge of the plays, but also to help you find the entertainment value they were intended to have.

References

Adler, John (ed.). *Responses to Shakespeare*. Vols 6 and 7. London: Routledge/Thoemmes Press, 1997.
Aristotle. *Poetics*. Trans. Richard Janko. Indianapolis: Hackett, 1987.
Armitage, David, Condren, Conal, and Fitzmaurice, Andrew (eds). *Shakespeare and Early Modern Political Thought*. Cambridge: Cambridge University Press, 2009.
Barber, C. L. *Shakespeare's Festive Comedy*. Princeton: Princeton University Press, 1959.
Bate, Jonathan (ed.). *The Romantics on Shakespeare*. New York: Penguin, 1992.
Bate, Jonathan. *The Genius of Shakespeare*. London: Picador, 2008.
Berry, Edward. "Laughing at 'others.'" In *The Cambridge Companion to Shakespearean Comedy*. Ed. Alexander Leggatt. Cambridge: Cambridge University Press, 2002. 123–138.
Bloom, Harold. *Shakespeare: The Invention of the Human*. New York: Riverhead, 1998.
Bradley, A. C. *Shakespearean Tragedy*. 1904; London: Macmillan, 1971.

Cavendish, Margaret. "Letter CXXIII" of *CCXI Sociable Letters*. In *Women Reading Shakespeare 1660–1900*. Ed. Ann Thompson and Sasha Roberts. Manchester: Manchester University Press, 1997.

Chambers, E. K. *William Shakespeare: A Study of Facts and Problems*. 2 vols. 1930; Oxford: Clarendon Press, 1966.

Cheney, Patrick. *English Authorship and the Early Modern Sublime*. Cambridge: Cambridge University Press, 2018.

Cohen, Adam Max. *Wonder in Shakespeare*. New York: Palgrave Macmillan, 2012.

Cowden Clarke, Mary. "Shakespeare as the girl's friend." In *Women Reading Shakespeare 1660–1900*. 101–103.

Dusinberre, Juliet. *Shakespeare and the Nature of Women*. 1975; London: Macmillan, 1996.

Dryden, John. "The grounds of criticism in tragedy." In *The Works of John Dryden*, vol. 13. Berkeley: University of California Press, 1984. 229–248.

Erne, Lukas. *Shakespeare as Literary Dramatist*. 2003; Cambridge: Cambridge University Press, 2013.

Fernie, Ewen. *Shakespeare for Freedom: Why the Plays Matter*. Cambridge: Cambridge University Press, 2017.

Gervinus, G. G. *Shakespeare Commentaries*. Trans. F. E. Bunnett. London: Smith, Elder, & Co., 1892.

Greer, Germaine. *Shakespeare*. Oxford: Oxford University Press, 1986.

Gurr, Andrew. *Playgoing in Shakespeare's London*. 3rd ed. Cambridge: Cambridge University Press, 2004.

Hammond, Paul. "The Janus poet: Dryden's critique of Shakespeare." In *John Dryden: His Politics, His Plays, and His Poets*. Ed. Claude Rawson and Aaron Santesso. Newark: University of Delaware Press, 2004, 158–179.

Hazlitt, William. *Characters of Shakespear's Plays*. In *Complete Works of William Hazlitt*, vol. 4. Ed. P. P. Howe. 1817; London: J. M. Dent, 1930.

Hegel, G. W. F. *Aesthetics: Lectures on Fine Art*. Trans. T. M. Knox. Vol. 2. Oxford: Clarendon, 1975; 2010.

Hobby, Blake (ed.). *Bloom's Literary Themes: The Sublime*. New York: Infobase Publishing, 2010.

Holbrook, Peter. *Shakespeare's Individualism*. Cambridge: Cambridge University Press, 2010.

Honigman, E. A. J. *Shakespeare: Seven Tragedies: The Dramatist's Manipulation of Response*. London: MacMillan, 1976.

Hopkins, David. *Conversing with Antiquity*. Oxford: Oxford University Press, 2010.

Horace. *The Art of Poetry*. Trans. D. A. Russell. In *Classical Literary Criticism*. Ed. D. A. Russell and Michael Winterbottom. 1972; Oxford: Oxford University Press, 1989. 98–110.

Howard, Jean. *Shakespeare's Art of Orchestration*. Urbana: University of Illinois Press, 1984.

Jameson, Anna. *Shakespeare's Heroines: Characteristics of Women Moral, Poetical, and Historical*. 1832; London: Bell, 1916.

Johnson, Samuel. *Johnson on Shakespeare*. Vol. 7 of *The Yale Edition of the Works of Samuel Johnson*. Ed. Arthur Sherbo. New Haven: Yale University Press, 1968.

Kern Paster, Gail, Rowe, Katherine, and Floyd-Wilson, Mary (eds). *Reading the Early Modern Passions*. Philadelphia: University of Pennsylvania Press, 2004.

Levin, Richard. "The relation of external evidence to the allegorical and thematic interpretation of Shakespeare." *Shakespeare Studies* 13 (1980): 1–29.

Logan, John. "Longinus and the sublime." In *The Cambridge History of Literary Criticism: Vol. 8. The Renaissance*. Ed. Glyn Norton. Cambridge: Cambridge University Press, 1999. 529–540.

Longinus. *On Sublimity*. Trans. D. A. Russell. In *Classical Literary Criticism*. Ed. D. A. Russell and Michael Winterbottom. 1972; Oxford: Oxford University Press, 1989. 143–187.

Marsden, Jean. "Shakespeare and sympathy." *Shakespeare and the Eighteenth Century*. Ed. Peter Sabor and Paul Yachnin. London: Routledge, 2008. 29–41.

McLuskie, Kathleen. "The patriarchal bard: Feminist criticism and Shakespeare: *King Lear* and *Measure for Measure*." In *Political Shakespeare*. Ed. Jonathan Dollimore and Alan Sinfield, 1985; Manchester: Manchester University Press, 1994. 88–108.

Meredith, George. "An essay on comedy." In *Comedy*. Ed. Wylie Sypher. New York: Doubleday, 1956. 3–57.

Montagu, Elizabeth. *An Essay on the Writings and Genius of Shakespeare…, 1769*. Vol. 1, *Bluestocking Feminism*. Ed. Elizabeth Eger. London: Pickering and Chatto, 1999.

Nietzsche, Friedrich. *The Birth of Tragedy*. Trans. Walter Kaufmann. New York: Random House, 1967.

Poole, Adrian. "Falstaff's belly, Bertie's kilt, Rosalind's legs: Shakespeare and the Victorian prince." *Shakespeare Survey* 56 (2003): 126–136.

Pope, Alexander. *Preface to Shakespeare*. In *Four Centuries of Shakespearian Criticism*. Ed. Frank Kermode. New York: Avon, 1965. 64–74.

Prince, Kathryn. "Shakespeare in the periodicals." *Shakespeare in the Nineteenth Century*. Ed. Gail Marshall. Cambridge: Cambridge University Press, 2012. 60–75.

Puttenham, George. *The Art of English Poesy*. Ed. Frank Whigham and Wayne A. Rebhorn. Ithaca: Cornell University Press, 2007.

Richman, David. *Laughter, Pain, and Wonder*. Newark: University of Delaware Press, 1990.

Roberts, Sasha. "Reading Shakespeare's tragedies of love…" In *A Companion to Shakespeare's Works, Volume 1*. Ed. Richard Dutton and Jean Howard. London: Blackwell, 2003. 108–133.

Rowe, Katherine. "Minds in company: Shakespearean tragic emotions." In *A Companion to Shakespeare's Works, Volume 1*. Ed. Richard Dutton and Jean Howard. London: Blackwell, 2003. 47–71.

Schlegel, Augustus William. *Lectures on Dramatic Art and Literature*. Trans. John Black. London: George Bell & Sons, 1879.

Schopenhauer, Arthur. *The World as Will and Representation*. 2 vols. Trans. E. F. J. Payne. 1958; New York: Dover, 1969.

Sidney, Sir Philip. *An Apology for Poetry*. In *Criticism: The Major Texts*. Ed. W. J. Bate. 1952; New York: Harcourt, 1970.

Skinner, Quentin. *Reason and Rhetoric in the Philosophy of Hobbes*. Cambridge: Cambridge University Press, 1996.

Steggle, Matthew. *Laughing and Weeping in Early Modern Theatres*. Aldershot: Ashgate, 2007.

Strier, Richard. *The Unrepentant Renaissance*. Chicago: University of Chicago Press, 2011.

Tillyard, E. M. W. *The Elizabethan World Picture*. New York: Macmillan, 1944.

Whitney, Charles. *Early Responses to Renaissance Drama*. Cambridge: Cambridge University Press, 2006.

1 Emotion

Plot

One of the main things that makes Shakespeare's plays special is their power to make people feel particular emotions: pity, sympathy, compassion, sadness, fear, horror. But what is it about the plays that enables them to do this? What is the source of this power? The most important aspect of the tragedies (and some of the histories, such as *Richard II*) that accounts for this power is the nature of the actions and events that are represented.

We sympathize with and pity some of the characters because they suffer and, in the end, die, but the depth of our sympathy for them depends in part on whether or not we feel they deserve such an end, whether or not it seems just. In those cases where we feel the suffering and death of the characters are in some way deserved or just, whatever sympathy we have for them may well be tempered. When the bodies of Goneril and Regan are produced at the end of *King Lear*, for example, Albany speaks for many when he observes, "this judgement of the heavens, that makes us tremble, / Touches us not with pity" (5.3.233–4); he continues to do so when, in response to the news that the villain Edmund is dead, he tersely states, "that's but a trifle here" (5.3.314). Because we feel they get what they deserve, we have little compassion for the suffering and death of these characters, even though Edmund does ultimately show signs of remorse. Even our sympathy for Gloucester and Lear may cool if we agree with Gloucester's son Edgar when he observes at the end of the play, "the gods are just, and of our pleasant vices / Make instruments to plague us" (5.3.182–3).

Similarly, in *Romeo and Juliet*, whatever sympathies we have for the dead Lady Montague and the surviving, grieving parents of the young lovers at the end of the play are tempered by the fact that, as the Prince observes, "heaven" has punished them for their long-standing enmity that has caused discord in Verona (5.3.300–4). Many have claimed that they sympathize with Macbeth, but do we not sympathize less for him than for other protagonists in light of the fact that his destruction seems fair enough in light of the terrible things he has done? And I think it is in part because we feel that he gets what he deserves that we feel little pity for Richard III when he is killed on the battlefield at the end of *Richard III*—that is one of the reasons most people now reject the early classification of the play as a tragedy (in the first printed editions of it) in favor of the 1623 folio's classification of it as a history play.

But in those cases where we feel they really do not deserve to suffer and die as they do, our sympathy for the characters can run deep: as Aristotle observes, we feel pity "for a person undeserving of his misfortune" (16). It is in part because the *casualties* of the main protagonists' actions are innocent and therefore do not deserve to suffer and die as they do that their deaths may move us so deeply—I'm thinking of Desdemona in *Othello*, Ophelia in *Hamlet*, and Portia in *Julius Caesar*. And since, even given their faults, it seems that protagonists who have served their political societies well and are deeply committed to them—such as Brutus and Coriolanus—do not deserve to be destroyed by those societies, we may well feel for them. The sweet prince, Hamlet, can move us in part because it seems so unfair that his efforts to set things right in his family and country end in his own death. Though he has his failings and commits a terrible murder, Othello, too, has moved audiences because he is the victim of Iago's plots against him and he does not deserve to be deceived and destroyed as he is. That the world in which the characters suffer is unjust is also arguably the case in *Lear*, in spite of Edgar's comment on the matter, and in spite of the fact that the cruel sisters and Edmund are all destroyed in the end. For as Lear observes, "I am a man / More sinned against than sinning" (2.2.56–7); Gloucester more directly asserts, "as flies to wanton boys are we to th' gods: / They kill us for their sport" (4.1.41–2). This perspective on human suffering and death seems confirmed by the mutilation and death of Gloucester (even if he is lecherous), the death of Lear (even if he is foolish), and the murder of Cordelia. Samuel Johnson was so deeply moved and upset by this ending because it seemed to him to bear out Gloucester's conviction that human suffering was the product of a universe that was *not* governed by principles of justice, much less benevolence to mankind.

In cases where the protagonists do not deserve to suffer and die, they are in an important sense innocent, victims of other people, even *sacrifices*. That our word "tragedy" derives from *tragos*, ancient Greek for goat (one of the animals used in ancient sacrificial ritual), is just one of many reasons scholars think that western tragedy originated in and represented some kind of sacrificial rite (Burkert, Frye). In some Shakespearean tragedies, this sacrificial dimension of the suffering and death of the protagonists and some of the other characters is explicitly asserted by the characters themselves. At the end of *Romeo and Juliet*, for example, Capulet refers to the dead lovers as "poor sacrifices of our enmity" (5.3.314). In the final scene of *Lear*, the old king observes, "upon such sacrifices, my Cordelia, / The gods themselves throw incense" (5.3.22–3). Because he thinks Desdemona is lying about the handkerchief, Othello regards what he intends to do as "a murder, which [he] thought a sacrifice"—as though if she *was* telling the truth, as indeed she was, it really would be a sacrifice (5.2.75). In *Julius Caesar*, Brutus encourages the conspirators and the audience to see Caesar as the sacrificial victim when, opposing Cassius' suggestions that they kill Antony along with Caesar, he exclaims, "let's be sacrificers, but not butchers, Caius" (2.1.173), and then, after the deed, encourages all the conspirators to stoop and bathe in Caesar's blood. But that Brutus himself may be the real sacrifice is suggested when, shortly before his own death, he sees himself as another kind of animal that served as a sacrificial victim in ancient ritual: a "lamb" (4.3.1009). So, too, does Menenius in *Coriolanus* describe his friend and hero, Coriolanus, as a "lamb" (2.1.5–10). That description is in line with the designation of Coriolanus as a single man who paid the price required to save the rest of the nobles, which Shakespeare may have found in one of his main sources for the play (Philemon Holland's English translation of the ancient historian Livy's *History of Rome*). This sacrificial aspect of the action may well give rise to experiences beyond sympathy, since sacrifice often involves ritual, purification, and the satisfaction of the gods. But be it sacrificial or no, the destruction of Shakespeare's protagonists can move us because they are in many cases innocent, and they do not deserve to be destroyed.

It would be bad enough if the protagonists injured and killed people they didn't know, or those who had always been their enemies, and if they themselves were destroyed by strangers or long-time enemies. But many of the acts of violence which cause pain and death in the tragedies are committed either by people against members of their own family with whom they had had decent relations, or by people against those with whom they are or had been friends. Tybalt is a Capulet, but he is also the newlywed Romeo's cousin-in-law, which is one reason Romeo protests just before he kills him, "I never injured thee, / But love thee better than thou canst devise" (3.1.56–7). Othello is fatally deceived by a fellow soldier, a man he promoted to the rank of lieutenant, a man he thinks has "such noble sense of [his] friend's wrong" (5.1.34); he then strangles his beloved wife who loves him until the bitter end. In *Hamlet*, Claudius kills his brother, marries his former sister-in-law, and conspires to have his nephew killed. Hamlet is cruel to Ophelia, whom he avers to have loved, and he speaks daggers to his own mother with whom he seems to have enjoyed a decent relationship before her hasty marriage with his uncle, whom he kills. He also kills Laertes, a man he claims ever to have loved, but who conspired to kill him in order to avenge his father Polonius' death.

In *Lear*, Gloucester's bastard son, Edmund, conspires against his own half-brother, Edgar, and is complicit in the mutilation and death of his father, which Edgar avenges by killing Edmund. Lear's own daughters mistreat him and their youngest sister in ways that result in the death of both of them; Goneril poisons her sister Regan before killing herself. Caesar appears to find the *coup de grace* so shocking because it is delivered by Brutus, who loved and admired Caesar (1.2.88), and who was loved by Caesar (1.3.301). In *Antony and Cleopatra*, Octavius Caesar weeps over the death of Antony that he himself has brought about, for Antony, his competitor, was also his

> Friend and companion in the front of war,
> The arm of mine own body, and the heart
> Where mine his thoughts did kindle....
> (5.1.50–4)

And in *Coriolanus*, Aufidius, who seems genuinely to have set aside his long-standing enmity and embraced the banished Coriolanus as a new friend and ally, soon turns against him and has him killed. It is all something out of a Greek tragedy, as they say.

But think about why Shakespeare, following the Greeks, sets it up this way. Do you hope and expect that those bound to you by blood and friendship will treat you well? When they do otherwise, are you more deeply injured than you would have been had strangers treated you in this way? If you know how painful it can be to have family and friends turn on you, how painful it can be to feel compelled to turn against your friends and relatives, then you know the pain of some of Shakespeare's protagonists. You may therefore be inclined to sympathize with and have compassion for them, which is one of the things Shakespeare wants you to feel.

In some of the tragedies, another aspect of the action that deepens the pathos is that the protagonists commit extreme acts of violence on the basis of mistaken beliefs—had they known better, they would not have acted as they did. Thus, Othello orders Cassio to be killed and he kills Desdemona in the mistaken belief that they are lovers. Poor Romeo kills himself thinking that Juliet, under the influence of the sleeping potion, is really dead, while Antony kills himself under the delusion that Cleopatra is dead. In *Julius Caesar*, Cassius orders his own death, mistakenly thinking his friend Titinius had been taken by Antony's forces, and unaware that Brutus' forces had in fact defeated those of Octavius. But at least Cassius and Romeo are spared an awareness of the mistaken belief on which they acted. Othello and Antony are not so lucky: they must also suffer, but not for long, the knowledge that they acted on erroneous beliefs.

Another aspect of the plot of the tragedies that accounts for their special power to pull at our heartstrings is the movement of the protagonist from states of integration with community to a condition of isolation. The isolation of the protagonist is often discussed in connection with *character*, but I think there is an important sense in which this isolation is part of the *plot* of Shakespearean tragedy: what *happens* in Shakespearean tragedy is that a person becomes isolated, and then perishes in that isolation. But you can end up being alone in a lot of different ways for a lot of different reasons, and it is crucial to see how and why Shakespeare's protagonists end up this way. Often, they do not seek their isolation. They end up this way because the societies in which they exist are diminished and corrupt, the protagonists themselves have various moral failings, and they are uncompromising in a commitment to a duty, an ambition, a love, an ideal, or the very society that excludes them. It is in part because we see them enter a condition of isolation *in this way* and *for these reasons* that we feel for them.

This movement is often officially proclaimed and enforced, imagined and described in the most graphic ways, and observed by the characters themselves. Thus, civic officials banish Romeo and Coriolanus from their cities, while in *Julius Caesar* Brutus is chased from his city by the plebeian mob. Hamlet is a little different, since he is isolated from the very start. But in *Romeo and Juliet*, we have a stark dramatization of the protagonist *becoming* isolated. After Juliet's mother has informed her that a match has been arranged with Paris, her father and the Nurse enter, so that all four are onstage. In the face of her opposition to the match, her father berates her and leaves the stage. In response to her appeal for pity, her mother rebukes her and leaves the stage. In response to her appeal for "some comfort," the Nurse recommends that she forget Romeo and go with Paris, and, after a few more words, she leaves the stage. Juliet remains on stage, alone, and though she would like to be on good terms with her family, she is separated from it from this time forth. True, she resolves to go to the Friar, but this scene is still a stark dramatization of a particular way in which a good person can end up alone—in this case, as a result of others physically leaving her. And even after she goes to the Friar, who counsels her and formulates a plan, she knows she is on her own: "My dismal scene I needs must act alone" (4.3.20). Her suicide is the final dismal scene, and it is all the more moving because, the Friar having fled the tomb, she acts alone.

In *Antony and Cleopatra*, we again observe people abandoning the protagonist, but for different reasons. Under the influence of the Egyptian queen, Antony makes what, in the eyes of the experienced military men around him, are poor military decisions; he then behaves shamefully at Actium, thereby giving "example" to his men to fly. Antony himself bids his attendants who remain to flee to Caesar: "Let that be left / Which leaves itself" (3.11.20–1). Though his closest follower and admirer Enobarbus stays behind for the moment, he too decides to "leave him" (3.13.233), and the soldiers who remain then hear music which they take to be a sign that "the god Hercules, whom Antony loved, / Now leaves him" (4.3.21–2). He still has one last hurrah on the battlefield, but when his fleet yields to Caesar, he again commands all who remain to leave him, and he falls on his sword alone.

In some of the other plays, the protagonists take a more active role in bringing about their own isolation, though it is still not the condition they really seek. Pursuing his ambition and driven by fear, Macbeth, for example, imagines himself as a man wading alone, of his own volition, further and further out into a sea of blood (3.4.157–9). In *Lear*, the enraged old king calls for horse, flees Gloucester's residence, charges out onto the heath, and rages alone in the storm (though still attended by the fool and Kent). At the end of this play, we have a variation on this kind of action. After Edmund commands officers to take Lear and Cordelia away, Lear imagines the condition of isolation as one of happiness: "Come, let's away to prison. / We two alone will sing like birds i'th'cage" (5.3.10–11).

In *Coriolanus*, before he is banished, the protagonist acts in a way that directly results in his isolation, though that is not the result he seeks: exercising his courage and valor, he leads the charge into an enemy city while his men, not as valiant as he is, stand back and watch him. The word "alone" then booms throughout the entire play, from these opening scenes in which a soldier observes, "He is himself alone, / To answer all the city" (1.4.59), through the banishment scene that results in the hero leaving Rome "alone, / Like to a lonely dragon" (4.1.31), up to the very end of the play where Coriolanus emphatically reminds the Volscians that "like an eagle in a dovecote, I / Fluttered your Volscians in Corioles. / Alone I did it" (5.6.130–2). Here we see that, in the minds of some characters, enduring isolation and acting alone is a mark of valor, dignity, and fortitude and therefore something of which one is rightly proud. Earlier in this play, Menenius explicitly makes this point: in response to the conniving tribune Brutus' observation that he is not alone in criticizing Martius, the patrician Menenius observes of the tribunes, "I know you can do very little alone, for your helps are many or else your actions would grow wondrous single: your abilities are too infant-like for doing much alone" (2.1.26). Seeing protagonists such as Juliet, Lear, Macbeth, Antony, and Coriolanus *respond* in valiant fashion to being alone, we perhaps admire them. But are you not also moved to strong feelings of sympathy when you see that, after suffering and responding heroically to an isolation they do not seek, they perish all alone?

Finally, Aristotle felt that if you are in the business of making people feel sympathy, compassion, and pity for your characters, it is essential not just to make them suffer and die in the end, but also to make that ending seem probable, if not necessary, given what goes before. So that if, at the end of what is billed as a tragedy, you are sitting there looking upon the dead protagonist and saying to yourself, "gee, I didn't see that coming," you could not feel the intense emotion that tragedy should make you feel. If this is so, then one last thing about the plots of Shakespeare's tragedies that qualifies them to make us feel this kind of intense emotion is that the endings seem probable, if not necessary, given what goes before (and given our own pre-existing ideas about how people behave).

One of the things that makes the catastrophes seem probable is just that many of the characters, including the protagonists themselves, often *say* they are going to occur. *Romeo and Juliet*, for example, begins with the chorus informing us that Romeo and Juliet will die. Even before he meets Juliet at the party, Romeo expresses a foreboding sense that he will suffer an "untimely death" (1.4.); after he kills Tybalt he claims, "this but begins the woe others must end" (3.1.106). On hearing Romeo is banished for having killed Tybalt, Juliet claims "I'll to my wedding-bed, / And death, not Romeo, take my maidenhead!" (3.2.140–1); after their one night together, she exclaims, "O God, I have an ill-diving soul! / Methinks I see thee, now thou art so low, / As one dead in the bottom of a tomb" (3.5.54–6). From then on, she repeatedly asserts she will exert her own "power to die" if she cannot be with Romeo (3.5.254). Upon being informed Juliet is dead, Romeo says, "Well, Juliet, I will lie with thee tonight" (5.1.36); having procured the poison, he commands it to go with him "to Juliet's grave, for there must I use thee" (5.1.89).

In *Macbeth*, both Lady Macbeth and Macbeth speak in the future tense throughout the play about their own demise. In *Antony and Cleopatra*, Antony may well be thinking of suicide when he commands his followers to leave him and announces he is "resolved upon a course" immediately after having turned tail at the battle of Actium (near the end of Act 3). When his fleet then defects to Octavius Caesar, he announces he will never see another sunrise and speaks much of dying before he finally does finally die at his own hands, at the end of Act 4. Even before he dies, Cleopatra announces from her monument, "I will never go from hence" (4.15.1), and repeatedly asserts from then on that she will kill herself before finally doing it. And in *Coriolanus*, after he has been banished, the protagonist foresees two possible outcomes, one of which is his own demise: he "will or [either] exceed the common, or be caught / With cautelous [deceitful] baits and practice" (4.1.29). Aufidius confidently predicts the latter outcome: "when, Caius, Rome is thine, / Thou art poor'st of all; then shortly art thou mine" (4.7.51). Immediately after his mother Volumnia persuades him not to sack Rome, Coriolanus observes, "Most dangerously you have with him [Coriolanus] prevailed, / If not most mortal to him. But let it come" (5.3.194).

True, saying that it will come does not necessarily mean it will come, but these dark prophesies that run throughout the tragedies make the final destruction seem a little more likely, I think. Moreover, in many cases, the protagonists are not merely saying their own destruction will occur; they are also asserting either a *resignation* to it, or an outright *will* to it, at least under certain conditions. And once we see that they are either resigned to death, or determined to bring it upon themselves, we feel it is highly likely that it will come.

The probability or necessity of the endings of the plays also derives from the way Shakespeare creates a certain kind of environment or world, and places characters of a certain kind within it: in many cases, he creates familial, social, and political environments that are corrupt, degraded, or extremely dangerous, and then places morally elevated, passionate, and uncompromising people within them (as we will see in more detail later). What are the chances that two high-minded, impetuous young lovers from two different families will do well in a city that is torn apart by the violent feuding between those families? What are the chances that Othello, a man who "is of a free and open nature, / That thinks men honest that but seem to be so" (1.3.388–89), will do well in a contained environment that is managed by a brilliant villain who hates him and who seems to be honest but isn't? What are the chances that a noble, young prince will do well in a corrupt court overseen by a voluptuous, cunning, ambitious, murderous king? What are the chances that intemperate, magnanimous lovers like Antony and Cleopatra are going to be a match for the ruthless and calculating Octavius Caesar? What are the chances that Coriolanus, a staunch aristocrat whose "heart's his mouth" (3.1.302) and who despises the populace of his city, will do well in that city when its fickle populace is subject to resentful, conniving, slanderous, self-serving demagogues such as Sicinius and Brutus? What are the chances that Brutus, a man who is honest to a fault, will do well in an extremely dangerous political environment where even his friends conspire against him?

I think your answers to these questions will depend in part on your view of the world: if you are an optimist and are seeing these plays for the first time, you might preserve hope for the protagonists until the bitter end. But many I think would respond to all of these questions with, "not good!" And if this is what we feel as we watch the action unfold, we have a growing sense of not just the *inevitability* of the protagonists' destruction, but also their *helplessness*: given what they are and what their world is, nothing can help them or prevent their destruction. True, we may well feel that they need not be destroyed in precisely the way they are destroyed, but it seems that, one way or the other, they will be destroyed. Seeing that they are doomed, in spite of their own freedoms, exceptional powers, and valiant efforts, we pity them.

As for *fear*, I think it is useful to distinguish between fear for the characters and fear for ourselves. Many of the aspects of the plot of the plays that account for our sympathy and pity for the characters also enter into the causes of the fear we experience when we read or see performances of Shakespeare's history and tragedies, insofar as that fear is fear for the characters. For if we did not develop at least some degree of sympathy for them before they are destroyed, we would not be apprehensive about and fear for them. Sympathizing with them for the reasons we have observed, we also see that they are threatened and endangered, and that it is highly probable if not necessary that they will be destroyed. And seeing this, we fear for them—though this fear is perhaps stronger the first time we read or see a performance of the play and may be diminished if we *know* they will be destroyed.

Hegel suggests that when he was discussing the function of tragedy, Aristotle was not, or at least ought not to have been, speaking of the audience's fear for a character; neither was he speaking of "mere fear" grounded in the perception of a specific, immediate danger to our own personal safety. Aristotle was or ought to have been speaking of "fear of the ethical order" that the protagonist has violated:

> what a man has really to fear is not an external power and oppression by it, but the might of the ethical order which is one determinant of his own free reason and is at the same time that eternal and inviolable something which he summons up against himself if once he turns against it.
> (1198)

If this is so, then the plots of Shakespeare's plays would be qualified to cause this feeling in the audience insofar as they intimate the existence of an eternal, mighty, and inviolable ethical order that opposes and punishes anyone who turns against it.

Over the last four hundred years, many have argued that the plots of the histories and tragedies often point to some kind of ethical world order. One reason for this is that many characters in the plays explicitly observe, often in light of their experience, that the world is ordered by certain basic laws, principles, or agents—be they natural or supernatural. In *Richard III*, for example, after having helped the villainous Richard to the throne, and immediately prior to being executed on Richard's orders, Buckingham observes that the world is governed by a "high All-seer." Having "dallied" with God, and seeing that he will now be executed, Buckingham concludes, "thus doth He [God] force the swords of wicked men / To turn their own points in their masters' bosoms" (5.1.23–4). In *Romeo and Juliet*, the Friar announces what seems to be an ethical law of the world when he observes that "these violent delights have violent ends / And in their triumph die, like fire and powder, / Which as they kiss consume" (2.5.11–13). At the end of the play, the prince sternly tells Montague and Capulet that the violent ends that have indeed materialized amount to a form of punishment meted out by heaven:

> See, what a scourge is laid upon your hate,
> That heaven finds means to kill your joys with love.
> And I for winking at your discords too
> Have lost a brace of kinsmen: all are punished.
> (5.3.300–4)

In *Julius Caesar*, the natural world seems to be responding to the situation in Rome since, while the conspirators meet during the night to plot the assassination of Caesar, "all the sway of earth / Shakes like a thing unfirm," and a number of strange, wondrous, fearful events are observed in the city (1.3.3–13). Casca and Cassius agree that these events in the natural world indicate that human affairs are indeed monitored by and subject to the heavens and the gods—but they argue over whether the problem is Caesar, the servility of Romans, or the conspirators themselves. When, in *Macbeth*, the protagonist is considering murdering the king, he speculates that the world is subject to "judgment" and governed by an "even-handed justice" according to which evil deeds in some way destroy those who commit them (1.7.7–12). Several characters observe that, on the night of the murder, the natural world is disrupted, something Ross takes to show that "the heavens, as troubled with man's act, / Threatens his bloody stage" (2.4.6–7). After ordering the murder of Banquo and seeing his ghost, Macbeth observes another ethical principle that seems to operate in his world: "it will have blood, they say: blood will have blood" (3.5.142). The virtuous Malcolm, meanwhile, sees himself and his allies as "instruments" that are put on by "the powers above" with the aim of destroying the tyrant, Macbeth (4.3.273–4).

In *Hamlet*, near the end, the young prince expresses his sense that things are not happening arbitrarily, but in accordance with some higher being or order: recounting his experience on the ship to Horatio, he observes, "there's a divinity that shapes our ends, / Rough-hew them how we will" and that "heaven [was] ordinant" in the affair (5.2.52). He later observes, "there's a special providence in the fall of a sparrow. If it be now, 'tis not to come: if it be not to come, it will be now: if it be not now, yet it will come" (5.2.150–2). And in the final scene of this play, Laertes twice observes that events are fulfilling some kind of natural justice: when he is wounded by his own poisoned sword, he exclaims "I am justly killed with mine own treachery" (5.2.251); when Hamlet finally kills Claudius by forcing the poisoned potion down his throat, Laertes observes, "he is justly served: / It is a poison tempered by himself" (5.2.273–4). And in *Lear*, Albany responds to the news that a servant has killed Cornwall for his cruelty to Gloucester by observing, "this shows you are above, / You justices, that these our nether crimes / So speedily can venge" (4.2.54–6). And we have seen that he also interprets some of the carnage at the end of the play as a "judgement of the heavens" (5.3.233). True, these assessments of the world may well provide us with a kind of *consolation*—the consolation of knowing that our world is in some way governed by basic principles of justice. But that kind of consolation can coexist with the fear of an impersonal, objective, and punitive world order that many characters in the plays themselves claim to feel, and that Hegel claims the best of tragedies make the audience feel.

We are of course free to question and reject these characters' assessments of the events that have transpired and the worlds in which they exist. Many have done so, and, as we have seen, some of the characters themselves do so as well. In *Lear*, for example, Gloucester finds little justice in the gods who make him suffer, and Lear himself feels that he is more sinned against than sinning. Immediately after Albany promises to reward friends and punish foes, Lear again poignantly questions the fairness of his world when, holding his dead daughter in his arms, he asks, "Why should a dog, a horse, a rat have life, / And thou no breath at all?" (5.3.323–4). Coming to realize the villainy of Iago, and incredulous that the heavens have not punished it, Othello roars, "are there no stones in heaven / But what serves for the thunder?" (5.2.268–9). In the end, Macbeth seems to retract his observations concerning how justice operates in the world when he responds to the news of his wife's death with that marvelous nihilistic vision of life as a tale told by an idiot that signifies nothing. And after all, is not one of the reasons we pity the protagonists simply that their misfortune is undeserved and therefore unjust in some important sense? Insofar as we find the world of the plays to be one that is at least in some respects unjust, our fear that we are subject to some kind of mighty ethical order may well be compromised. But it is perhaps replaced by other fears, ones that also surface in the history of audience response to the plays: the fear of a world that is malevolent to us, the fear of a world that is not subject to any principles of justice, the fear that existence is meaningless and our lives ultimately amount to nothing.

Character

Hegel claims that in order for the misfortune of the protagonist "to arouse a tragic sympathy, he must be a man of worth and goodness himself. For it is only something of intrinsic worth which strikes the heart of a man of noble feelings and shakes it to its depths" (1198). I think the destruction of Shakespeare's protagonists—both men and women—has shaken to the depths the hearts of so many because they are all people of great worth or goodness. But of what does their great worth and goodness consist? One of its major components is *moral* goodness, or virtue. A good way of understanding this dimension of Shakespeare's characters is by considering them in relation to some of the virtues the ancient Roman, Cicero, identifies in one of the most respected and widely printed works of ethical thought in Shakespeare's England: *Of Duties*.

34 *Emotion*

None of Shakespeare's protagonists is a dope. As we will see in chapter 3, they possess, express, and in some cases acquire a considerable degree of wisdom. All of them are people of high spirit and courage: if they experience fear—and some of them do—they overcome it and ultimately go through with their plan, be it to drink a potion, kill someone, confront witches and ghosts, fight on the battlefield, or kill themselves. The military men—Brutus, Macbeth, Othello, Coriolanus, Antony—display the closely related virtue of fortitude: the ability to withstand pain and to carry on in spite of it. With the exception of Macbeth, the protagonists are generally honest (at least with their allies), and averse to engaging in forms of duplicity and deceit, though they will do so against their enemies and in the service of their dominant passions. Most of the protagonists—including Juliet, Romeo, Brutus, Lear, Othello, Antony, and Coriolanus—have a keen sense of justice, and most are motivated by it, however mistaken they may be in their views of what justice is and how best to serve it. None of them is covetous: those who have or acquire wealth and property (such as Lear, Coriolanus, Othello, Cleopatra, and Antony) liberally share it, give it away, or scorn it. With the exception of Antony and Cleopatra, none is licentious. Though Brutus might be a touch self-righteous and Antony and Cleopatra melodramatic and self-aggrandizing, I would not say that any of them are vain or arrogant.

Cicero sees wisdom, courage, fortitude, justice, liberality, and honesty as virtues for human beings in part because he thinks human beings need them in order to fulfill their natural inclination to fellowship and their duties to their political society. Many of Shakespeare's heroes display this civic-mindedness and patriotism, and they often act with what Cicero regards as the best of intentions—those of serving one's political society. Thus in *Julius Caesar*, Brutus participates in the conspiracy to assassinate Caesar and then raises an army against Rome, with the intention of saving the republic which he sees as the foundation of Roman freedom, justice, and greatness. As Antony claims at the end of this play, Brutus acted not out of envy of Caesar but "in a general honest thought / And common good to all" (5.5.76–7). Coriolanus fights so well and opposes the plebeians and their tribunes out of a genuine concern to serve Rome, which he thinks ought to maintain the *original* republican constitution.

Though he acts in part to avenge his father's murder, Hamlet also acts with the intention of setting things right in the corrupt court that governed his nation, Denmark. Othello modestly observes that he "has done the state some service" (5.2.382), and he at least says that one reason he killed his wife was to serve justice and prevent her from betraying more men: "naught I did in hate, but all in honor," he avers before killing himself (5.2.333). Lear divides and parcels out his kingdom in order to divest himself of "all cares and business" (1.1.30), but also to prevent "future strife" between his children (1.1.35). As Cordelia later observes of herself and her father, "We are not the first / Who with best meaning have incurred the worst" (5.3.4–5). The "tyrant" Macbeth is an exception here, as are Romeo and Juliet, since they are almost entirely preoccupied with their passion for each other, yet even they display some awareness of Friar Laurence's perspective on their match as a means of ending the feud and improving civic life in their city, Verona. Almost all of these protagonists act at least in part with the intention of benefiting their political societies, and they exercise a wide range of virtues in doing so. That they often not only fail to achieve that intention but also destroy themselves and damage their political societies in pursuing them makes this destruction all the more lamentable.

Shakespeare's protagonists also display some of the Christian virtues, as laid out in the New Testament. One of the things some of the minor scenes away from the main action of these plays do is to fill out the emotional profile of the protagonists and serve as occasions for them to display their capacity for love, charity, care, friendship, and affection for others. Though he gets what he deserves, I must say that I start to feel sorry for Richard II when, after he has been deposed and is being led as a prisoner through the streets of London to the Tower, he displays such affection and compassion for his wife, the Queen—it is a very touching scene of parting. In *Julius Caesar*, the scenes with his wife Portia and his boy Lucilius, show that the "gentle" Brutus is capable of these more tender passions, and he displays his capacity for friendship with other men throughout the play. The hard man Coriolanus displays care and affection for his wife, mother, and son, as well as mercy towards Rome at large: as Menenius observes in the face of the Volscian onslaught led by Coriolanus, "we are all undone, unless / The noble man have mercy" (4.6.129–30). He ultimately does "show mercy to his country" that banished him, as Cominius puts it (5.1.82), mainly because Volumnia's eloquence makes his "eyes to sweat compassion" (5.3.209). Lear is, as Kent observes, an "old kind king" (3.1.22) who at the outset cares for all of his daughters and who displays profound affection and love for Cordelia in the end. His compassion for his fool and, indeed, all "poor naked wretches" during the storm out on the heath endears him to us, as does his regret that he had "taken too little care" of them while king (3.4. 31–6). We see the softer side of Hamlet when he fondly remembers his childhood happiness with Yorick; while sharp-tongued and ultimately deadly to his false friends, Rosencrantz and Guildenstern, he displays his affability with the players, and shows admiration and affection for his true friend, Horatio. And in *Antony and Cleopatra*, Antony's capacity for friendship and amity with other men is ever-present, and it sets him apart from Octavius Caesar, while the imperious Cleopatra still displays care and affection for her "noble girls" throughout the play (4.15.96).

While it might not figure in the old tables of virtue, a sense of humor is for many an endearing quality. I think it is important to notice the lively sense of humor that is displayed by some protagonists in the histories and tragedies. Though Hal in *Henry IV, part 1*, is cold and calculating, and his humor is often at the expense of others, he still appreciates Falstaff's wit and gaiety. When Romeo is Romeo, and not groaning for love, he is, as Mercutio observes, "sociable," witty, and fun to be around (2.3.67–9). One of the ways Hamlet deals with the corruption of the court is by joking and exercising his dark and cynical sense of humor, often at the expense of others. At times even Lear has to laugh along with his fool. In *Antony and Cleopatra*, the good old boy, Antony, knows how to drink and have a laugh with his men, while Cleopatra finds humor in practical jokes, her lovers, sexual banter with her servants, catty insults of her competitors, and her own melodramatic self.

So Shakespeare's protagonists are thus morally good, but they are not too good to be human. Many obviously come up short on the count of justice. *Ignoring* the acute sense of justice he expresses early in the play, Macbeth, for example, proceeds to commit gross acts of injustice; Lear unfairly divides his kingdom; Othello commits an act of gross injustice. The justice of other protagonists is questionable, and, indeed, a matter of ongoing debate in the plays themselves: Coriolanus has a highly contentious view of what a just distribution of political power and corn would be, while Brutus in *Julius Caesar* debates with himself and others the justice of the assassination of Caesar.

As many of the characters in the plays themselves observe, the protagonists also often come up short on the count of temperance or moderation, another important virtue that Cicero discusses under the heading of *decorum* (seemliness). Thus, seeing the lovers' inclination to excessive, extreme passion and behavior, Friar Laurence cautions Romeo "to love moderately" (2.5.14); later, when he sees Romeo ready to kill himself after he has been banished, he chastises him and says, "I thought thy disposition better tempered" (3.3.118). In *Coriolanus*, Sicinius the tribune observes that Coriolanus "cannot temp'rately transport his honours / From where he should begin and end" (2.1.187); "you are too absolute" Volumnia quite reasonably tells her son (3.2.49), as she and Menenius attempt to persuade him to behave "mildly" (3.2); the tribunes know very well that "being once chafed, he cannot / Be reined again to temperance" (3.3.34–5); after Coriolanus has been banished, Menenius laments that things might have been much better "if / He could have temporized" (4.6.17–18). And in the opening scene of *Antony and Cleopatra*, Antony's follower, Philo, observes how Antony's excessive passion for the Egyptian queen governs him: "His captain's heart... reneges all temper / And is become the bellows and the fan / To cool a gipsy's lust" (1.1.6–10). Commenting upon her affairs with other men, Antony says to Cleopatra, "though you can guess what temperance should be, / You know not what it is" (3.13.146–7). Drawing on the English lexicon that served to translate ancient Roman ethical treatises such as Cicero's *Of Duties*, all of these characters identify ways in which the tragic protagonists are lacking in the virtue of temperance.

As we will see in chapter 3, these protagonists possess, express, and in some cases acquire a considerable degree of wisdom, another of the principal virtues for Cicero, but they are also unwise and imprudent in important respects, or they at least act against their better wisdom on many occasions, as those around them often point out. Thus, the impassioned young lovers lack the wisdom that might allow them to negotiate successfully their dangerous situation in Verona. Macbeth lacks the wisdom to understand how he, his wife, and the world will react to the killing. "Brutus is wise," Portia says to her husband (2.1.269), yet Brutus is also unwise and imprudent in thinking that all will be well if he spares Antony, allows him to speak at Caesar's funeral, and takes him on at Phillipi—Cassius is wiser and more prudent on all three counts. In *Antony and Cleopatra*, Antony knows he needs to break his Egyptian fetters, but he doesn't, and he proceeds to make a series of bad military decisions in violation of the better wisdom of his officers. Coriolanus is wise to both the moral failings of the plebeians and the machinations of the tribunes against him, he has well-developed views on the Roman constitution, and he knows that his own behavior is endangering his own life—yet we would not say he is a wise man given the impetuous, reckless way in which he behaves. Othello lacks the wisdom to see what Iago is, and as he confesses at the end, he "loved not wisely" (5.2.387). In *Lear*, the fool sums up the situation rather well when he tells Lear shortly after he has divided his kingdom, "thou shouldst not have been old till thou hadst been wise" (1.5.33).

And while many of them display considerable capacities for charity, compassion, and kindness, Shakespeare's tragic protagonists are generally a far cry from being paragons of Christian virtue. None of the protagonists of the Roman plays of course is a hero of Christian faith, but neither are any of the protagonists of the plays set in Christian societies, such as fair Verona, medieval Scotland, early sixteenth-century Denmark, and Renaissance Venice—somewhat surprising from a playwright operating in Protestant Tudor and Stuart England. Patience is not the strong point of the tragic protagonists, most of whom are intemperate, impassioned people who are much more inclined to avenge injuries committed against them than to forgive them. Though he has some reservations grounded in Christian perspectives on prayer and the soul, and though he and Laertes forgive each other in the end, Hamlet finally avenges the death of his father by killing Claudius.

Romeo immediately avenges the death of Mercutio by killing his murderer, Tybalt, and when Paris later gets in his way, he kills him as well. Thinking of himself and his men as Christians who are superior to the "Turks" and "Ottomites," Othello appeals to his men's sense of "Christian shame" to end the "barbarous brawl" that breaks out between them on Cyprus (2.3.152–4). Yet as soon as Iago leads him to believe that Desdemona has committed adultery with Cassio, he is overcome by hatred and anger that drive him to cry for "revenge" and "vengeance" on both of them (3.3.487–527). Coriolanus avenges himself on his native city by leading its enemies against it—though he does finally relent. Neither do these protagonists display much in the way of Christian hope: Romeo, Juliet, Antony, and Cleopatra all hope that they shall be re-united with their lovers in death; Hamlet, Macbeth, and Othello display some Christian anxieties about the afterlife, but none displays much hope for salvation or a Second Coming.

Two more important characteristics that make the protagonists human and qualify them for our sympathies are the *potential* for outstanding achievement, and *actual* outstanding achievement. Because they are so young, Romeo, Juliet, and Hamlet have no record of outstanding achievement, but they show tremendous potential for it. As Ophelia laments in the face of the apparent madness of Hamlet,

> O what a noble mind is here o'erthrown!
> The courter's, soldier's, scholar's, eye, tongue, sword,
> Th' expectancy and rose of the fair state,
> The glass of fashion and the mould of form,
> Th'observed of all observers, quite quite down!
>   (3.1.148–52)

And as the young Fortinbras observes at the very end of the play, "he was likely, had he been put on, / To have proved most royal" (5.2.351–52). That richly endowed young people of whom so much is expected are destroyed makes their destruction seem such a terrible *waste*, and so perhaps even more punishing than the destruction of other older protagonists who at least have fulfilled much of their potential for greatness and been duly rewarded and honored for having done so. Most of these older male protagonists—Macbeth, Coriolanus, Othello, Brutus, Antony, and perhaps even Lear (5.3.288–9)—have actually achieved great things in the military and political arenas and in some cases continue to do so up until the end.

The worth and goodness of Shakespeare's protagonists also consist of their tremendous capacity for *emotion*, emotion so strong that, as we have seen, it can get the better of them. It might be an obvious point, but it is a very important one: one reason people are wiping away their tears at the end of a good performance of *Romeo and Juliet* is that Juliet shows them that she is animated not by what she calls "light love," but by what she calls "my true love's passion" (2.1.153–4). We feel so much for her because *she* feels so much—but also because she places supreme importance upon her passion and it governs her life. But it is not just love that she feels: she displays hope and anger on several occasions, and after having arranged with Friar Laurence to take the potion, she observes, "I have a faint cold fear thrills through my veins, / That almost freezes up the heat of life" (4.3.16–17). Realizing that she must go through with the plan all alone, she then for a moment fears that the Friar might be plotting against her, and that she might awaken in the tomb before Romeo gets there: "a fearful point!" she exclaims, as she then imagines dying of suffocation in the vault, going mad, or dashing her own brains out "with some great kinsman's bone, / As with a club" (4.3.15–55). Though she is hopeful, courageous, and resolute, the young Juliet is also beset by *fear*—and a powerful imagination—which further enriches her emotional and intellectual profile and qualifies her even more for our sympathies.

Shakespeare's other tragic lovers, Antony and Cleopatra, are also driven by a grand passion, though we might feel less for them because theirs is not a true love passion in its earliest stages, but the true love passion of people who have been around the block a few times and who have already gratified and enjoyed their passion for each other. Even though they lose political power, social standing, honor, glory, wealth, fame, and prestige that Romeo and Juliet never had, they perhaps evoke our sympathies less than the inexperienced, more idealistic young lovers who would never describe their one night together as man and wife as a "gaudy night," which is how Antony describes one of his many nights with Cleopatra (3.13.214).

That they are capable of such powerful and wide-ranging emotional experience also enters into our sympathy for those protagonists who commit terrible deeds—such as Macbeth and Othello. One of the reasons we might not have much sympathy for the main character in *Richard III* is that his emotional range is so limited: Richard displays so little fear, so few feelings of remorse, grief, depression as he lies, slanders, marries, and murders his way to the throne. True, in the end he displays some fear and remorse and is tormented by "conscience," but up until then he goes merrily on his way. This is not the case with Macbeth: right from the start he is prone to fear, and for some time following the murder he is tormented by fear, regret, even sorrow. Though, by the end, he claims "I have almost forgot the taste of fears" (5.5.9), how sad and desolate he sounds when he observes that he has "lived long enough," that his life is "fall'n into the sear, the yellow leaf," and that he will have no friends in his old age! (5.3.24–30). And rather than coldly going about the business of killing his adulterous wife, Othello is emotionally devastated by it, both before and after he does it: before, he is of course tormented by jealousy, wrath, anger, hatred; after, he is tormented by guilt, shame, grief, self-loathing, and as he weeps just before he kills himself, "the melting mood" (5.2.392). It is in part because he is subject to such a wide range of intense, overwhelming emotions, many of which are painful to him, that people can sympathize with him in spite of what he does.

Our word "compassion" derives from the Latin *com* (with) and *pati* (to suffer). As this derivation suggests, we pity and have compassion for others who suffer and experience pain. So that if we feel people are insensitive, thick-skinned, incapable of suffering or feeling pain, we might feel sorry for them, or perhaps look down on them, but we will not have much compassion for them: it takes two sufferers to suffer together. Though it might be clear from what has been said already, it is perhaps worth noting, finally, that another thing about Shakespeare's tragic protagonists that qualifies them as objects of our compassion is their capacity for exceptional pain and suffering, a capacity that is realized to the full. The enabling conditions of this pain and suffering are complex and manifold, but it is in part because they are so emotional, have such a strong sense of justice and self-worth, think so intently and relentlessly, are hyper-sensitive in some ways, and are so uncompromising and intemperate, that they can and do suffer in the extreme. Note that in many cases, the other characters in the plays observe this fact. At the end of *Romeo and Juliet*, for example, the Prince observes the suffering of those around him and observes that "never was a story of more woe / Than this of Juliet and her Romeo" (5.3.316–20). At the end of *Lear*, the remaining characters share and express an overwhelming sense that the old man has suffered more "upon the rack of this tough world" than anyone else has or will (5.3.290). It seems that one reason Hamlet wants Horatio to tell his story is that it is a story of *unusually* intense suffering and pain. And as Othello observes of himself at the end of the play, once made jealous he was "perplexed in the extreme" (5.2.389). The protagonists, in short, are not your average sufferers. It is because they have a capacity for *extreme* suffering and pain, one that is realized, that we may be stirred.

Our *fear* for the protagonists is to an important extent a function of these aspects of their character, but it is also a function of Shakespeare's graphic representation of another kind of character: individuals who embody unique combinations of cunning, intelligence, passion, linguistic brilliance, and malice and who lead both characters in the plays and critics over the centuries to use the terms "villain," "monster," and "evil" to describe them. Thus Hamlet must face the cunning, incestuous fratricide, Claudius, whom Hamlet regards as a "villain" and his "mighty opposite" (5.2.66). In *Othello* the principal external danger to the protagonist is embodied in Iago, a consummate villain whose resentment at being passed over for the rank of lieutenant and suspicions that Othello has committed adultery with his wife, Emilia, do not quite plumb the depths of his motives for destroying the Moor and injuring others around him. In *Lear* we have the evil sisters, Goneril and Regan, but also the bastard Edmund, another wonderful, highly intelligent and cunning villain who is driven by ambition, greed, resentment of his brother and a society that is governed by primogeniture. Shakespeare succeeds in making us fear for his protagonists in part because he succeeds in creating these magnificent villains who seek to destroy them. But though evil, they are not evil forces from another planet: Shakespeare endows them with thoughts, rationales, motives, feelings (that in some cases include remorse and shame for their evil deeds) in such a way that they still come across as being human, all too human.

In other plays, the extreme dangers that are faced by the tragic protagonists and that make us fear for them derive not so much from single individuals as from broader socio-political environments that are afflicted by deep-seated enmities and deadly conflicts. Though in *Romeo and Juliet* we have the hothead Tybalt, he is just part of a diminished socio-political environment at large, one in which "ancient grudge" has broken out "to new mutiny" with the result that "civil blood makes civil hands unclean" (1.1.3–4). That this ancient grudge was caused by merely "an airy word" (1.1.74) and that no one really seems to know or care about the causes of the enmity between the two families is just one more aspect of the situation that makes it seem so dangerous for the beautiful young lovers. In *Coriolanus*, the leader of Rome's official enemy poses a major threat to him, especially when, after Coriolanus has defeated him yet again in battle, Aufidius resolves to resort to dishonorable means in order to destroy him: "for where / I thought to crush him in an equal force, / True sword to sword, I'll potch at him some way / Or wrath or craft may get him" (2.1.13–16). The cacophonous, colloquial "potch," meaning to poke, is such a powerful linguistic expression of Aufidius' new determination to play dirty in order to destroy his long-standing enemy. But what is even more dangerous to Coriolanus is the socio-political condition of his city: Rome is an extremely dangerous place for a hot-headed, outspoken aristocrat such as Coriolanus since, as Shakespeare shows us from the opening scene of the play onwards, it is afflicted by the Conflict of the Orders (the conflict between the aristocrats and the plebeians)—and Shakespeare does not seem to share Machiavelli's view that that conflict was beneficial to the republic. Shakespeare rather shows that the plebeians are fickle and subject to demagoguery, and that their new-won official representatives in government, the tribunes, are cunning, slanderous, resentful demagogues who hate Coriolanus. The result is that even the situation *within* his own city is fraught with danger for him.

In *Julius Caesar*, we fear for Brutus, too, in part because we see how dangerous *his* Rome is, especially to men of integrity like him: the opening scenes of the play brilliantly evoke a city in which the fickle plebeians, having recently celebrated the republican Pompey, now celebrate the arrogant general who defeated him at Pharsalus and who, according to the tribunes, is now aspiring to "soar above the view of men, / And keep us all in servile fearfulness" (1.1.71–2). The danger of opposing such a man is brought home by the fact that these tribunes who refused to celebrate him are immediately "put to silence" (1.2.275). The conspiracy to assassinate him is thus, as Cassius says, "an enterprise / Of honourable dangerous consequence" (1.3.128–9). But the situation remains extremely dangerous for Brutus and all of the conspirators after the deed is done, for though Brutus might not think so, "the multitude" (3.1.182) is still fickle, prone to violence, and subject to the force of oratory, while Caesar's ambitious, eloquent, aggrieved ally, Antony, is determined to make the conspirators pay for their assassination. As Antony himself rightly observes, "here is a mourning Rome, a dangerous Rome" (3.1.307), one that is indeed deadly for the conspirators once Antony has turned the populace against them. Thus it is in part because Shakespeare is so good at embodying extremely potent threats and dangers to the protagonists—mainly in the form of individual villains or broader socio-political forces and circumstances—that we fear for them.

Aristotle thinks of tragic fear mainly in terms of *fear for ourselves*, and he claims that what makes us experience it is the representation of the destruction of "a person like ourselves" (16). He does not explain why this is the case, but he seems to think that, concerned for our own welfare, we fear that we ourselves may be destroyed when we see someone like us destroyed. If this is the case, then one thing that would account for the experience of this kind of fear is the basic verisimilitude of Shakespeare's characters—their truth to what humans are—which we have already observed, and which for Samuel Johnson and many others is *the* achievement of Shakespeare.

Thought

Shakespeare's protagonists' capacities to think, reason, and argue account in part for the power of the plays to give us the impression that we learn and acquire wisdom when we watch them (as we will see in more detail in chapter 3). But would we become so *emotionally* involved with them if they did not think, reason, and argue with themselves and others as they do—if they did not provide such marvelous displays of what Aristotle identifies as one of the six main components of tragedy and calls *dianoia* (usually translated as "thought," "reason," or "intellect")? Surely not. Rather than giving us automatons or goons who have no life of the mind, Shakespeare gives us characters who think, reason, and argue with themselves and others, in some cases to excess. This is one reason they come across to us as being real human beings who are interesting, engaging, and therefore candidates for our compassion.

But the particular way in which they think, reason, and argue also enters into their powers to move us. For one thing, characters such as Hamlet, Macbeth, Othello, and Brutus are *afflicted* by their wonderful minds. Even before he commits the murder, Macbeth observes to himself, "my thought, whose murder [enactment] yet is but fantastical, / Shakes so my single state of man / That function is smothered in surmise"; then he says to Banquo that "my dull brain was wrought with things forgotten" (1.3.149–63). Immediately after committing the deed, he tells his wife of his inability to say "amen" and of a voice he heard crying "sleep no more." She attempts to calm him by telling him that "these deeds must not be thought / After these ways," and that "you do unbend your noble strength to think / So brainsickly of things" (2.2.40–54). Later, Macbeth himself observes it is better to be dead "than on the torture of the mind to lie / In restless ecstasy" (3.2.21–4); "O, full of scorpions is my mind" he then exclaims (3.3.40). Othello, too, is afflicted by his mind. Once Iago has incited doubt and suspicion in him, Othello is indeed "on the rack" and will never again have a "tranquil mind" (3.3.372, 386).

In *Julius Caesar*, even before Cassius has sounded him out about Caesar, Brutus observes that he has been "vexed" by not just "passions" but also "conceptions only proper to myself," and that "Brutus has been with himself at war" (1.2.44–51). His wife, Portia, knows and says so: "you have some sick offence within your mind" (2.1.279). And even after having resolved to participate in the conspiracy, he observes, "Between the acting of a dreadful thing / And the first motion, all the interim is / Like a phantasma, or a hideous dream" (63–65). As for Hamlet, well, the young courtier seems incapable of calming his hyperactive mind until the very end. Seeing how these characters suffer as a result of their own thinking and reasoning that is intense, serious, powerful, and in some cases relentless and beyond their control, we feel for them—even if the scorpions of the mind are the result of contemplating foolish or terrible deeds, committing them, lacking self-control, or being in the grip of an all-consuming jealousy.

But the thinking of Shakespeare's characters also qualifies them to engage our sympathies because they often think and reason about their own particular situations and problems in light of propositions about a condition that they claim to share with us. They often claim to speak for and about humans in general. Consider, for example, Hamlet's famous soliloquy that begins with "To be or not to be…" (3.1.62–96). Hamlet here does not think in the first-person singular—"I" or "me" or "my." Neither does he think about a situation that only he is in. He thinks in the first-person plural—"we" and "us." And he concludes his meditation not with "thus conscience doth make a coward of *me*," but with "thus conscience doth make cowards of *us all*" (3.1.89). However much of a unique individual we may think he is, Hamlet thinks that he is typical, an individual who shares an ethical condition with *all* other human beings. This is one small reason so many readers and audiences find his thinking engaging and relevant to them.

This is also the case with Macbeth, even if he is a butcher and a tyrant. When, for example, he is thinking about killing Duncan, he thinks about a specific act which it would seem *he* would commit:

> If it were done when 'tis done, then 'twere well
> It were done quickly; if th'assassination
> Could trammel up the consequence and catch
> With his surcease success; that but this blow
> Might be the be-all and the end-all—here,
> But here, upon this bank and shoal of time....
> (1.7.1–6)

Surely Macbeth will continue with "I," to indicate what *he* would do if the act of killing the king would have no significant consequences. But no! He completes this long conditional sentence by saying what *we* would do:

> We'd jump the life to come. But in these cases
> We still have judgment here, that we but teach
> Bloody instructions, which being taught, return
> To plague th'inventor: this even-handed justice
> Commends th'ingredients of our poisoned chalice
> To our own lips.
> (1.7.7–12)

Suddenly not just Macbeth but "we" are involved: if killing the king had no long-term consequences, *we* would risk/overlook the afterlife. True, he might be using "we" to refer to just himself, or to himself and his wife, but that he is speaking of people in general becomes clear when he then refers to "these cases." This phrase indicates that he is thinking about not just one particular evil deed—killing Duncan—but evil deeds in general, and that his case is not unique but merely an instance of a *kind* of case that other people experience: his case is just one of "these cases" that other people encounter. Continuing to use first-person plural pronouns and adjectives ("we" and "our"), he then asserts a general proposition: judgment and justice are here, in this world, with the result that those who commit evil deeds in this world, such as assassinating kings, will suffer serious consequences: they will be plagued and poisoned. That goes not just for the Macbeths, but for all of us.

Similarly, in *Julius Caesar*, when Brutus is considering his participation in the conspiracy to assassinate Caesar, he does so in light of several general propositions. He begins with the old adage, "it is the bright day that brings forth the adder, / And that craves [requires] wary walking." After drawing the analogy between an adder drawn from its lair on a bright day and a crowned Caesar, Brutus then observes that "th'abuse of greatness is when it disjoins / Remorse from power," and that

> 'tis a common proof
> That lowliness is young ambition's ladder
> Whereto the climber upward turns his face.
> But when he once attains the upmost round,
> He then unto the ladder turns his back,
> Looks in the clouds, scorning the base degrees
> By which he did ascend.
>   (2.1.10–34)

It is in light of these general propositions about the way ambitious men achieve power, and the way they behave once they have it, that Brutus confirms his resolution to participate in the pre-emptive strike against the particular individual who in his opinion is ambitious: Julius Caesar. Later in the play, before the battle of Philippi, Brutus thinks in a similar manner:

> There is a tide in the affairs of men
> Which, taken at the flood, leads on to fortune:
> Omitted, all the voyage of their life
> Is bound in shallows and in miseries.
> On such a full sea are we now afloat,
> And we must take the current when it serves,
> Or lose our ventures.
>   (4.2.300–6)

Brutus here again thinks about his particular situation in light of general propositions about the human condition, propositions that I dare say ring true for many. Isn't it true that whether or not you seize a particular opportunity can be decisive for the rest of your life? Isn't it true that situations of this kind arise in our affairs? In light of this observation that a certain kind of situation recurs in human experience, and that he and the republican forces are indeed in this kind of situation, Brutus resolves, as it turns out against the better wisdom of Cassius, to meet Antony and Octavius Caesar at Phillipi.

A final example from *Lear*. The old king objects to his daughters' claim that he really does not *need* to have any retainers, and he attempts to persuade them to allow him to keep, as agreed, his entourage of one hundred knights. He does this by forwarding a remarkable array of propositions about human existence in general:

> O, reason not the need! Our basest beggars
> Are in the poorest things superfluous:
> Allow not nature more than nature needs,
> Man's life is cheap as beast's. Thou art a lady:

If only to go warm were gorgeous,
Why, nature needs not what thou gorgeous wear'st,
Which scarcely keeps thee warm.
(2.2.453–9)

Granted, few of us will find ourselves in the situation of having to persuade our children to allow us to keep a hundred knights when we retire. But we may well find ourselves in the position of being denied something we want on grounds that we do not really need it, or denying something to others (our children perhaps) on grounds that they do not really need it. If so, then Lear's words may come to mind, and perhaps even be useful to us, because he thinks about and argues from his particular situation in light of his understanding of this kind of situation. We can "identify" with, "relate" to, and sympathise with Lear and these other characters not just because, like us, they think, but also because they think of and present themselves as individuals who are not in unique situations but in the kinds of situation that arise in the lives of other people. They are continually observing that they have something important in common with other people. I think this way of thinking about themselves can also make us fear for ourselves, since it implies that the characters are *like* other people, including those who are watching or reading the play. Seeing the destruction of people who, though in some ways extraordinary, are nevertheless also like us, we sympathize with them, but perhaps also fear for ourselves.

Moral goodness, the potential for outstanding achievement, actual outstanding achievement in some field (often military), deep and powerful emotion, exceptional capacity for suffering, actual suffering in the extreme, a sense of humor, intense and powerful thought and reasoning (often informed by wild imagination), and (as we will see) spectacular powers of linguistic expression—these are the main grounds of the outstanding worth and goodness of Shakespeare's characters that qualify them to make us fear for them, fear for ourselves, and feel for them when we see them destroyed. But however exceptional and extraordinary they may be in these respects, these protagonists rarely cease to come across to us as real human beings. Many of us feel compassion and sympathy for animals and non-human agents that suffer. But we perhaps experience these feelings most intensely when confronted by the suffering and annihilation of agents who are most like ourselves, agents who are human. What is it to be human? It might seem presumptuous to attempt to answer such a question, but I think most of us have beliefs about the nature of humanity, and that we rely on such beliefs not just to assess the verisimilitude and quality of representations of the human, but to get through life. I think a good part of our humanity consists of moral imperfection, the capacity to experience emotion and passion, the ability to think, imagine, remember, and argue, and the capacity to suffer and feel physical and mental pain. Shakespeare endows his morally good but imperfect and fallible protagonists with powerful emotion and intense thought, and he endows them with emotions and thoughts that are for the most part appropriate to the kinds of people they are and the situations in which they find themselves. In short, he makes them human and thereby empowers them to make us feel pity, fear, sympathy, and compassion.

Language

But how does Shakespeare manage to create characters who seem so real and impassioned and who are therefore qualified to move us? Certainly what they do reveals and expresses their passions, but it is their *language* that is the main thing here. One of the basic things about some of their words that makes them seem real and life-like is that they are not organized into phrases of a set number of syllables or words, nor are they organized into patterns of stressed and unstressed syllables (they don't have *meter*), nor is there a recurrence of the same sound at regular intervals (they don't *rhyme*). Because they do not have these unusual qualities, the sound of these spoken words (which are printed as prose in the script) is close to the sound of everyday speech.

Most of the time, though, the words spoken by the main characters in the plays are not printed as prose but as verse, and the standard form of that verse is *blank verse*: unrhymed *iambic pentameter*. This means that most consecutive printed lines of Shakespeare's dramatic verse do not rhyme with each other. And most printed lines have five feet, where a foot is a sequence of stressed and unstressed syllables, with most feet in each line made up of an unstressed followed by a stressed syllable. So an example of a fairly regular iambic pentameter line is Juliet's "this **dismal scene I needs** must **act alone.**" When read aloud, these words might sound formal and contrived to us, but just imagine how much further from everyday speech it would sound if the characters always spoke in rhymed couplets—as they do in seventeenth-century French tragedy and Elizabethan translations of Seneca. Just imagine how much further from everyday speech it would sound if they spoke in sequences of *trochaic* (stressed/unstressed) or *dactylic* (stressed/unstressed/unstressed) feet—as we will see some of the witches in *Macbeth* do.

A few other features bring Shakespeare's blank verse even closer to everyday speech:

- though the prevailing meter is *iambic*, there are often *trochaic, spondaic* (stressed/stressed) and *pyrrhic* (unstressed/unstressed) feet in the lines, which disrupt this meter and bring the lines closer to the irregular sequences of stressed and unstressed syllables of everyday speech
- some lines are *end-stopped* (the end of the line corresponds with the end of a phrase, clause, or sentence), while some lines are *enjambed* or display *enjambment* (the end of the line does not correspond with the end of a phrase, clause, or sentence; we therefore must read through the end of the line into the next line to get to the end of a phrase, clause or sentence). When properly read, this mixture of *end-stopped* lines and *enjambment* prevents the language from sounding like an artificial listing of clauses and phrases of the same length
- there are many *caesurae* (pauses in mid-line), which also prevent the language from coming across as an artificial list of phrases and clauses of the same length.

So, yes, the characters' delivery of blank verse can sound different from everyday English in many countries, and may at times sound rather formal and artificial to us. But it is still closer to everyday language than many other verse forms.

As for the impassioned dimension of Shakespeare's tragic protagonists, many scholars emphasize the importance of bearing in mind that Shakespeare was educated in ancient Graeco-Roman writings about rhetoric, such as Aristotle's *Rhetoric*, Cicero's *Orator*, the *Ad Herennium*, and Quintilian's *Institutes of Oratory*. Shakespeare probably also read Renaissance rhetorical manuals based on these ancient writings (Joseph, Baldwin, Vickers, Mack, Keller, Skinner). In the ancient world, rhetoric was a broad field of study, the main ends of which were to praise or blame another person and to persuade others to believe something, make a decision about the guilt or innocence of a defendant, or do something (such as adopt a policy or course of action in foreign relations or domestic government). A commonplace of these ancient and Renaissance writings on rhetoric was that *unusual linguistic usage* was empowered to represent emotion, to express emotion, and to cause emotion in the audience and reader. The rhetoricians felt this was of the utmost importance in part because they believed that expressing, representing, and evoking emotion were extremely powerful means of achieving the ends of rhetoric. They identified two major ways in which we can make our linguistic usage differ from common, standard usage, and thereby connect it with passion:

- using words to mean or refer to something other than what they are usually used to refer to or mean—the term many of them used to refer to this type of unusual usage was translated into English as *trope*
- placing our words in unusual sequences, orders, or grammatical structures—the term they used to refer to this type of unusual usage was often translated into English as *figure* (or *scheme*).

A common selling point of books like this one is that they provide "plain-language" accounts of Shakespeare's plays. Though I am committed to clarity, I also wish to move beyond plain language in some ways because I think learning how to use the special, technical vocabulary which the Greeks and Romans devised in order to identify these tropes and figures is so beneficial. Learning this vocabulary first of all helps us to *describe* with precision Shakespeare's language. And ask yourself this: is language just a tool that you use to express thoughts you would have even if you had no language to formulate and express them? I don't think so. I think that acquiring and mastering vocabularies is in some fundamental way bound up with our ability to think and to understand. Thus, I think learning the special rhetorical vocabulary helps us to think about Shakespeare's language and improves our understanding of it. Also, since much of the commentary on this vocabulary deals with its *effects*, studying it can also improve our ability to describe and understand the effects of Shakespeare's words. In addition, I think studying and knowing how to use this vocabulary improves our ability to read and deliver the lines well in performance. So over the course of this book I propose to use this vocabulary not just to describe but also to understand and account for some the major achievements of the Shakespearean script. One of these achievements is the representation of characters who, because they are impassioned, move us.

One of the important tropes at the heart of Shakespeare's representation of impassioned people who engage our sympathies is *metaphor* (and *simile*, which has traditionally been lumped in with *metaphor* because both are grounded in perceptions of resemblance). Why are *Shakespeare's* Romeo and Juliet, but not the Romeo and Juliet of his Italian sources, celebrated the world over as great young lovers? In part because their love-talk is filled with *metaphor* and *simile*! That is to say they often use words that are usually used to describe one thing, in order to describe something else that resembles it (*metaphor*). And they often compare things and assert perceptions of resemblance between them by using the words "like," "as," or "so" (*simile*). Thus, for example, the first time Romeo sees Juliet he says, "O she doth teach the torches to burn bright! / It seems she hangs upon the cheek of night / As a rich jewel in an Ethiope's ear" (1.4.161–3). Soon after, when he sees her on her balcony, he says,

> But soft, what light through yonder window breaks?
> It is the east, and Juliet is the sun.
> Arise fair sun....
>
> (2.1.47–9)

Love-struck, Romeo seems to be struck by Juliet's *resemblance* to bright, precious, rare, magnificent things, such as a jewel and the sun, and he expresses these perceptions by using words which are usually used to refer to those things in order to describe and refer to her. That is one of the things about his language that makes us think he is so mad about her. But notice, too, that they are not just any old metaphors and similes. How unusual and striking it is for the lover to see his beloved as a teacher of torches, or a jewel in an Ethiopian's ear!

Similarly, Juliet on her balcony observes that just as "a rose / By any other word would smell as sweet, / So Romeo would, were he not Romeo called" (2.1.90–2). Having fallen madly in love, Juliet, too, perceives resemblances between her beloved and something that is beautiful and sweet—a rose—and she asserts that perception by way of a *simile*, one that is a little unusual since it was more conventional for the male lover to describe the beloved woman as a rose. As the play proceeds we have an ever stronger impression of her "true love's passion" (2.1.153), in part because she continues to produce *similes* and *metaphors* that assert a resemblance between Romeo and a falcon, a little bird, day, snow on a raven's back, and stars. We should also note that when she is *angry* with him for killing her cousin, Tybalt, she produces a rather different set of *similes* and *metaphors*: he is or is like a serpent, a dragon, a tyrant, an evil angel, a "dove-feathered raven," etc. (3.2.75–87). As for her own love for him, well, Juliet has *similes* for that as well: "My bounty is as boundless as the sea, /

My love as deep: the more I give to thee, / The more I have, for both are infinite" (2.1.184–6). One of the reasons the world has such an overwhelming sense of Juliet's profound, all-consuming love for Romeo is that she uses words which are usually used to refer to something that is vast, bountiful, and deep—the sea—in order to describe something that in her mind resembles it—her love.

Juliet sometimes expresses her feelings by way of another trope: *irony*. The ancient rhetoricians define this trope as the use of words to mean the opposite of what they are usually used to mean. This is what Juliet does at the end of that great scene we discussed earlier in connection with her isolation. After her parents have demanded that she marry Paris and left her, Juliet turns to the nurse for comfort and counsel. The nurse advises her to forget about her new husband, Romeo, and to marry Paris. After all, Romeo is a "dishclout" compared to Paris. When Juliet asks the nurse if she really means it, the nurse says she does. Juliet replies, "Well, thou hast comforted me marv'llous much." But we know that the nurse has not comforted Juliet at all. So I think Juliet here uses words which are usually used to mean one thing—that the nurse has comforted her—to mean the opposite of what they are usually used to mean. Speaking *ironically*, Juliet manifests her sharp mind, but also her anger and disgust at the nurse for disparaging Romeo and recommending that she forget about him and marry Paris. That anger and disgust, as well as a new resolution, become more clear when she then addresses the nurse in her absence: "go, counsellor, / Thou and my bosom henceforth shall be twain" (3.5.214–4).

Hyperbole is another important trope that gives us the impression of characters who are impassioned and who therefore engage our own feelings. Strictly speaking, we have this trope when a person uses words which are usually used to describe large things to describe smaller things, but it is often used as a label for any kind of exaggerated description. In the *Rhetoric*, Aristotle claims "hyperboles are characteristic of youngsters; they betray vehemence. And so they are used, above all, by men in an angry passion" (216). Aristotle cites some of the wrathful Achilles' words in Homer's *Iliad* as his example, but angry old men, such as Lear, also resort to them. Flying into a rage in the face of his daughter Cordelia's inability to heave her heart into her mouth, he exclaims,

> For by the sacred radiance of the sun,
> The mysteries of Hecate and the night,
> By all the operation of the orbs
> From whom we do exist and cease to be,
> Here I disclaim all my paternal care,
> Propinquity and property of blood,
> And as a stranger to my heart and me
> Hold thee from this for ever. The barbarous Scythian,
> Or he that makes his *generation messes*   [children food]
> To gorge his appetite, shall to my bosom
> Be as well neighboured, pitied and relieved
> As thou my sometime daughter.
>
> (1.1.109–13)

Lear saying that he will treat his daughter in the same way he would treat barbaric Scythians and cannibals seems a little over the top! And that is one reason we have such a strong sense of the old king's terrible wrath.

This trope also enters into Shakespeare's representation of other passions. In *Macbeth*, for example, we have a sense of Macbeth's overwhelming guilt and fear in part as a result of his *hyperbolic* description of his own bloody hand immediately following the murder:

> Will all great Neptune's ocean wash this blood
> Clean from my hand? No, this my hand will rather
> The multitudinous seas incarnadine,
> Making the green one red.
>
> (2.2.68–74)

Similarly, our sense of the mad Lady Macbeth's soul-destroying guilt comes through when she exaggerates the bloody stench of her hand: "Here's the smell of the blood still. All the perfumes of Arabia will not sweeten this little hand. O, O, O!" (5.1.37–8). In chapter 4 we will see that, in *Antony and Cleopatra*, we have a sense of Cleopatra's love for the dead Antony as a result of her *hyperbolic* description of him. But in that case the trope also accounts for our sense of Antony as a towering, sublime character.

One of the figures that goes to Shakespeare's representation of impassioned characters is evident in the passage from *Lear* cited above. We have such a strong sense of the old king's mounting anger on this occasion in part as a result of an *anaphora*: a series of consecutive phrases or lines all beginning with the same word or words. Beginning his curse by repeating the word "by the" at the beginning of consecutive phrases—"for *by the* sacred radiance of the sun ...," then "*by all the* operation of the orbs...,"—Lear momentarily retards forward motion, and winds himself up for his terrible, wrathful act of disowning his daughter. Later in this play, when he is out on the heath, our sense of Lear's anger is enhanced by a well-known instance of another figure, *aposiopesis*. This is where a speaker interrupts the normal sequence of words and leaves it unfinished. Thus, addressing his cruel daughters, he says,

> No, you unnatural hags,
> I will have such revenges on you both,
> That all the world shall – I will do such things –
> What they are yet I know not, but they shall be
> The terrors of the earth!
>
> (2.2.467–71)

Lear seems to be so overwhelmed by his disgust and anger that he is incapable of thinking straight or managing the grammar of his sentences.

Another figure that can have the effect of intensifying emotion is *epistrophe*: the repetition of words at the ends of consecutive phrases or sentences.

Consider, for example, how Friar Laurence's anger with the despairing Romeo comes through as a result of this type of unusual structure:

> Thy Juliet is alive,
> For whose dear sake thou wast but lately dead:
> There art thou happy. Tybalt would kill thee,
> But thou slew'st Tybalt: there art thou happy.
> The law that threatened death became thy friend
> And turned it to exile: there art thou happy.
> (3.3.138–43)

And we really must observe *hyperbaton*, one of the most common and powerful figures in Shakespeare's script. This is essentially just an inversion or reversal of common word order, as in "apple red" instead of "red apple." In *On Sublimity*, here's what Longinus has to say about this figure: it "is a very real mark of urgent emotion. People who in real life feel anger, fear, or indignation, or are distracted by jealousy or some other emotion ... often put one thing forward and then rush off to another, irrationally inserting some remark, and then hark back again to their first point" (166–7). This is what Juliet does when, before drinking the Friar's potion, she is terrified she might awaken in the vault before Romeo comes to her. A common sentence structure would be something like, "If I live I will probably be distraught finding myself with Tybalt and all my dead ancestors in the vault!" But after beginning the sentence with "if I live," Juliet rushes off to imagine all the horrors of the vault, before beginning the sentence again with "O, if I wake" and then completing it by saying how distraught she would be (4.3.31–59). A massive *hyperbaton* that conveys to us her fear.

Finally, let's observe the importance of *apostrophe* on this count. This is where a speaker directly addresses a person, thing, or god that may or may not be present. In so doing, the speaker often turns from one addressee to another, and speaks to the new addressee as though it were sentient and can hear the spoken words. Since it need not involve any unusual order of words, I've never liked the classification of *apostrophe* as a figure, but that is the traditional classification, so we'll go with that for now. Note that many of the great soliloquies in the tragedies begin with or include *apostrophes*. Alone in her chamber, for example, Juliet fearfully addresses the vial that contains the potion she will drink, her dagger, and the ghost of Tyablt (4.3.21–59). Alone in his bedchamber with the sleeping Desdemona, the angry, jealous Othello addresses his own "soul," the "chaste stars," the candle/torch he holds, and the sleeping Desdemona (5.2.1–22). Standing alone before the enemy city of Antium, the banished Coriolanus directly addresses it: "City, / 'Tis I that made thy widows"; after being informed which house belongs to Aufidius, alone on stage he opens his grim meditation on the nature of friendship with another *apostrophe*: "O world, thy slippery turns!" (4.4.1–15). Alone in his orchard, awaiting the conspirators, Brutus in *Julius Caesar* exclaims, "O conspiracy..." (2.1.80). In his solitude out on the heath,

Lear cries out *to* the winds, cataracts, hurricanoes, fires, thunder, and elements (3.2.1–24). But perhaps Macbeth is the greatest apostrophiser of all: in his terrible isolation, he speaks *to* the Stars (1.4.55), the dagger, the "sure and firm-set earth," and, indeed, his intended victim, Duncan (in his absence) before murdering him (2.1.40–71). After doing it, we feel his fear, remorse, anguish, and desperation as he addresses Duncan again (2.2.85), his next victim, Banquo, in his absence (3.1.145–6), "seeling night," (3.2.51), "Time" (4.1.157), "brief candle" (5.5.23), "wind" and "wrack" (5.5.54).

Cut off from people around them, these characters turn from them and address something else, with the aim of making something happen, venting their passions, expressing their thoughts, coping with isolation. In some cases they perhaps think their addressees can hear them and may respond in some way (perhaps by obeying their commands). But I think that in most cases, even though these characters address these things as though they were sentient, they do not really expect a reply—they know that they are really beyond *com*munication and *dia*logue. In addition to expressing their wishes and states of emotion, these *apostrophes* thus also often serve to deepen the pathos of their isolation.

Some have claimed that we of the post-Renaissance, modern age respond to this kind of ornate language in ways that differ from the ways in which people in the Renaissance did, because they thought language was essentially *speech*, whereas we think of it as *writing*, and they saw ornate language as a kind of delightful craft, whereas we see it as a kind of duplicity (Hope, MacDonald). I'm not sure about this, since the ancient authorities on rhetoric taught the Renaissance humanists that naturalness was persuasive, while conspicuous linguistic artifice was unpersuasive because it made audiences suspicious. Also, I would say that some modern speeches did and still do come across to many as impassioned utterances that are deeply moving, memorable, and pleasurable. One of the reasons for this is that these speeches are highly tropological and figurative.

Consider, for example, Winston Churchill's "We shall fight on the beaches" speech (1940), John F. Kennedy's 1961 inaugural address, and Martin Luther King's "I have a dream" speech (1963). In the Churchill speech, the great, defiant passage is a massive *anaphora*: a series of consecutive sentences all beginning with the phrase, "we shall fight." In the Kennedy speech, we get the famous imperative: "ask not what your country can do for you; ask what you can do for your country." This sentence is based on the unusual abba sequence of words (country/you, you/country) that the rhetoricians identified as the figure, *antimetabole*. In King's passionate speech, we get more *anaphora* with groups of consecutive sentences that begin with "Now is the time...," "We can never...," "I have a dream...," and "Let freedom ring...." And in the description of a nation in which King's children "will not be judged by the color of their skin but by the content of their character," we have a *parallelism*, a repetition of a grammatical structure (definite article/noun/preposition/possessive adjective/noun). Since the meaning of "the color of their skin" is contrary to the meaning of "the content of their character," the whole phrase also qualifies as an *antithesis*. It is because tropological and figurative language still has a strong hold on us, and their language is so highly tropological and figurative, that Shakespeare's protagonists seem to be driven by such grand passions and that we sympathize with them when they suffer.

If we also wish to understand what it is about the plays that qualify them to make us feel horror and fear for ourselves, we must add a few further observations about their language. Let's take *Macbeth* as an example. In this play we see that the language of the witches differs in important ways from the blank verse that prevails in the discourse of the other characters:

FIRST WITCH: Here I have a pilot's thumb,
    Wrecked as homeward he did come.
THIRD WITCH: A drum, a drum:
    Macbeth doth come.
ALL: The weyard sisters, hand in hand,
    Posters of the sea and land,   [swift travellers]
    Thus do go about, about,
    Thrice to thine and thrice to mine
    And thrice again, to make up nine.
    Peace, the charm's wound up.

(1.3.29–38)

The numerous rhymed couplets (29/30; 31/32; 33/34; 36/37) make the language of the witches more incantatory and charm-like. That *end-stopped* lines predominate and there is little *enjambment* makes it more terse, oracular, formal. The meter of many lines is *trochaic* rather than *iambic*: that the first syllable of many lines, feet, and words is stressed makes the utterance darker, more menacing. Many of the trochaic lines also end in a stressed syllable and are therefore *catalectic* (the final unstressed syllable is missing), with the result that the lines seem even more oracular and sharp. All of the lines are shorter than the pentameter that prevails in the rest of the play: there are *trochaic tetrameters* (29, 30, 34, 35, 36), *trochaic trimeters* (38), *iambic dimeters* (31, 32), and *iambic tetrameters* (33, 37). These shorter lines further align the dialogue with our idea of spells and incantations. The simple repetition of many words (come, drum, thrice, hand) is one more aspect of this highly repetitive linguistic discourse that makes it scary.

Song

Song is another aspect of performances of the plays that can intensify the emotions that Shakespeare wanted his audience to experience and that many have claimed to have experienced when witnessing performances of them on stage and screen. When reading the script, we perhaps skim over the lyrics—in part because the musical settings for them are usually not included. Our editions of Shakespeare are abridged! For Shakespeare had particular musical settings for his lyrics in mind, and in some cases those settings were composed by the leading composers and musicians of his day. So I, and many other lovers of both Elizabethan song and Shakespeare's plays, think that before cutting them or substituting their own music for the songs, directors should realize what they are dealing with and treat them as integral components of the plays that are there for a reason (Sternfeld, Duffin, Henze). Since the musical settings for these songs are probably not included in your text, I'll provide a few examples here and in later chapters to show you what I mean and give you a chance to sing or play them for yourselves. To hear performances of them, you can google the song titles or consult Ross Duffin's *Shakespeare's Songbook* (which includes a CD).

A well-known example of song from the tragedies is Desdemona's song in *Othello* (4.3.42–59). Speaking with Emilia in her chamber, Desdemona observes that her mother's maid, Barbary, used to sing a song of unrequited love, a "song of willow," which she died singing, and which would not go from Desdemona's mind that night. Recalling and singing the sad song, Desdemona displays her own gentle nature and capacity for compassion. Duffin claims that the lyrics to Desdemona's song might have been sung to a plaintive, D minor melody, in 6/4 time, set out in a sixteenth-century collection of music for the lute (467–70).

When sung well, this song can indeed come across as a sad, sweet song that is all the more moving for arising in the calm, intimate moment Desdemona

Figure 1.1 "Willow, willow," from *Othello*
Source: *Shakespeare's Songbook* by Ross W. Duffin. Used by permission of W. W. Norton & Company, Inc. Copyright © 2004 by Ross W. Duffin.

shares with Emilia just before the storm we know is coming. Indeed, Desdemona seems to set the scene for sadness and weeping when, apparently deeply moved by her own rendition, she observes, "mine eyes do itch" and asks, "Doth that bode weeping?" (4.3.60–61). Just before she dies, Emilia answers this question in the affirmative, singing the sweet song one last time:

> What did thy song bode, lady?
> Hark, canst thou hear me? I will play the swan,
> And die in music:—
> Willow, willow, willow—   *Sings*
> (5.2.281–4)

Similarly, the pathos of Ophelia's mad scenes in *Hamlet* can be greatly enhanced by a performance that is sensitive to the way in which her discourse is a patchwork of lyrics and that incorporates the music to which those lyrics may have been set in Shakespeare's time. Ophelia enters singing lines from the Walsingham ballad in which the main speaker, an old man, tells another man of how his young female love has abandoned him—but Ophelia's version then modulates into an elegy for a male lover who "is dead and gone" (4.4.30–1). Duffin surmises the song may have been sung to William Byrd's beautiful setting of the ballad in "My Ladye Nevells Booke" (1591). Ophelia's distracted state is forcefully brought home to us when she then suddenly launches into the more sprightly "Tomorrow Is St. Valentine's Day," a maid's slightly ribald tale (perhaps set to an up-tempo 6/4 jig) of how a man "tumbled" her in bed and then does not marry her because she allowed him to do it. By the time she finishes, I think we should see why, at the very beginning of this scene, Horatio says, "her mood will needs be pitied" (4.4.3). When, after having departed, she then returns to find her brother Laertes, she sings a few lines from "Bonny sweet Robin" (4.4.171–4) in which the singer bids farewell to the dead Robin who was all her joy. These lyrics may have been set to another very beautiful, simple melody in a minor key with descending melodic lines which appeared in several Renaissance collections of music for the lute (Duffin: 72).

Laertes then observes that such songs are more affecting/persuasive than mere words, and perhaps gives a cue to the audience when he says to his sister, "hadst thou thy wits and didst persuade revenge, / It could not move thus" (4.4.175–6). Citing a further fragment from "Bonny Sweet Robin" in her exchange with her brother, Ophelia then sings another sad song, "And will he not come again?," which asserts that "he is dead" and will never come again. She then exits, leaving Laertes distraught and the king demanding to "commune" with him in his "grief" (4.4.202).

Shakespeare thus discretely introduces simple, sad, plaintive, beautiful songs into the tragedies to represent the emotions, mental states, and moral qualities of his characters. But he also dramatizes the power of music to move

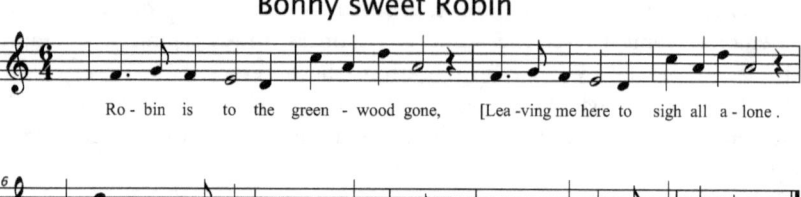

Figure 1.2 "Bonny sweet Robin," from *Hamlet*
Source: *Shakespeare's Songbook* by Ross W. Duffin. Used by permission of W. W. Norton & Company, Inc. Copyright © 2004 by Ross W. Duffin.

the passions by staging the emotional responses of other characters to these songs and often having these characters explicitly describe and remark upon their responses. Song thus enters into the causes of our pity and sadness as we watch the tragedy unfold.

We should also note here that song functions in this way not only in the tragedies but also in the comedies and romances. As we have seen, Shakespeare aims in these plays to provide the pleasures of laughter and delight, but he also aims to enrich and enhance this experience by including a wide range of lovely songs that tell of inconstancy, death, betrayal, and heartache. In *Much Ado About Nothing*, for example, there is a pause in the comic action when Balthasar sings, "Sigh no more, ladies…," a song that advises women to cease making "sounds of woe" and to let men go in light of the fact that "men were deceivers ever" and "to one thing constant never" (2.3.50–62). Things get even more serious and moving when, at what those on stage take to be the tomb of Hero, Balthasar sings "Pardon, goddess of the night." This is a "solemn hymn" that asks the goddess to pardon Claudio and Don Pedro for having slain Hero by falsely accusing her of infidelity (5.3.11–21). In *As You Like It*, we have a similar moment when, after Amiens tells Jaques that the song he has been singing, "Under the greenwood tree…," will make him melancholy, Jaques nevertheless asks him to sing more of it (2.5.1–36). A few scenes later, Amiens sings another sad song, "Blow, blow, thou winter wind…," that tells of man's ingratitude and the falsity of friendship—something the inhabitants of the forest know all too well (2.7.178–94). And in *Twelfth Night*, the raucous late-night partying scene that includes several rowdy songs is something of a compensation for the sadness Toby and Sir Andrew seem to experience in response to Feste's rendering of the plaintive "O Mistress mine…" (2.3.26–39). Feste later sings what Orsino refers to as an "old and plain" song, "Come away, come away, death" (2.4.53–68), perhaps to an exquisite tune that appears in two sixteenth-century English manuscripts (Duffin: 98):

Figure 1.3 "Come away, come away, death," from *Twelfth Night*
Source: *Shakespeare's Songbook* by Ross W. Duffin. Used by permission of W. W. Norton & Company, Inc. Copyright © 2004 by Ross W. Duffin.

Sung to this simple melody in a minor key, this broken-hearted lover's request to die and be lain in an unknown grave is such a sad, moving song. This play comes to a close with Feste singing another rather plaintive song, "When that I was..." (5.1.371–90). If only for a moment, these songs—especially if they are sung to their simple, beautiful musical settings of Shakespeare's day—may well leaven our good cheer and move us to sadness and even pity for some of the suffering characters who are on the scene.

Spectacle

By "spectacle" I mean what we *see* when we are watching a performance of the plays on stage or screen. Like music and song, spectacle is thus not, strictly speaking, a dimension of Shakespeare's script (the text intended to govern performance). When we silently *read* the Shakespearean script, we do not *see* any stage, screen, characters, props, physical actions, facial expressions, lighting, or setting in which the characters exist and act, nor do we *hear* any music or songs—though we can *imagine* the settings of the action and the physical appearance of the characters, and we might hear in our mind's ear the music and song to which the characters allude.

Given our concerns here, it is worth noting that many over the years have claimed that even though they perceive neither spectacle nor song when they read, they nevertheless have greater enjoyment and more intense emotional experiences when they read the Shakespearean script than they do when they see performances governed by that script. Madame de Staël, for example, claimed that Shakespeare's plays "have so much depth that the rapidity of theatrical action makes us lose a great part of the ideas which they contain; in this respect his pieces deserve more to be read than to be seen" (Bate: 82). The Romantic essayist, Charles Lamb, claimed that there was very little connection between Shakespeare's "mastery over the heart and soul of man" and the performance of his plays on stage. This is mainly because this mastery lies in the "poetry" of the script that provides us with "sublime images" and a "knowledge of the inner structure and workings of mind in a character" (357–9, 368). Hazlitt, for similar reasons, also claimed that "we do not like to see our author's plays acted, and least of all, *Hamlet*" (237), while Bloom has recently expressed his aversion to seeing performances of the plays, mainly on grounds of the ways in which he feels directors with particular moral-political agendas diminish them. Whether or not the reading experience is more emotionally intense than the experience we have at the theatre or in the cinema is a matter I won't try to address. But I do think the remarks of de Staël, Lamb, Hazlitt, Bloom, and many others suggest that the Shakespearean script on its own, without any song or spectacle, is sufficient to provide us with strong emotional experiences. And we have noted that it seems that Shakespeare was writing and publishing his plays with the aim of entertaining not just theatre audiences, but also readers (Erne). All of which I think suggests that, whether we are reading the script of any given Shakespearean play, or seeing a performance based upon that script, the *main* sources of the plays' power to move us are plot, character, thought, and language.

Still, spectacle can affect our emotional response to scenes in very powerful ways. Because the script of the plays provides so few explicit stage directions and so little explicit detail as to the nature of the spectacle, and because there is an infinite number of ways one can stage and direct any given play, it is difficult to assess how this dimension of performances of Shakespeare's plays affects us—so much depends on how directors stage and film their performances. So I will limit my discussion of this aspect of the plays here, and in the rest of the book, but I do want to make just a couple of remarks on this count.

The histories and tragedies are filled with descriptions of the outstanding physical strength, martial prowess, and physical beauty of many of the heroes. Sensitive to this aspect of the script, modern directors usually cast men known for their manly good looks in the title roles—Richard Burton, Marlon Brando, Kenneth Branagh, Lawrence Fishbone, Mel Gibson, Leonardo DiCaprio, and Tom Hiddleston, to name just a few of the heart-throbs cast in western, post-war productions of the plays. The physical beauty of the protagonists is thus often an aspect of the spectacle of the plays, and it is another thing that can enhance our compassion for them when they are destroyed. For, at least according to the German poet, Friedrich Schiller, even the gods lament the death of *beautiful* heroes: beginning his great poem, *Nänie*, with "also the beautiful must die," Schiller observes that upon the death of Thetis' glorious son Achilles in front of the gates of Troy, "the gods weep, all the goddesses weep, / That the beautiful perishes, that the perfect dies" (Browning: 88). The exceptional physical beauty of the heroines also commands florid description and praise from many characters throughout the plays in which they appear, which is why the actresses cast for these roles are also usually women known in their societies for their physical beauty: Elizabeth Taylor and Josette Simon (Cleopatra), Jean Simmons (Ophelia), Kate Winslet (Ophelia), Irene Jacob (Desdemona), Olivia Hussey and Claire Danes (Juliet), to name a few in western, post-war productions of the plays. At least if we are like Schiller's gods, we weep for Shakespeare's dead heroes and heroines in part because they are beautiful.

In some cases, the suffering and death of these beautiful heroes and heroines is not part of the spectacle but is reported or described by another character. In *Julius Caesar*, for example, we are spared the sight of Portia's gruesome suicide. Shakespeare also spares us the sight of Cordelia being hanged, and Ophelia drowning, though Gertrude's famous lavish description of it draws tears from her brother Laertes, if not from the audience (4.4.165–86).

But in most cases, Shakespeare makes us *see* the suffering and death of his heroes and heroines:

- Romeo drinks poison and dies, and Juliet kills herself by plunging a dagger into her breast
- Macduff kills Macbeth in a sword-fight and displays his severed head
- The conspirators kill Coriolanus
- Lear breathes his last
- Iago stabs Rodorigo and his wife Emilia to death; Othello strangles Desdemona, stabs himself, and dies
- Hamlet is wounded by Laertes' poisoned sword and dies
- the conspirators stab Caesar to death and bathe in his blood; Pindarus kills Cassius; Brutus falls upon his sword and dies
- Antony falls upon his sword, bleeds a lot, and then dies; Cleopatra applies the asps to her breast and dies.

All of this occurs on stage. In ancient Greek and Roman tragedy, the death of the protagonist usually occurs offstage and another character reports it. Shakespeare thus departs from ancient precedent in making violence, suffering, and death part of the spectacle. Certainly second-hand accounts of this kind of thing can evoke our sympathies, and in the *Poetics* Aristotle claimed that "the plot should be constructed in such a way that, even without seeing it, someone who hears about the incidents will shudder and feel pity at the outcome." But he also observes that "that which is terrifying and pitiable can arise from spectacle" (17). Seeing the pain and death of Shakespeare's beautiful protagonists, we are moved.

Spectacle can enter into the causes of our fear when Shakespeare follows the ancient Roman playwright, Seneca, and Thomas Kyd's very popular *Spanish Tragedy*, which was published in 1592 and performed on the London stage throughout the decade: he puts supernatural agents on stage and dramatizes the terror and horror of those to whom these agents appear. Thus, in *Richard III*, the ghosts of Richard's deceased victims appear on stage at the end of the play to curse the dreaming, fearful Richard and bless his adversary, Richmond (5.3). *Hamlet* begins with an appearance of the ghost of old Hamlet, a "dreaded sight" first seen at night by Marcellus and Barnardo, a "thing," an "apparition," an "image," a "spirit" that then "harrows" Horatio "with fear and wonder" and makes him "tremble and look pale" the first time he sees it (1.1.29–61). This "dead corpse" then appears to Hamlet, "making night hideous and we fools of nature / So horridly to shake our disposition / With thoughts beyond the reaches of our souls" (1.4.33–7). "Look you how pale he glares!," Hamlet exclaims when it revisits him later in his mother's bedchamber and again makes his hair "start up and stand on end" (3.4.125–8). In *Julius Caesar*, the ghost of Caesar appears to Brutus at Philippi: it is "a monstrous apparition" that, as Brutus avers, "makes my blood cold and my hair to stare" (4.2.367–70).

And then there is *Macbeth*, a play which I think is more invested in providing the pleasures of fear, dread, and horror than the other tragedies are. Opening with the three witches, thunder and lightning in the background, plotting to intercept Macbeth (1.1.1–13), they shortly thereafter do indeed appear out on the heath, thunder again in the background, to Macbeth and Banquo, who observes that they are "so withered and so wild in their attire" that they "look not like th'inhabitants o'th'earth" (1.3.41–2). After the witches hail Macbeth as Thane of Cawdor and tell him he shall be king, Banquo asks of him, "why do you start and seem to fear / Things that do sound so fair?," and the "weyard sisters" then vanish (1.3.33). After the murderers have carried out Macbeth's order to kill Banquo, the ghost of Banquo appears at the banquet hosted by the Macbeths: he shakes his "gory locks" at Macbeth, who describes it as "that which might appal the devil," a "horrible shadow" who glares at him with "no speculation" in his eyes and who terrifies him and leaves his cheeks "blanched with fear" (3.4.58–132). Resolved to overcome his "initiate fear" (3.4.164)—the fear of a novice in crime—Macbeth then visits the "black and midnight hags" (4.1.47) whom he finds mixing a repulsive "hell-broth" and who present Macbeth with a series of gruesome apparitions. Observing the way these scenes with the "weyard sisters" are combined with other scenes of madness and gore, Schlegel observes that "nothing can equal this picture in its power to excite terror" (410).

In Shakespeare's day, when many theatre-goers believed in devils, angels, spirits, demons, witches, and ghosts, their appearance on stage seems to have caused experiences of fear and horror that were especially intense. But even if we do not believe in these supernatural agents, they may well still frighten us. This is because, as Schlegel observes, "no superstition can be widely diffused without having a foundation in human nature: on this the poet builds [in *Macbeth*]; he calls up from their hidden abysses that dread of the unknown, that presage of a dark side of nature, and a world of spirits, which philosophy now imagines it has altogether exploded" (407). Evoking terror and horror in those to whom they appear, appealing to our sense of the dark side of nature, these ghosts, witches, spirits, and apparitions hold infinite possibilities for imaginations and spectacles of gore, grotesquerie, monstrosity, and dark ritual which may heighten our experience of fear as we read, or observe what passes on stage and screen. Violence, mutilation, atrocity, suffering, death, ghosts, spirits, witches—they do not just happen to be there. Shakespeare puts them there in order to make us experience pity, fear, horror, dread, and the pleasures he knew some members of his audience took in witnessing acts of violence and cruelty, both real and fictional.

References

Aristotle. *Poetics*. Trans. Richard Janko. Indianapolis: Hackett, 1987.
Aristotle. *Rhetoric*. Trans. Lane Cooper. 1932; Englewood Cliffs: Prentice Hall, 1960.
Baldwin, T. W. *William Shakspere's Small Latine and Lesse Greeke*. 2 vols. 1944; Urbana: University of Illinois Press, 1956.
Bate, Jonathan. Ed. *The Romantics on Shakespeare*. New York: Penguin, 1992.
Bloom, Harold. *Shakespeare: The Invention of the Human*. New York: Riverhead, 1998.
Browning, Robert. Ed. *German Poetry from 1750–1900*. New York: Continuum, 1984.
Burkert, Walter. *Savage Energies*. Trans. Peter Bing. Chicago: University of Chicago Press, 2001.
Cicero. *On Duties*. Ed. M. T. Griffin and E. M. Atkins. Cambridge: Cambridge University Press, 1991.
Duffin, Ross. *Shakespeare's Songbook*. New York: Norton, 2004.
Erne, Lukas. *Shakespeare as Literary Dramatist*. 2003; Cambridge: Cambridge University Press, 2013.
Frye, Northrop. *Anatomy of Criticism*. Princeton: Princeton University Press, 1957.
Hazlitt, William. *Characters of Shakespear's Plays*. In vol. 4, *Complete Works of William Hazlitt*. Ed. P. P. Howe. 1817; London: J. M. Dent, 1930.
Hegel, G. W. F. *Aesthetics: Lectures on Fine Art*. Trans. T. M. Knox. Vol. 2. Oxford: Clarendon, 1975; 2010.
Henze, Catherine. *Robert Armin and Shakespeare's Performed Songs*. New York: Routledge, 2017.
Hope, Jonathan. *Shakespeare and Language*. London: Arden Shakespeare, 2010.
Joseph, Sister Miriam. *Shakespeare's Use of the Arts of Language*. 1947; New York: Hafner, 1966.
Keller, Daniel. *The Development of Shakespeare's Rhetoric*. Tübingen: Francke Verlag. 2009.
Lamb, Charles. "On the Tragedies of Shakespeare." In *Selected Essays, Letters, Poems*. Ed. J. Lewis May. 1953; London: Collins, 1966. 356–373.
Longinus. *On Sublimity*. Trans. D. A. Russell. In *Classical Literary Criticism*. 1972; Oxford: Oxford University Press, 1989. 143–187.
Mack, Peter. *Reading and Rhetoric in Montaigne and Shakespeare*. London: Bloomsbury, 2010.
McDonald, Russ. *Shakespeare and the Arts of Language*. Oxford: Oxford University Press, 2001.
Schlegel, Augustus William. *Lectures on Dramatic Art and Literature*. Trans. John Black. London: George Bell & Sons, 1879.
Skinner, Quentin. *Forensic Shakespeare*. Oxford: Oxford University Press, 2014.
Sternfeld, Frederick. *Music in Shakespearean Tragedy*. London: Routledge, 1963.
Vickers, Brian. *In Defence of Rhetoric*. Oxford: Oxford University Press, 1989.

2 Laughter and delight

Plot

Shakespeare's comedies—but also many scenes in the histories, tragedies, and romances—are special because they do one of the things Shakespeare wanted them to do: they make people laugh. But what is it that enables them to do so? One of the main things is the action they represent. In some cases, the comic incident consists in nothing more than incompetence, people doing things badly. Thus, at least one of the reasons the mechanicals' performance of the Pyramus and Thisbe play in *A Midsummer Night's Dream* can be so funny is just that, as their audience remarks, they are such bad actors! One of the reasons Orlando in *As You Like It* is funny is that, as many other characters remark, he is such a bad love poet. In *Henry IV, part 1*, Falstaff makes for a pretty poor soldier when, instead of producing his pistol to give Prince Henry in the midst of battle, he pulls out a bottle of sack. And one of the reasons Dogberry and his men are funny in *Much Ado About Nothing* is that they are rather sad watchmen, and not very good at legal proceedings either (though in the benign world of that comedy, they still manage to apprehend some of the bad guys).

Another type of comic incident we get in all genres of Shakespearean drama is action that results in injury or pain, but nothing so serious that we are moved from laughing to feeling outrage or profound pity. This is the kind of thing you see in the old Three Stooges skits and Charlie Chaplin films when someone smacks somebody, slips on a banana peel, gets scared and runs away, runs into a door, pulls another person's hair, tweaks somebody's nose, kicks someone in the behind. In some cases this kind of slapstick comedy is called for or described in the script. In *A Midsummer Night's Dream*, for example, the artisans panic and flee their ass-headed friend Bottom, and Puck describes how their clothes were scratched and torn as he chased them "through bog, through bush, through brake, through brier" (3.1.76). We then see Helena physically accost the taller Hermia, who runs away. In *Twelfth Night*, the duped, cowardly Sir Andrew Agucheek and Viola/Cesario, swords drawn, attempt to avoid fighting each other (3.4); this ridiculous incident is shortly followed by another in which Sir Andrew, thinking Sebastian is the cowardly Viola/Cesario, strikes Sebastian, who responds by striking Sir Andrew several times (4.1). Sebastian then roughs up both Sir Andrew and Sir Toby.

In *The Tempest*, Stephano smacks Trinculo a few times because he thinks that Trinculo, not the invisible Ariel, has been calling Caliban a liar (3.2). And in the final act of the play, Stephano, Trinculo, and Caliban get scratched up running through briars and thorny shrubs, they fall into a pool of horse-pee, they are distracted from their plot by some shiny clothes, they are chased through the bush by dog-like spirits, and they finally reappear onstage drunk and rather worse for wear. Shakespeare also includes this kind of lower comic incident in the histories and tragedies. In *Henry IV, part 1*, for example, after Falstaff and the other thieves have robbed the travellers, Poins and Prince Hal set upon them; roughed up and afraid, they run away and leave the booty to Poins and Prince Hal to take back to London: "argument for a week, laughter for a month and a good jest for ever," as Hal says (2.2.62–3). And one of the great scenes in *Antony and Cleopatra* is a serio-comical scene in which Cleopatra, unable to contain her jealous rage, unfairly berates and strikes the messenger who informs her that her lover Antony has married Octavia (2.5).

In this kind of comic incident, the characters often act in ways that are morally diminished—they behave in ways that are rather cowardly, hypocritical, dishonest, cruel, selfish, boorish, greedy, intemperate, and unfair. But because this kind of behavior usually results in only minor forms of pain and injury, it can move us to amusement rather than indignation or compassion. And if we have read or seen the play before, we know things will turn out well in the end, and we are more inclined to laugh at incidents of this kind than we would be in the absence of that knowledge. But even if we haven't seen the play before, just knowing we are watching a comedy which will be governed by the conventions of that genre—one of which is that things will turn out well in the end—will incline us to laugh at incidents of this kind. The script of Shakespeare's plays sometimes *explicitly* calls for this type of comic incident, but it also provides endless possibilities to include it in imagination and performance. Though the script might not explicitly call for the characters to walk into a tree, pull someone's pants down, or trip somebody, one can always insert such things in performance to great comic effect, as modern directors usually do so.

In all genres of Shakespearean drama we also find a wide range of comic mimicry—people playfully imitating or pretending to be someone else. Thus, at the opening of the great tavern scene after the robbery in *Henry IV, part 1*, Hal has some fun mimicking both his opponent, Hotspur, and his wife. Hotspur, Hal playfully says, is the man who

> kills me some six or seven dozen of Scots at a breakfast, washes his hands, and says to his wife 'Fie upon this quiet life! I want work.' 'O my sweet Harry,' says she, 'how many hast thou killed today?' 'Give my roan horse a drench,' says he, and answers 'some fourteen,' an hour after, 'a trifle, a trifle.'
>
> (2.4.80–4)

64 *Laughter and delight*

Note that the mimicry here takes on a playful, comical, but also derisory edge in part because of the tropological language Hal uses to imitate Hotspur. We get an exaggerated description (*hyperbole*) of Hotspur's exploits—he has killed six or seven dozen men at breakfast. And we also get an understated description (*meiosis*) of them—for Hotspur, it is a mere trifle. The comedy continues as Falstaff then plays Hal's father, King Henry IV, and is then "usurped" by Hal who plays the same role, though a little more ominously (2.4). In *Much Ado*, Don Pedro mimics Dogberry's incoherent listing of the villains' offences (5.1.191–196), and in *A Midsummer Night's Dream*, Puck mimics the voices of both Demetrius and Lysander in order to lead them astray and prevent a more serious fight between them.

An example of this kind of thing in the tragedies is when, in *Romeo and Juliet*, Mercutio tries to make Romeo come forth by making fun of him and mimicking the conventional love-talk Romeo has been spouting over Rosaline (2.1.8–23). Hamlet also does it occasionally, even in the most deadly of situations, as when he mimics the language of diplomacy in telling Horatio how he composed the commission requesting England to put Rosencrantz and Guildenstern to death (5.2.41–50). And we have the great opening scene of *Antony and Cleopatra* in which the Egyptian queen taunts her man by mimicking the young, imperious Octavius Caesar with whom Antony supposedly shares power. She saucily commands him to hear the ambassadors from Rome, for

> Fulvia [Antony's wife] perchance is angry, or who knows
> If the scarce-bearded Caesar have not sent
> His powerful mandate to you: 'Do this, or this;
> Take in that kingdom, and enfranchise that:
> Perform't, or else we damn thee.'
>
> (1.1.21–5)

Note that our editors place the command in quotation marks, to make clear to us that Cleopatra is mimicking Octavius Caesar.

In some cases, this mimicking is really an instance of a broader kind of comic action, one that Shakespeare frequently represents in his plays with the aim of providing the pleasures of laughter to his audience: ridicule. In *Henry IV, part 1*, for example, we have Hal's ongoing and rather sharp ridicule of Falstaff, and Falstaff's more playful and affectionate ridicule of Hal. We also find a fair bit of this kind of thing in the tragedies. Hamlet, for example, mocks Polonius on several occasions. He has some fun with his false friend Rosencrantz when he *metaphorically* describes him as a "sponge" and then explains why (4.1.10–17), and he has another go at the servile Osric later in the play (5.2.87–140). At the opening of *Coriolanus*, Menenius can get a laugh when he *metaphorically* describes the second citizen as "the toe of this great assembly" on grounds that "being one o'th' lowest, basest, poorest / Of this most wise rebellion, thou goest foremost" (1.1.136–8). And in addition to noting Cleopatra's ridicule of Antony for being answerable to his wife and the young hot-shot Octavius Caesar, we might also note a later scene in this play. After having been beaten by the queen for having told her Antony has married Octavia, the messenger is recalled, and he tells Cleopatra what she wants to hear about her rival, Octavia: she is not very tall, she is "low-voiced," she has little majesty in her movement but "creeps," and she has a face that is "round, even to faultiness." This derisory description of the noble Octavia of course enables Cleopatra to indulge in a little gleeful, self-serving ridicule of her own: Octavia is "dull of tongue and dwarfish!," "there's nothing in her," she must be foolish since "they are foolish" who have round faces, and, to conclude, "this creature's no such thing" (3.3). A great scene of catty ridicule and scorn (in the absence of the object of scorn) that is funny because everyone, including Cleopatra, knows it is not deadly serious but constructed to console the haughty, furious, jealous queen whose lover has just married another woman.

But comic ridicule is more common in the comedies. We have, for example, the four lovers' wild exchange of insults in the middle of *A Midsummer Night's Dream*; Feste's mockery of the main characters in *Twelfth Night*; Rosalind's open insults to the haughty Phoebe, and Touchstone's derision of pretty much everyone in *As You Like It*. But perhaps the ridicule that runs through the early scenes of *Much Ado About Nothing* is the most distinguished instance of this kind of incident: the "merry war" between Beatrice and Benedick includes countless acts of ridicule and insult such as the ones in their first encounter in the play:

BEATRICE: I wonder that you will still be talking, Signior Benedick: nobody marks you.
BENEDICK: What, my dear Lady Disdain! Are you yet living?
BEATRICE: Is it possible disdain should die while she hath such meet food to feed it as Signior Benedick? Courtesy itself must convert to disdain, if you come in her presence.
BENEDICK: Then is courtesy a turncoat. But it is certain I am loved of all ladies, only you excepted: and I would I could find in my heart that I had not a hard heart, for truly I love none.
BEATRICE: A dear happiness to women: they would else have been troubled with a pernicious suitor. I thank God and my cold blood, I am of your humour for that. I had rather hear my dog bark at a crow than a man swear he loves me.
BENEDICK: God keep your ladyship still in that mind, so some gentlemen or other shall scape a predestinate scratched face.
BEATRICE: Scratching could not make it worse an 'twere such a face as yours were.(1.1.79–93)

Pretty sharp, isn't it! And if we thought that the two were tearing strips off each other out of nothing but malice, cruelty, scorn, and hatred, it would not be very funny. But even at this early stage in the play (which we may know is a comedy from its title page and billing), we have seen Beatrice inquire rather persistently into "Signior Mountanto" and heard her quip that he is "a good soldier to a lady" (1.1.36). And so we suspect that there is something more between them, that their ongoing "skirmish of wit" is not deadly serious, that it has a playful dimension and is informed by more generous sentiments. This impression is enhanced by *the way* in which they ridicule each other. You can insult, mock, deride, and ridicule another person in a lot of different ways: in a crude, unimaginative way, such as calling them nasty names; in a cold, dispassionate way, such as calmly and literally ascribing faults and weaknesses to them; in an impassioned way, such as angrily yelling obscenities at them; and in a refined, intelligent way, such as speaking to and about them with wit, eloquence, and linguistic sophistication.

Though they sometimes exchange rather crude insults, Beatrice and Benedick often ridicule each other in a way that is eloquent, witty, imaginative, and refined, as they do in this opening clash. What makes it so?

- they both invent names for each other—"Signior Mountanto" and "Lady Disdain"(*antonomasia*)
- there are sexual connotations (*double entendre*) to some of their expressions, such as the meaning of having sexual intercourse deriving from the fencing term, *montanto* (an upward thrust)
- Benedick seems to assert his indifference to the welfare of Beatrice, and perhaps that she is so old and nasty that she might well have died, by way of a question that literally expresses his surprise to see her still alive (a kind of *rhetorical question*)
- Beatrice describes Benedick *metaphorically* as food for her disdain
- they often begin their utterances by repeating and playing on the other's words (to form the figure of *asteismus*).

In other words, the characters ridicule each other by using the highly figurative and tropological language that the ancient Greek and Roman rhetoricians identified as a means of ridiculing and raising laughter (Skinner: 199–211). Because the characters often ridicule each other in this way, no matter how scornful they may be, they are still talking *with* each other, they are engaging with each other and having a *conversation* and *dialogue*. And because they ridicule each other in this way, their ridicule is witty and refined, as opposed to boorish, vulgar, obscene, or crude. While certainly having an edge, it can and I think should still come across as being in some degree playful and humorous.

In other cases, I think audiences laugh not because some characters are mocking and ridiculing other characters in a certain way, but simply because they know that the characters are deceiving other characters, sometimes by way of disguise. In *As You Like It*, for example, we are amused if not driven to laughter when we see Rosalind, disguised as a man called Ganymede, engage in an ongoing deception of Orlando and the other characters in the forest. In *Twelfth Night,* the spirit of laughter is enabled not just by the merrymaking of Sir Toby but also by Viola who disguises herself as a man called Cesario who deceives both the man she loves (Orsino) and the woman who loves her

(Olivia). We also get Feste disguising himself as Sir Topaz the curate in order to make fun of Malvolio at the end of this play. Perhaps we have a little compassion for the characters who are deceived, but again, their suffering is bearable and fleeting, with the result that our compassion can give way to amusement. There are further occasions for mirth when these comic heroines find it difficult to play their parts and, so, verge on blowing their disguises: Viola/Cesario cuts a comical figure as she shrinks from playing the role of a man who has been challenged to fight by another, and wittily exclaims, "Pray God defend me! A little thing [i.e. a penis] would make me tell them how much I lack of a man" (3.4.223–4). Similarly, in *As You Like It*, there is some good fun to see Rosalind almost blow her disguise when she feints at the sight of the handkerchief covered in her dear Orlando's blood: as Oliver observes, "be of good cheer, youth. You a man! You lack a man's heart." Indeed she does, because as she and we, but not Oliver knows, "he" is a woman (4.3.164).

True, some of this comedy depends on generalizations about men and women that the characters themselves explicitly state and that we might not find to be so funny. But I think modern western audiences find humor in this kind of thing because these generalizations are also often made in a playful spirit and are indeed challenged and undermined in many ways. Though dressed as a man and playing the part of a man, for example, Viola in *Twelfth Night* objects to Orsino that women "are as true of heart as we [men]" and that "we men may say more, swear more, but indeed / Our shows are more than will [our desires], for still we prove / Much in our vows, but little in our love" (2.4.108–21). And the action of this play bears out this claim: Orsino forgets about his supposed love of Olivia and ends up with Viola, while Viola remains true to Orsino from the moment she lays eyes on him. More generally, the strength, dominance, and complexity of female comic protagonists such as Viola and Rosalind challenge the commonplaces about men and women on which some of the role-playing depends, and so further enhance their comic potential.

In many cases, those characters who are deceived or misled—be it by disguise, magic, conspiracy, alcohol, love, or drugs—do silly, ridiculous, mad, vulgar, boorish, or irrational things. In *A Midsummer Night's Dream*, for example, Bottom is such a great comical character in part because in the middle of the play Puck places an ass's head on him and he then acts in a way that is half human, half ass. When, in response to Titania's inquiry into what he would like to eat, he coolly responds, as though he is what he has always been but has inexplicably developed a new appetite, "Truly, a peck of provender [fodder]; I could munch your good dry oats. Methinks I have a great desire to a bottle of hay: good hay, sweet hay, hath no fellow" (4.1.24–5). That really cracks me up! Titania makes for a comical character when, under the influence of the love juice Oberon administers to her eyes, she falls for and puts herself and her attendants at the service of the transformed Bottom. Lysander seems loony when, awakening after Puck has administered the love juice in his eyes, he falls for Helena and scorns his real love, Hermia. Demetrius, too, becomes a serio-comical lover once, under the influence of the same love juice, he suddenly renounces Hermia and falls for Helena. We get a similar kind of incident in *Twelfth Night*. Sir Andrew makes himself a laughing stock in part because Sir Toby and Fabian dupe him into thinking Olivia is interested in him and that he could gain her favour by challenging Viola/Cesario to a duel. And having been misled or "gulled"—not by love juice but by a forged letter—into believing that Olivia loves him, wants him to wear yellow stockings and cross-garters, and would like to see him smile and be surly with the members of her household, Malvolio does just that. He thereby causes Olivia to think he is mad and ought to be looked to—a cue for the others to lock him up in a dark room.

In *Much Ado about Nothing*, we have an elegant and refined variation on this type of comic incident when some of the characters conspire to deceive and trick other characters in order to believe something that is true. I'm thinking of the parallel scenes in which Benedick overhears Don Pedro, Leonato, and Claudio speak of him as a proud man who would never requite Beatrice's love for him, and Beatrice overhears Hero and Ursula speak of her as a proud woman who would never requite the love of Benedick. These scenes can be hilarious, first, because they provide the possibility of showing the two main characters going to ridiculous lengths (like dressing up as a gardener, climbing a tree, hiding in a hole, putting a bucket over their head, or just running around) in order not to be seen as they overhear the contrived conversation. Second, they show the two main characters being tricked into some rather serious soul-searching, a resolution to change their behavior, and a belief in something that really is the case: Beatrice really does love Benedick, and Benedick really does love Beatrice! That their love for each other compels them to break their earlier staunch vows never to love and marry is just one more detail that slightly humiliates them and makes the whole thing comical.

Incompetence, morally diminished action, slightly injurious behavior (slapstick), mimicry, ridicule, deception, mistakes, errors, and unexpected events are thus the mainstay of Shakespearean powers to raise laughter through incident in all genres of drama. But what about the overall action or plot of the plays: is Shakespeare trying to make us laugh by representing larger sequences of events, and bringing them to a close as he does in the comedies and romances—with a "happy ending"?

It has been said that while the incidents in the tragedies seem to follow one after the other up to the bitter end with probability, if not necessity, the incidents in the comedies and romances seem more loosely connected, improbable, accidental, surprising, and therefore qualified to make an audience feel a little festive and given to laughter. There is certainly some truth to this claim, as some of the characters themselves observe. In *A Midsummer Night's Dream*, for example, Puck is enjoying himself so much because "those things do best please [him] / That befall preposterously," which is precisely how he finds things are befalling (3.2.120–21). Later on, Oberon refers to the events as "this night's accidents" which all will consider as merely "the fierce vexation of a dream" once they have returned to Athens (4.1.57–60). In *Twelfth Night*,

Fabian says of the prank on Malvolio that "if this were played upon a stage now, I could condemn it as an improbable fiction" (3.4.97–8). In *As You Like It*, both Rosalind and Orlando speculate on how unlikely it is that Oliver and Celia should have met, fallen for each other, and resolved to marry so quickly (5.2.1–29). And this play ends with many other improbabilities: Duke Frederick encounters a religious man who "converts" him; Oliver and Orlando happen to come across a snake and a lion; the god Hymen appears to clear up all of the confusion.

At the same time, though, the happy endings of these plays often come as no surprise, and for several reasons. First, if when we are watching, say, *A Midsummer Night's Dream*, we know we are watching a certain kind or genre of play—comedy—we *expect* it will have some kind of happy ending, with the result that the happy ending of the play does not surprise us but is consistent with our expectations. And, as we have noted, our knowledge that it *is* this kind of play and will have this kind of ending affects our response to some of the pain and suffering we see earlier in the play: we are inclined not to take so seriously, and perhaps even to find humorous, the suffering of the characters if we know that it is transitory and will be superseded by long-term happiness. The happy endings seem probable, if not necessary, also because whereas the socio-political environment of the tragedies is so dangerous and menacing, the socio-political environment of the comedies is either more benign or, in cases where it is dark, one that may be temporarily left for another more benign green world. And because many of the characters, as we will see, are more inclined to make compromises and do not pursue their aims with deadly seriousness, we feel they are more likely to be happy.

Moreover, many of the characters in this relatively benign world keep on saying that things are going to turn out well. Thus, at the very beginning of *A Midsummer Night's Dream*, Hippolyta, speaking in the future tense, says the four days and nights will pass quickly, "And then the moon, like to a silver bow / New-bent in heaven, shall behold the night / Of our solemnities" (1.1.9–11). Theseus then claims "I will wed thee in another key, / With pomp, with triumph and with reveling" (1.1.19–20). The artisans' preparations for their performance is all predicated upon the occurrence of this wedding, and in the middle of the play the rather benevolent Oberon prophesies that the four human lovers shall return to Athens in friendship, that he shall release his dear Titania from her delusion, and that "all things shall be peace" (3.2.385–90). The scene concludes with Puck addressing Lysander and reaffirming this rosy prediction:

> Jack shall have Jill,
> Naught shall go ill,
> The man shall have his mare again, and all shall be well.
> (3.2.474–9)

True, the fact that characters say things will turn out well does not necessarily mean they will. But their optimism and up-beat prophecies throughout the play make it seem more likely that there will be a happy ending.

70 *Laughter and delight*

To be sure, when that ending occurs, some characters are laughing and they invite us to do so as well. At the end of *Twelfth Night*, for example, Fabian hopes that the whole Malvolio affair "may rather pluck on laughter than revenge," and Olivia seems to fulfil his hope (5.1.351). But the fact that these endings meet our expectations does not really make us laugh so much as merely provide the satisfaction and pleasure of having expectations met. And, as we saw in the Introduction, many of the characters at the endings of the comedies are not so much laughing as feeling joyous, delighted, and happy. They often say this is what they are feeling and encourage others—including the audience—to do the same. And there is considerable evidence in the critical tradition (and most of the contemporary performances of the comedies I have seen) that this is at least part of what many people in the audience do experience.

The endings of the comedies and romances can affect us in this way because they include a wide range of actions that are different from the comic actions we have observed. In some cases the main characters marry: by the end of *Twelfth Night*, Olivia has married Sebastian and Sir Toby has married Maria; at the end of *As You Like It*, all the couples seem to be married in a kind of pagan rite presided over by Hymen, the ancient Greek god of marriage; the three couples in *A Midsummer Night's Dream* appear to have been married at the "temple" before the final act of that play. But the actual marriage ceremony often occurs off-stage, and in some cases the wedding is not part of the action of the play proper but is foreseen as an event that will take place in the immediate future, *after* all of the action represented by the play. At the ends of the comedies and romances, the main characters thus often *confess* their love for each other, *commit* themselves to each other for the long term, and *state their intention* to marry, usually openly and in public. The characters "do purpose to marry" as Benedick announces at the end of *Much Ado* (5.4.104). This is the case with Benedick/Beatrice and Claudio/Hero in *Much Ado*, Orsino/Viola in *Twelfth Night*, and the lovers in some of the other comedies and romances, including *The Tempest* and *The Winter's Tale*.

Be it an actual or anticipated wedding, it is described as a serious, rather solemn event. At the beginning of *A Midsummer Night's Dream*, for example, Hippolyta makes clear that the "nuptial hour" which brings the play to a close will be "the night of our solemnities" (1.1.10–11). In the final scene of *Much Ado*, Friar Francis takes Claudio and Hero off to chapel in order to perform "holy rites" (5.4.69). In the fifth act of *Twelfth Night*, the priest describes the marriage of Olivia and Sebastian over which he has just presided as

> A contract of eternal bond of love,
> Confirmed by mutual joinder of your hands,
> Attested by the holy close of lips,
> Strengthened by interchangement of your rings,
> And all the ceremony of this compact
> Sealed in my function, by my testimony.
> (5.1.149–54)

Speaking to Viola/Cesario at the very end of the act, Orsino claims that "when golden time convents, / A solemn combination shall be made / Of our dear souls" (5.1.364–5). And in *The Tempest*, Prospero foresees the wedding of Miranda and Ferdinand as "sanctimonious ceremonies" that will "with full and holy rite be ministered" (4.1.16–17).

These weddings are solemn and rather serious events, first, because as many characters themselves observe, they are intended to mark the end of one stage of life—call it courtship—and the beginning of another stage of life—call it marriage—which will never end or which, at least, will last until death do the lovers part. In *A Midsummer Night's Dream*, for example, Theseus refers to his wedding as an event that marks an "everlasting bond of fellowship" (1.1.87), and he later observes that he and Hippolyta along with the other four lovers "shall eternally be knit" (4.1 176). Second, the wedding is presided over by a priest, a minister, or a god, and it usually takes place in a church or a temple. Third, in most cases the wedding also marks the loss of a condition that many of the characters take seriously, the condition of virginity. For, as many of the leading characters of these plays believe and in some cases explicitly state, premarital sex is immoral and they therefore have not engaged in it. The full gratification of the sexual desires that have to an important extent been driving the action is thus also not strictly speaking included in the ending of many of the plays: sexual desire is restrained, and its gratification is foreseen and anticipated by the characters as a pleasure they shall know in the immediate future, after the wedding. Finally, if "marriage is the control of human sexuality by law" (Bates: 104), then the ceremony that marks the entrance of lovers into the state of matrimony is in some sense a show of respect for the law and the limitations it places on the gratification of sexual desire.

This of course means that the bearing of children and formation of new families is also not part of the action of the plays, but is foreseen as something to come in the longer term. Thus, in *As You Like It*, Hymen, the god of marriage, sings that wedlock should "be honoured" because "'Tis Hymen peoples every town" (5.4.114–17). In *Much Ado*, Benedick is perhaps not entirely joking when, early in the play, he justifies his resolution to love and marry Beatrice on grounds that "the world must be peopled" (2.3.174). And in *A Midsummer Night's Dream*, the fairies sing that "the issue" created in the bridal bed "Ever shall be fortunate" (5.1.375–6). So while the conflicts and confusions represented earlier in the comedies are resolved by characters who confess love, promise, commit, and sometimes marry at the ends of the plays, these main characters usually do not have sex, they do not have children, and they sometimes do not marry—all of this is in the offing. The prevailing mood at the end of the comedies is thus powerfully informed by hope, optimism, and great expectation.

In addition, in cases where the main characters have assumed disguises, they shed them and resume their former appearances, however much they may have changed as people (though in *Twelfth Night*, Viola remains Cesario until they can find women's clothes for her). The other characters might hold something against those who have deceived them, but they usually don't: they *forgive* those who have deceived them, just as other characters who have suffered more substantial injuries forgive those who have caused them. And in some cases, supernatural deities intervene, announce the matches and impending weddings, and perform another quite important act: they *bless* the couples. Thus, at the end of *As You Like It*, Hymen invites the four couples to sing "a wedlock-hymn" that includes the lines, "Wedding is great Juno's crown, / O, blessed bond of board and bed!" (5.4.101–15). In *A Midsummer Night's Dream*, once he has made up with Titania, Oberon says that the next night they will "bless" Theseus' house "to all fair prosperity" (4.1.81–2). At the end of the play, Titania tells the fairies, "Hand in hand, with fairy grace, / Will we sing and bless this place," and this is what they do: "to the best bride-bed will we, / Which by us shall blessed be" (5.1.373–4).

It is also important to note that ridicule tends to fade out in the final acts of the comedies and romances. True, in *A Midsummer Night's Dream*, the aristocrats make fun of the mechanicals' theatrical performance. But Theseus softens the derision beforehand when he observes that though the play might well be a matter for their "sport," the aristocrats should accept it kindly because the mechanicals present it out of simplicity, fearful duty, modesty, and even love (5.1.93–109). And as Oberon observes earlier in connection with the four lovers, "when they next wake, all this derision / Shall seem a dream and fruitless vision" (3.2. 383–4). This is generally what happens at the end of the comedies and romances: instead of calling for more derision and ridicule of particular individuals, someone usually calls for festivity and celebration that will include most characters.

Sure, it is possible to stage this festivity as wild, Dionysiac revelry, and some of the characters do indeed use the word "revelry" to describe the proceedings: Duke Senior calls all to join in "rustic revelry" (5.4.151), and Theseus asks "what revels are in hand?" (5.1.37). If, like Jan Kott and some directors, you think *A Midsummer Night's Dream* is really about brutal eroticism in the woods, then you might well stage the final revelry in this way. But "revel" could mean simply a masque or play, and there are many indications that the final festive activity is on the ceremonious, orderly side. Note, first of all, that no one is walking around at the end of Shakespeare's comedies and romances with a big rubber phallus, much less an erect one—as characters in Aristophanic comedy sometimes do. There is little to suggest that this revelry includes any significant sexual activity, and no one is calling for drinking wine or liquor. The call is rather for music, singing, dancing, and some kind of entertainment. Thus, after calling all to join in revelry, Duke Senior calls on "brides and bridegrooms all, / With measure heaped in joy, to th'measures fall," where "measure" means both moderation and stately dance. He then observes, "We'll begin these rites, / As we do trust they'll end, in true delights" (5.4.152–3; 171–2). At the end of *A Midsummer Night's Dream*, Theseus asks "How shall we beguile / The lazy time, if not with some delight?" (5.1.42–43), and Quince claims that his play is "all for your delight" (5.1.118). Oberon says to Titania, "Now thou and I are new in amity, / And will tomorrow midnight solemnly / Dance in Duke Theseus' house triumphantly" (4.1.79–81). Theseus thrice refers to the "solemnity" of the feast to celebrate the wedding of the three couples (4.1.126, 179; 5.1.339). At the end of *Much Ado*, Benedick says, "let's have a dance ere we are married, that we may lighten our own hearts and our wives' heels" (5.4.112–13). The words "measure," "delight," "lighten," "rite," "solemnity"—not to mention the music and song—all suggest that there ought to be a ceremonious, refined, sober, ritualistic, beautiful side to the festivity and celebration at the end of Shakespearean comedy.

These endings, though, are not sickly sweet, for there are also elements that qualify the happiness and festivity. In *A Midsummer Night's Dream*, for example, the fairies make us aware that their blessing and promise are intended to protect the lovers' children from the "blots of Nature's hand," such as "mole, hare-lip, [and] scar" and "mark prodigious, such as are / Despised in nativity" (5.1.379–84). In *Twelfth Night*, Antonio is left alone without his dear Sebastian, Malvolio storms off vowing revenge, and Feste sings a rather sad song. In *As You Like It*, Oliver and Celia will not return to court but will remain in the forest. Duke Senior will regain his dukedom, but he and the others are bound to leave the forest and return to what Jacques refers to as "the pompous court" (5.4.156). Jaques declines the invitation to join the dancing measures in favor of remaining in the forest in order to converse with Duke Frederick who "hath put on a religious life" (5.4.156). While foreseeing happy, well-deserved futures for the lovers, he "bequeaths" Touchstone and Audrey "to wrangling, for thy loving voyage / Is but for two months victualled" (5.4.165–6). And *Much Ado* concludes with Benedick advising the good but sad Don Pedro to get a wife on the rather dubious grounds that it will qualify him to experience cuckoldry (5.4.116).

The endings of Shakespeare's comedies are thus occasions not so much for laughter as for feelings which Sidney felt were different from laughter (at least laughter of a certain kind) but still ought to be called forth by comedy: delight, joy, and that warm fuzzy feeling many people get when they see their friends and family graduate, announce an engagement, or get married. This is because these endings consist of characters confessing love for each other, making long-term commitments to each other, promising, blessing, forgiving, singing, dancing, celebrating, getting married, looking forward to getting married, restraining sexual desire while anticipating its gratification, hoping for happiness and children, announcing intentions to return to and take up various roles in the societies they had left. The characters who perform these actions are for the most part happy in their good fortune and chances, and as Sidney observes, "we delight in good chances," and "we delight to hear the happiness of our friends" (103). And though the characters perform these actions in a world that is in many ways benign, it is still a world in which there is sadness, solitude, unrequited love, corruption, natural depravity, death, and evil. There is thus a precariousness to the joy and happiness. It is not guaranteed, even if it may be blessed by supernatural agents, but that in a way makes it all the more precious and sweet. These actions are thus also ones that in important ways resemble an initiation rite, as some critics have claimed: having been separated from their societies and undergone forms of confusion, conflict, and change, the characters are in the end incorporated back into their societies (Barber, Salingar, Berry). Representing this kind of rite as he does, Shakespeare wants to make you laugh along the way, but like Duke Senior, he also wants it all to "end, in true delights."

Character

The ancient Greeks and Romans associated comedy with the representation of people who are inferior to other people in terms of physical appearance, morality, social standing, and intelligence. Many characters in Shakespeare's comic scenes fit this bill. For ugly, monstrous, unusual physical appearance we have, for example,

- the "monstrous" Bottom once he is transformed into an ass
- the corpulent Falstaff who describes himself as one whose "skin hangs about [him] like an old lady's loose gown. I am withered like an old apple-john" (3.3.2–3)
- Falstaff's drinking buddy, Bardolph, whose nose is so red from drinking that it makes Falstaff think of hell-fire whenever he sees him (3.3.21)
- the "monstrous" Caliban
- the fools and clowns in their strange clothing.

There are also many characters who are slightly inferior on the count of intelligence:

- courtiers such as Sir Andrew Aguecheek in *Twelfth Night*
- simpletons and country bumpkins, such as Silvius, William, and Audrey in *As You Like It*
- some of the artisans in *A Midsummer Night's Dream*
- Dogberry and his men in *Much Ado*.

Many characters in comical scenes in all genres of Shakespearean drama are also from lower socio-economic ranks of society. And as we have seen, many of the funny characters in all genres of Shakespearean drama are also a little short on some of the moral virtues as well: we see a wide range of rather unwise, cowardly, dishonest, selfish, rude, vain, greedy, intemperate, unfair characters.

Nietzsche observed that the human race will always decree that there are some things at which it is forbidden to laugh (75), and the list of those things can change over time. Given modern moral sensibilities and the ways in which they differ from the prevailing moral sensibilities of earlier periods in western society, you might feel that the kinds of characters mentioned above are not so funny and ought not to be laughed at. In that case, Shakespearean comedy would fail to achieve one of its principal aims, and if enough people felt that way, it might well be deemed to be second-rate comedy. But judging from modern criticism, reviews, and audience responses to many performances on stage and screen, I think the moral sensibility of many people today has enough in common with the moral sensibility of many who came before them to qualify these characters as comical characters, ones who can make audiences laugh.

The ancient Greeks and Romans also felt that in order to be funny, you had to avoid creating characters, or singling out people for ridicule, who were *too* inferior. If the "inferiority" of characters was so pronounced that they were really evil, they experienced or inflicted on others serious pain, or were pathological, they would not make us laugh but would arouse our indignation, compassion, or anger. I think Shakespearean comedy generally conforms with this idea as well. It is because we have many characters who, though inferior in some ways, are not so diminished that we think they are evil, cruel, malicious, wretched, or pathological that many scenes in the comedies and other genres of Shakespearean drama appeal to our sense of humor. True, there are some exceptions to this generalization. Richard III, for example, is a villain who can nevertheless be played to great comic effect, as can Aaron the Moor in *Titus Andronicus*, and even Iago in *Othello*. A rich potential for black comedy is created by the ways in which these characters make light of their own villainy, wittily deride others, engage in sinister wordplay, trivialize the suffering of their victims, cynically comment on the action, deprecate themselves, shamelessly brag and joke with the audience. But our laughter in these cases is sporadic and tempered by our comprehension of the real malevolence of these villains and the terrible pain and suffering they bring upon others and themselves.

If Shakespeare's comic characters were simply inferior people, we might well laugh *at* them, but we would not be so inclined to laugh along *with* them, to experience the more generous, joyful kind of laughter that Hegel experienced when he read Aristophanes and that he found again in Shakespearean comedy. One reason we might share Hegel's experience is that, like many characters in the Old Comedy of Aristophanes, many of Shakespeare's comic characters are not deadly serious in their aims. This, I think, is what Hazlitt sees about Falstaff when he observes the *motives* of the big man's pursuit of worldly pleasures: "he is represented as a liar, a braggart, a coward, a glutton, etc. and yet we are not offended but delighted with him; for he is all these as much to amuse others as to gratify himself" (279). Yes, Falstaff enjoys his drinking, eating, and sex, but rather than engaging in them with deadly seriousness, solely for his own gratification, he does so at least in part for fun—his own and that of others. He does so because, as Hazlitt also observes, besides loving sensual pleasure, Falstaff has a "love of laughter and good fellowship" (278–9). As we will see in a moment, this playfulness also enters into the way Falstaff pursues his arguments aimed at justifying and excusing himself—something he is frequently called upon to do.

This playful manner of pursuing aims is also evident in the romantic comedies. Take, for example, Beatrice and Benedick in *Much Ado*. In the opening scene of the play Beatrice says, "I had rather hear my dog bark at a crow than a man swear he loves me" (1.1.90); later, in response to her uncle Leonato's expression of his hope that she one day find a husband, she responds, "not till God make men of some other metal than earth. Would it not grieve a woman to be overmastered with a piece of valiant dust?" (2.1.39–41). Similarly, Benedick in the opening scene emphatically asserts, "I will live a bachelor" (1.1.162–3); later he claims "I would not marry her [Beatrice], though she were endowed with all that Adam had left him before he transgressed" (2.1.175–6). Both of them assert that at least part of their aim in life is to stay single, and certainly never to marry each other. Yet they are hardly deadly serious in the pursuit of this aim. We feel this right from the start because they use such exaggerated (*hyperbolic*) language to assert it, and they seem to be attracted to each other in some way. And we see how easily they give up this aim. Upon overhearing others speak of Beatrice's love for him, Benedick immediately resolves to requite her love, and he provides what both he and the audience know is some specious, playful argument in defence of his capitulation (2.3.171–5). Beatrice, too, suddenly abandons her aim to remain a maid when she overhears others speak of Benedick's love for her (3.1.109–16). And so we see the not-so-serious side of the lovers' determination to remain single. Sure, we might look down on them as hypocrites, or weaklings who have caved, and laugh *at* them. But we might also warm to them and share their good humor as they acknowledge their affections, eat humble pie, and see the lighter side of the way they relinquish earlier resolutions.

But this is not always the case. In *Twelfth Night*, the playful side of the main lovers' aims is evident from the fact that while Orsino simply must have Olivia, he ends up being perfectly happy with Viola, and while Olivia simply must have Cesario, she is happy with Sebastian. But I think Malvolio is a character who might be said to be serious in his aims and who therefore may cause in both other characters and the audience the more scornful kind of laughter Hegel associated with Molière and modern comedy at large (though some have also felt compassion for him). And some characters in the comedies, such as Viola in *Twelfth Night* and Rosalind in *As You Like It*, pursue their love interests with constancy and determination. But because there is a playful and even ridiculous dimension to the way many characters, including Viola and Rosalind, pursue their aims, and because they can see the humorous side of their experiences, they are not laughing stocks as Malvolio is. They are rather characters *with* whom we can laugh. They can evoke in us that softer kind of laughter Hegel liked, the kind of laughter recent scholars describe as "carnivalesque laughter" and see as an occasion for "communal merriment" (Berry 2002: 123).

This also holds to some extent for the "fools" in Shakespeare's comedies, such as Feste and Fabian in *Twelfth Night* and Touchstone in *As You Like It*. While they might dress up in silly ways, and do some silly things, they are really "wise men under camouflage" (Salingar: 246), who are also well endowed with wit, intelligence, musical ability, and powers of expression. They display some interest in money and women, but they are not very serious in the pursuit of these goals and are content to play along with whatever game is on. Far from being laughing stocks, they are more inclined to expose and sing of the folly of the world in which they find themselves, and to respond to it all with wit, good humor, a song, but also a little cynicism and melancholy.

Good humor and merriment are on the way to what I mean by "delight," and there are a few other basic features of Shakespeare's characters that account for this experience that I think Shakespeare was aiming at, and which I think can still make his plays special for us. One is just that, unlike pretty much all of the western playwrights who preceded him, Shakespeare provides us with characters who have complex inner lives of thought and emotion and who change and develop over the course of the plays (Salingar, Berry, Bloom). He does so, moreover, in a way that, at least for many, makes his characters seem like real human beings. Because they are like us, because they seem real, we can sympathize with them, get interested in them, and care for them. So what? Well, if we care for them, we may well feel joy and delight when, in the end, they are happy.

Another thing about the characters that enables this response is that, contrary to the ancient Graeco-Roman recipe for comedy, they are *superior* in many ways. In *Much Ado*, for example, Don Pedro supports his plan to match Benedick with Beatrice by observing that Benedick, the Paduan lord, "is of a noble strain, of approved valour and confirmed honesty" (2.1.260); he might have added that Benedick is wise, extremely intelligent, linguistically brilliant, handsome, emotionally alive, and not too proud to follow his heart. Beatrice, niece to Leonato, governor of Messina, is a loyal friend to Hero and every bit as wise, intelligent, good-looking, emotional, and witty as he is. Claudio, a Florentine lord, is not so impressive, but Hero is nothing short of noble. In *As You Like It*, Rosalind, the daughter of a duke, is wiser than anyone else in the play, she is in command of a superior intellect, she displays courage and a strong sense of justice in the way she objects to Duke Frederick's banishment of her father and herself, she is compassionate and benevolent, she is a faithful friend to Celia, her physical beauty shows through her disguise, and she loves her Orlando truly and deeply. While not her equal, Orlando is a good man who stands up for himself against his unjust brother, cares for old Adam, is kind and forgiving even of those who have injured him, and truly and deeply loves his Rosalind—he must also be something of a hunk, given that he physically overpowers his older brother, defeats the court wrestler, Charles, and takes on a lion. In *Twelfth Night*, Viola is superior across the board, and Olivia and Orsino, though far from perfect, are better than your average aristocrats. In the romances, we have a wide range of superior figures, including the near-perfect young lovers, Miranda and Ferdinand in *The Tempest*, and Perdita and Florizel in *The Winter's Tale*. Many of the protagonists of the comedies and romances are thus superior in terms of virtue, intellect, linguistic power, socio-economic standing, physical appearance, and some other skills and abilities. Such characters are not really necessary if all you want to do is to make people laugh; neither are playful and benevolent supernatural characters such as Puck, Hymen (the god of matrimony), and Ariel. But such characters are useful if you are also in the business of providing people with more complex emotional experiences that include joy and delight.

Thought

Have you ever seen or attended those comedy shows which are set up as formal debates where one team argues for, and another team argues against, a general proposition—such as "the single life is better than married life"—and where the team that presents not just the most compelling but also the zaniest, funniest arguments for their side "wins"? If so, you will have seen that some people find this kind of show funny. I think this confirms one of the claims Aristotle makes about *dianoia* (thought, intellect, or reasoning). In the *Poetics*, Aristotle identifies *dianoia* as the third most important element of tragedy (after plot and character), and he thinks of it in terms of "that with which people demonstrate that something is or is not, or make some universal statement" (9–10). In the last chapter we saw that *dianoia* is indeed an important element of Shakespeare's tragedies and histories, one that in part accounts for the *emotional* response we have to the characters and their suffering. But in Richard Janko's reconstruction of *Poetics II*, Aristotle also makes the following claim, one that I think is borne out by modern comedy debate shows:

> hence character too is a part of comic representation; but so also is reasoning [*dianoia*], since actions are caused by the reasoning as well as the characters of the people acting. Therefore laughter can also arise from reasoning, when the argument for an action is disjointed and lacking any sequence.
>
> (51)

All genres of Shakespearean drama also bear out this claim, as does western comedy from Aristophanes on (Herrick). One of the main reasons for this is that, as opposed to being conducted in a way that is intense, serious, and logical, reasoning and arguing can be conducted in a way that is playful, light-hearted, illogical, spurious, and specious.

Take, for example, *Henry IV, part 1*. After the serious opening scene, we get the first comic scene of the play which begins with Falstaff asking the young Prince Hal what time of day it is. Hal then responds:

> Thou art so fat-witted with drinking of old sack and unbuttoning thee after supper and sleeping upon benches in the afternoon, that thou hast forgotten to demand that truly which thou wouldst truly know. What a devil hast thou to do with the time of the day? Unless hours were cups of sack and minutes capons and clocks the tongues of bawds and dials [sun dials] the signs of leaping-houses [brothels] and the blessed sun himself a fair hot wench in flame-coloured taffeta [silky fabric], I see no reason why thou shouldst be so superfluous to demand the time of the day.
>
> (1.2.2–8)

And so the comedy (in this history play) begins! What makes it funny is the way in which Hal makes fun of his portly drinking buddy. He begins with some pretty basic insults and ridicule: because Falstaff drinks so much, eats so much, and sleeps on benches in the daytime, Falstaff's mind has gone soft (he is "fat-witted"), he doesn't know what really concerns him, and he asks stupid questions. But Hal then presents a kind of zany but also highly imaginative argument, premises of which remain unstated but implied, and the conclusion of which is the accusation he makes in the beginning:

1   We all know that sack, capons (chickens for roasting), and prostitutes are the things that really concern you.
2   It follows that if hours were cups of sack, minutes capons, clocks the tongues of prostitutes, and the sun a hot wench, then you might well be concerned about the time of day and have a good reason to ask me about it.
3   But we all know that hours are not cups of sack, minutes are not capons, clocks are not prostitutes, and the sun is not a hot wench.
4   Therefore you have no good reason to ask me what time of day it is—what a stupid question!

Falstaff might well have retorted that actually it is Hal who is fat-witted, since Hal's argument is invalid: the premises could be true and the conclusion false! For, even if hours were not cups of sack, etc., Falstaff might well have some *other* reason for asking what time of day it is—maybe he has to get out of town by noon in order to avoid being arrested! But, like the audience, Falstaff knows that Hal is not seriously reasoning with him, that it is a playful, and a little scornful, kind of argumentative banter, and so he goes along with it. He concedes that Hal has a point, but then provides his own reason for it by admitting that he is also a petty thief: "for we that take purses go by the moon and seven stars, and not by Phoebus" (1.2.9–10). And so the playful reasoning and arguing continue.

And it is Falstaff who, as the play proceeds, proves to be the master of comic *dianoia* in this play. Perhaps the best-known instance of it is his "reasoning" with himself about honor:

> Well, 'tis no matter, honour pricks me on. But how if honour prick me off when I come on? How then? Can honour set to a leg? No. Or an arm? No. Or take away the grief of a wound? No. Honour hath no skill in surgery, then? No. What is honour? A word. What is that word 'honour'? Air. A trim reckoning! Who hath it? He that died o' Wednesday. Doth he feel it? No. Doth he hear it? No. Is it insensible, then. Yea, to the dead. But will it not live with the living? No. Why? Detraction will not suffer it. Therefore I'll none of it. Honour is a mere scutcheon [heraldic shield]: and so ends my catechism.
> (5.1.129–36)

Falstaff here claims to be thinking seriously and rationally about something—as one would in a catechism (a series of questions and answers used to teach and learn Christian doctrine). What makes it funny is that he is really only mimicking the form of a catechism in order to construct a pretext for not fighting in the war and excuse his own dishonourable behaviour. It is a playful, lively, mock self-justification, one that neither Falstaff nor the audience takes seriously. But we see here another important aspect of his comic reasoning: the reasons Falstaff provides for not fighting in an "honourable" fashion are not entirely specious. In a way, honor *is* useless, it cannot heal the wounded, it does consist in the words others say about one, those who die honorably are insensible of the honor they have won, and the envy and resentment of others may well lead them to detract and thereby diminish the honor some men deserve for having fought well and died in battle. Indeed, Falstaff here invents a rather searching critique of honor defined in terms of military valor. So part of the wit and humor of the soliloquy derives from the way in which, though aiming mainly to excuse his own dishonorable behaviour in a way he knows is duplicitous, Falstaff manages to provide some good reasons for it. We laugh at his reasoning, and the way he is using it to excuse himself, but we are also perhaps a little discomfited by it, because, however specious and self-serving it may be, there is still some truth to it.

But the best and to my mind the funniest case of comic *dianoia*, combined with figurative language and comic incident, comes later in the play. Seeing Falstaff lying motionless on the battleground, and believing him to have been killed, Prince Hal observes, "Embowelled will I see thee by and by: / Till then in blood by noble Percy lie" (5.3.110–11). The Prince leaves, "*Falstaff riseth up,*" and he then exclaims,

> Embowelled! If thou embowel me to-day, I'll give you leave to powder me and eat me too to-morrow. 'Twas time to counterfeit, or that hot termagant Scot had paid me scot and lot too. Counterfeit? I am no counterfeit; to die is to be a counterfeit, for he is but the counterfeit of a man who hath not the life of a man. But to counterfeit dying, when a man thereby liveth, is to be no counterfeit, but the true and perfect image of life indeed. The better part of valour is discretion, in the which better part I have saved my life. I am afraid of this gunpowder Percy, though he be dead. How, if he should counterfeit too and rise? I am afraid he would prove the better counterfeit: therefore I'll make him sure, yea, and I'll swear I killed him.
> (5.3.112–23)

Such a hilarious moment, kicked off by an action (Falstaff's rising up) that shows he has fooled the Prince, and a figure (*anadiplosis*) that displays the big man's linguistic brilliance and wit: Falstaff *begins* his sentence by repeating one of the words with which Prince Henry *ends* his speech: "embowelled." He then admits that, having faked death, he counterfeited—and by implication was cowardly—in order to avoid being killed by the Scot, Douglas. But Falstaff then retracts this admission on the basis of reasoning that might be schematized as follows:

1   The counterfeit of a man is a dead man.
2   If you counterfeit (fake) death in order to avoid being a dead man, you are not a counterfeit.
3   I counterfeited death in order to avoid being a dead man.
4   Therefore I am no counterfeit.

Here the argumentation depends on what we might call a "pun" but what Shakespeare and the ancient Greeks and Romans called the figure, *antanaclasis*, for Falstaff reasons by repeating a single word, "counterfeit," but using it to mean different things: he uses it to mean both a faker or duplicitous man, and a dead man. This allows him to argue that while in one sense he might be a counterfeit—a faker—he is not a counterfeit in another more important sense—a dead man. On the contrary, he is the true and perfect image of life! And so he justifies the retraction of his initial admission that he is a counterfeit (and by implication a duplicitous, dishonest, and even cowardly man). Again, what makes this reasoning funny is that it is spurious, it allows Falstaff yet once more to evade a moral accusation, it includes wordplay, and, I would suggest, it includes an element of reason and a grain of truth, as great comic argument usually does: the basic argument (premises 2–4) is valid, and a dead man *is* in one sense the counterfeit of a man! And we note that Falstaff doesn't leave the argument there: his fast-and-loose, self-serving reasoning continues as he then adopts the standard definition of the verb "to counterfeit" as to fake, fears that Percy might be counterfeiting in this sense, and fears that Percy would then be a better counterfeit (faker) than he himself has been. With the word "therefore," Falstaff gives the impression that his final dishonorable resolution to stab Percy (who lies dead beside him) and falsely claim that it was he who killed him in the first place is entirely rational. But since both he and the audience know how playful and spurious the reasoning behind this conclusion is, we laugh, even if we find the scene rather grisly.

This kind of reasoning and argumentation pervades the romantic comedies. In *Twelfth Night*, for example, the Countess Olivia's clown, Feste, asks Olivia, who is grieving for her deceased brother, "leave to prove you a fool." When she tells him to "Make your proof," the following exchange ensues:

FESTE: I must catechize you for it, Madonna. Good my mouse of virtue, answer.
OLIVIA: Well, sir, for want of other idleness, I'll bide your proof.
FESTE: Good Madonna, why mourn'st thou?
OLIVIA: Good fool, for my brother's death.
FESTE: I think his soul is in hell, Madonna.
OLIVIA: I know his soul is in heaven, fool.
FESTE: The more fool, Madonna, to mourn for your brother's soul being in heaven. Take away the fool, gentlemen.

(1.5.42–54)

Again a "catechism" and "proof," but one that is light-hearted, playful, witty, humorous. Olivia and we smile, perhaps, because Feste does not really mean to show that Olivia is a fool and thereby ridicule her and make of her a laughing stock, but to cheer her up and to comfort her with a playful but not entirely silly argument. We then see Sir Toby justify staying up late and drinking by arguing that to be up late is not to be up late (2.3.3–6). Feste, Olivia's fool, argues that he is not Olivia's fool, "but her corrupter of words" (3.1.25). And it is important to see that one of the funniest scenes in the whole play is really one in which a character is reasoning: we and the other characters laugh as we see Malvolio find and read the planted letter and draw a false inference from it: "every reason excites to this, that my lady loves me" (2.5.121). The good times only continue when, after he has presented himself to Olivia in his yellow stockings and she orders Toby and others to look after him, he mistakenly thinks to himself that her behaviour bears out the letter and that "everything adheres together" (3.4.61).

In *As You Like It*, we find another court jester—Touchstone—arguing playfully, not so much to console his auditor as to pass the time in an amusing way and perhaps to make fun of the shepherd, Corin, whom he has encountered in the forest of Arden. From the fact that Corin has never been at court, Touchstone infers that he is damned. What "reason" does Touchstone have for making such a ridiculous argument, Corin asks. "Why," Touchstone replies, "if thou never wast at court, thou never saw'st good manners. If thou never saw'st good manners, then thy manners must be wicked, and wickedness is sin, and sin is damnation." Notice the highly conspicuous, unusual linguistic form the argument takes: it is really several *anadiploses* strung together to form the figure that the ancient and Renaissance rhetoricians called a *gradatio* and that might be represented as follows: ab, bc, cd, de (court/manners, manners/wicked, wicked/sin, sin/damnation). In this context, this unusual grammatical structure is one of the things that makes the utterance seem contrived and artificial, and that makes the argumentation seem fast and loose.

Corin plays the game, but he defends himself in a rather sophisticated manner that includes the proposition that different kinds of behaviour are appropriate for different situations: "those that are good manners at the court are as ridiculous in the country as the behaviour of the country is most mockable at the court." A wise, if playful, general claim about life! He then provides an example or "instance" that supports it: at court, kissing hands is regarded as good manners, but to do so in the country would be ridiculous because people in the country are often handling the greasy fleeces of animals. Touchstone counters with the claim that the hands of courtiers are sweaty, and that the grease from an animal is "as wholesome" as the sweat of a courtier. So he challenges Corin to provide "a better instance" to show that shepherds ought not to adopt the manners of court and kiss hands as courtiers do. Corin responds by observing that shepherds' hands are hard, and often covered in tar, whereas courtiers' hands "are perfumed with civet." But Touchstone shoots these "instances" down by observing that the perfume made from civet is "the very uncleanly flux of a cat" (since it is a musk obtained from the anal glands of a cat), and is therefore "baser" than tar. Touchstone's argument is humorous because it is rather ingenious, but also because it suggests that courtiers are dirtier and baser than shepherds. Though in a way Touchstone is displaying respect for the shepherd by suggesting he is cleaner than your average sweaty, perfumed courtier, Corin at this point surrenders: acknowledging that it has not been a serious argument, he observes that "you have too courtly a wit for me. I'll rest." Touchstone, whose playfulness perhaps also includes an element of scorn, concludes by getting a few last digs in and reaffirming his initial accusation: Corin is damned! (3.2.24–60).

Several scholars have recently claimed that one of the things Shakespeare's rhetorical training at grammar school included was practice in arguing *in utramque partem*—on both sides of a question. And they suggest that this kind of training in part accounts for Shakespeare's dramatization of political debate, his elusiveness, and his cynicism and skepticism on moral and political matters (Armitage). I would add that this kind of training is also on display in Touchstone's comic argumentation, and much of the comic argumentation in Shakespearean drama at large—his characters can come up with arguments for *anything*! Shakespeare's rhetorical training also included following instructions on how to find or invent arguments (Joseph, Baldwin, Mack, Skinner). Those instructions were based on a set of "topics" or "places," which were understood as regions or general concepts from which arguments are drawn. In his highly influential account of them, the *Topics*, Cicero identifies definition and similarity as two such topics. But it is perhaps from the genus/species topic that Shakespeare draws some of the comic argument in *The Tempest*. For in one of the funniest scenes in this play, much of the comedy derives from the way in which characters reason and argue on the basis of their perception of properties and their ideas of kinds of thing.

Thus, when the jester Trinculo stumbles upon Caliban who is lying on the ground under his cloak, he reasons with himself concerning what kind of thing Caliban is:

What have we here? A man or a fish? Dead or alive? A fish, he smells like a fish: a very ancient and fish-like smell: a kind of not-of-the-newest poor-John. A strange fish! Were I in England now—as once I was—and had but this fish painted, not a holiday fool there but would give a piece of silver: there would this monster make a man: any strange beast there makes a man: when they will not give a doit [small coin] to relieve a lame beggar, they will lay out ten to see a dead Indian. Legged like a man and his fins like arms! Warm, o' my troth! I do now let loose my opinion, hold it no longer: this is no fish, but an islander that hath lately suffered by a thunderbolt.

(2.2.18–30)

84 *Laughter and delight*

The scene can be funny because of the disjointed, erroneous, but not entirely irrational way in which Trinculo reasons about the kind of thing Caliban is. He starts off by identifying Caliban as a fish, on grounds that Caliban smells like a stale kind of dried hake that poorer Englishmen ate at the time. Trinculo then digresses to make a rather unflattering observation about Englishmen in general: in England, though people will not give any money to aid lame beggars, they will pay to see a dead North American Indian, or any "strange beast" such as the strange fish or "monster" before him. But observing that Caliban has legs like those of a man, fins like human arms, and is warm, Trinculo then retracts his initial classification and concludes—mistakenly as the audience knows—that Caliban is a human islander who had been struck by lightning. This kind of reasoning continues when, after Trinculo joins Caliban under his cloak to avoid the storm, Stephano comes along and mistakenly identifies the two of them as "some monster of the isle with four legs, who hath got, as I take it, an ague" (2.2.55–6). When Caliban mistakenly identifies Stephano as one of Prospero's spirits and Trinculo mistakenly identifies Stephano as a devil, Stephano reasons that this thing that has "four legs and two voices" must be "a most delicate monster!" But no! When it then calls Stephano by name, he exclaims, again mistakenly, "this is a devil, and no monster." The reasoning is fast-and-loose, erroneous, and based on observations of similarity and definitions of fish, monsters, and humans in terms of specific properties and parts. It concludes with Stephano and Trinculo finally recognising each other and apparently settling on the classification of Caliban as a monster. As for Caliban, well he provides one last laugh by mistakenly classifying Stephano as a god on grounds that he bears and shares "celestial liquor" (2.2.90).

Some of the comic scenes in the tragedies are also grounded in reasoning that is playful, spurious, unsound, disjointed—but also not entirely removed from truth. One of my favorite instances of this is the scene near the end of *Coriolanus*: Coriolanus has been banished from Rome, joined forces with his arch-enemy Aufidius, and agreed to lead the Volscian army against Rome. Aware that war is imminent, Aufidius' servingmen converse with each other as follows:

SECOND SERVINGMAN: Why, then we shall have a stirring world again. This peace is nothing but to rust iron, increase tailors, and breed ballad-makers.
FIRST SERVINGMAN: Let me have war, say I: it exceeds peace as far as day does night: it's spritely walking, audible, and full of vent. Peace is a very apoplexy [paralysis], lethargy, mulled, deaf, sleepy, insensible: a getter of more bastard children than war's a destroyer of men.
SECOND SERVINGMAN: 'Tis so: and as wars in some sort may be said to be a ravisher, so it cannot be denied but peace is a great maker of cuckolds.
FIRST SERVINGMAN: Ay, and it makes men hate one another.
THIRD SERVINGMAN: Reason: because they then less need one another. The wars for my money: I hope to see Romans as cheap as Volscians.

(4.5.200–10)

Here we have characters from the lower social orders all reasoning in favor of the general proposition that war is better than peace and expressing their enthusiasm for the imminent war between the Volscians and the Romans. Though the scene might be played seriously, there is a comic potential here, one that derives from the way in which these men reason and the kind of conclusion they reach. The comical side of the *evidence* derives from the way in which it takes the form of exaggerated, *hyperbolic* descriptions of the downside of peace and the upside of war. In peace, weapons rust, men occupy themselves with trivial things such as clothing and ballads, they become weak and corrupt, they sleep with other men's wives, they beget bastards, and they come to hate each other. In war, men are healthy, vigorous, faithful to their wives, and, because they rely on each other, friends with each other. The one man's *simile* says it all: as day is better than night, so war is better than peace! But while this description of war and peace may well strike us as being distorted and inaccurate in some ways, are there not some grains of truth in it? The comical side of the *conclusion* this evidence is supposed to support lies in the fact that, at least on the face of it, it is ridiculous: surely war is not better than peace! Seeing these weaknesses and affronts to common sense in the servingmen's reasoning, we may well allow ourselves a moment of laughter in this grim play, even if we are also a little chastened by the uncomfortable truths lurking in the consensus of the participants.

There is one final dimension of the kind of reasoning and argument that accounts for our experience not so much of laughter as of merriment and delight in Shakespearean drama. Like the more serious reasoning we have already considered, it often involves propositions about life and human existence in general. I venture to say that, like the general propositions we have considered in the tragedies and histories, those in the comedies and romances are often true and wise. And like the characters in the tragedies and histories, those in the comedies and romances also often consider themselves as instances of or in light of these propositions. In *Much Ado About Nothing*, for example, when Claudio thinks (mistakenly) that his friend Don Pedro has wooed Hero for himself, he considers the experience as one that bears out the general claims that "friendship is constant in all other things / Save in the office and affairs of love," and that "beauty is a witch / Against whose charms faith melteth into blood" (2.1.122–27). But when he finds, to his surprise, his match with Hero has been arranged, he observes, "Time goes on crutches [slowly] till love have all his rites" (2.1.246). Having heard others censure and detract him for being too proud to accept the affections of Beatrice, Benedick observes "happy are they that hear their detractions and can put them to mending," and he proceeds to mend his fault by resolving to requite her love. Moreover, he defends his resolution by affirming claims about appetite and men in general: "doth not the appetite alter? A man loves the meat in his youth that he cannot endure in his age" (2.3.163–73). When, in her turn, Beatrice overhears others censure her for being proud and scornful, she, too, changes and immediately resolves to requite Benedick's love, in light of the general proposition that "no glory lives behind the back of such [women who are proud and scornful of love]" (3.1.110–12). Friar Francis justifies the strategy of pretending that the slandered Hero is dead on grounds that "we" don't know what we've got until it is gone (4.1.222–6). Antonio objects to his brother's attempt to counsel and comfort him because while "men" who do not feel grief can counsel those (such as himself) who do, once those counselors feel that grief themselves, "their counsel turns to passion" and they become incapable of giving counsel (5.1.1–33).

General claims such as these often enter into the kind of reasoning and arguing that is playful, specious, self-serving, and therefore empowered to make us laugh. But in many cases this dimension of the characters' *dianoia* is also a little more serious and encourages us to see them as people who find themselves in situations in which *other* people find themselves, people with whom we have important things in common, people about whom general propositions apply. If we see them in this way, we may well become interested in them and care about them, with the result that they become candidates for not just our compassion when they suffer but also our delight and joy when they are happy in the end. I think, finally, that this kind of *dianoia* is another thing that tends to diminish any inclination we might have to feel superior to the characters and, so, to laugh *at* them. For if we feel we are in some basic way the same as those characters, if we feel we are all in the same boat, then we know that their experiences are at least possible for us. We know that in laughing at them, we are also laughing at ourselves, or at least the follies to which we humans are prone. Comic *dianoia* that includes general claims about life is thus another aspect of the comedies that can give rise to carnivalesque laughter and communal merriment.

Language

Shakespeare's English is Modern English—the kind of English that came into being after Old English (450–1066) and Middle English (1066–1500) and that we speak now. But it still differs in some ways from the English spoken by most twenty-first century anglophones:

- some words had different meanings from the ones they have today
- some words have disappeared from modern usage
- Renaissance English pronunciation differs from modern pronunciation
- Renaissance English spelling was less systematic than modern spelling
- Renaissance English grammar was slightly different from modern English grammar.

This poses some real problems for understanding and enjoying the plays. In particular it poses problems for understanding and enjoying the humor that depends on forms of wordplay and erroneous or unusual linguistic usage. Here I think a little work is required: we need to read the plays carefully and take a little time to read some of the brief notes in good editions of the plays. But I think this work is worth it: doing it enables us to experience the laughter, merriment, and delight Shakespeare wanted to provide us by way of his words.

In some cases, the *sounds* of his characters' words enter into the causes of our laughter. In *A Midsummer Night's Dream,* for example, Quince introduces the mechanicals' play by describing how Pyramus thinks his beloved Thisbe has been killed by a lion, and so,

> with blade, with bloody blameful blade,
> He bravely broached his boiling bloody breast.
> (5.1.149)

Alliteration (the repetition of consonant sounds at the beginning of consecutive words) is not necessarily comical, and can indeed make for forceful and elevated expression, but here, because it is so excessive and harsh, it comes across as being comical. So, too, does some of the rhyme in this play and others. When, for example, he is about to do what Quince describes, Pyramus says,

> Out, sword, and wound
> The pap of Pyramus,
> Ay, that left pap
> Where heart doth hop:
> Thus die I, thus, thus, thus.
> Now am I dead,
> Now am I fled.
> (5.1.276–82)

A little more alliteration, along with short, two-foot lines (*dimeters*), some imperfect rhyme on the more colloquial terms "pap" and "hop," and then "dead" and "fled" all make for *sounds* that I think go to enhance the comic dimension of these lines.

In other cases, we have linguistic usage that is ungrammatical, improperly punctuated and pronounced, or erroneous in some other way. Quince, for example, has an ongoing struggle with his actors' delivery: he has to tell them that it should not be "odious savours sweet" as Bottom says, but "odours savours sweet"; the place where Pyramus and Thisbe meet is not "Ninny's tomb," but "Ninus' tomb" (3.1.54–69). I know, kind of silly, but note that it is still rather clever, since it is not just mispronunciation or verbal deformation, but mispronunciation and deformation that change the meaning of the original word into one that is incongruous with or contrary to its standard meaning. This kind of *malapropism* often marks the diction of the mechanicals (and is also a conspicuous feature of Dogberry's language in *Much Ado*). But Quince himself displays another type of comical linguistic error when he delivers the prologue to his play:

88 *Laughter and delight*

> If we offend, it is with our good will.
> That you should think, we come not to offend,
> But with good will. To show our simple skill,
> That is the true beginning of our end.
> Consider then, we come but in despite.
> We do not come as minding to content you,
> Our true intent is. All for your delight
> We are not here.
> (5.1.112–19)

In delivering this prologue, Quince mistakenly places full stops at the end of line 112 and in the middle of lines 114 and 118, while he reads as though there is *enjambment* in lines 118–19. The result is that he seems to say that he and the other players intend to offend his audience and that they are not there for their delight—the opposite of what the lines, properly punctuated would mean, and what he wants to say. Funny, yes, but if you are acting or directing, take note! A valuable lesson in how important it is to be sensitive to *end-stopped lines, enjambment*, and *caesurae* when reading and performing the Shakespearean script.

The ancient rhetoricians and their European Renaissance devotees caution the orator against overusing tropes and figures, for they felt that this would make him or her an ineffective speaker at best, a buffoon or laughing stock at worst. This perception was just part of their more general recognition that any particular trope or figure could be used (or abused) to do and to mean many things, and to induce a wide range of thoughts and feelings in the audience. Shakespeare knew all of this, and he sometimes aims to raise a laugh by having some of his characters go overboard with tropes and figures—as Bottom, for example, is required to do by his role as Pyramus in the play:

> O grim-looked night! O night with hue so black!
> O night, which ever art when day is not!
> O night, O night! Alack, alack, alack,
> I fear my Thisbe's promise is forgot.
> And thou, O wall, thou sweet and lovely wall
> That stands between her father's ground and mine!
> Thou wall, O wall, O sweet and lovely wall,
> Show me thy chink, to blink through with mine eyne!
> (5.1.169–76)

In the last chapter, we saw that *apostrophe* is one of the aspects of the tragic protagonists' linguistic usage that makes us think they are alone and impassioned and that can therefore strengthen our sympathy for them. Here we have the same figure, but rather than arousing sympathy, it makes Bottom's immediate audience and us laugh. Why? In part because Bottom overdoes it—there are just too many addresses beginning with "O" for it to seem real or serious. But notice that the potential for comedy here is a function of many other things about the utterance.

In addition to its overall comical context, we need to observe the rather silly addressee of the second apostrophe (the wall, played by Snout); the silly description of night as the time when day is not; the repetition of the colloquial "alack" without any words in between (an *epizeuxis*); the *metaphorical* description of both night and the wall as people (also a *personification*); the rhyme; the *double entendre* of "chink" (vagina/anus). These are just some of the aspects of the utterance that render the *apostrophes* comical.

This kind of excessive, over-the-top, highly conspicuous employment of tropological and figurative language at the expense of the person who uses it is common in the comedies. In *As You Like It*, for example, Silvius makes for a somewhat comical lover because he speaks as follows:

> If thou rememb'rest not the slightest folly
> That ever love did make thee run into,
> Thou hast not loved.
> Or if thou hast not sat as I do now,
> Wearing thy hearer in thy mistress' praise,
> Thou hast not loved.
> Or if thou hast not broke from company
> Abruptly, as my passion now makes me,
> Thou hast not loved.
> O Phoebe, Phoebe, Phoebe!
> (2.4.26–35)

The repetition of words ("if thou") at the beginnings of three consecutive sentences makes for an obvious *anaphora*, while the repetition of words ("thou hast not loved") at the endings of three consecutive sentences makes for an obvious *epistrophe*. The concluding repetition of "Phoebe" makes for another *epizeuxis* (as in Bottom's "alack, alack, alack"; his "die, die, die, die, die"; and Flute's "adieu, adieu, adieu"). Like lovers' "actions most ridiculous" to which he refers before, Silvius' language is ridiculous, and it is ridiculous because it is overtly figurative—but also because it is uttered by this character in this situation. The same might be said of Orlando's love poetry: laced with *hyperbole*, but also written in labored *trochaic tetrameter* couplets, it is obviously bad love poetry that Touchstone can't resist ridiculing by producing a ribald imitation of it—a brilliant little *parody*, since it is a debased imitation intended to ridicule the original (3.2.74–85). We should note, too, that sometimes the kinds of linguistic repetition that makes for conspicuous, corny figures is shared by several characters, as when Silvius, Phoebe, Orlando, and Rosalind all repeat each other's words and grammatical structures in a general lamentation. Rosalind finally calls an end to all the *anaphora* and *parallelism* since "'Tis like the howling of Irish wolves against the moon" (5.2.84).

This kind of comical tropological and figurative language at the expense of the speaker also arises in the histories and tragedies. In *Henry IV, part one*, for example, one of the things that makes Falstaff so funny is his ongoing *hyperbole*: claiming that he and his accomplice had stolen "a thousand pound" in the Gadshill heist, for example, he then tells Hal that "a hundred" other men stole it from them, but not before he had fought "with a dozen of them two hours together." "If I fought not with fifty of them, I am a bunch of radish," he boasts, and adds that "I have peppered [killed] two of them: two I am sure I have paid, two rogues in buckram suits." As Hal observes, and as the audience knows, "these lies are like the father that begets them, gross as a mountain." After Hal confronts Falstaff with a more accurate account of what happened, it seems that Falstaff will not be able to avoid the "shame" to which his exaggerations expose him—but no! He claims that he knew all along that among those who took the money from him was Hal, "the heir apparent," and exclaims, "hear ye, my masters, was it for me to kill the heir-apparent?" With this brilliant *rhetorical question*—it looks like a question but is really an emphatic statement meaning that it was *not* for him to kill the heir apparent—Falstaff excuses his cowardice and wild exaggerations in a way that can bring down the house (2.4.119–205).

A well-known example of this kind of thing in the tragedies is displayed by Polonius in *Hamlet*. Why does he come across as a rather silly man who is something of a laughing stock to both other characters in the play, and us? Well, one of the reasons is that he cannot help himself from playing with words and indulging in unusual linguistic usage. Early in the play, for example, he informs Gertrude that Hamlet is mad by using far too many words (*periphrasis*), repeating the same grammatical structures (*parallelism*), and beginning one sentence with the same word that completes the previous sentence (*anadiplosis*). When Gertrude impatiently interjects, "more matter, with less art," Polonius cannot help but continue to use this overly figurative, "artful" language:

> Madam, I swear I use no art at all.
> That he is mad, 'tis true: 'tis true 'tis pity,
> And pity it is true: a foolish figure,
> But farewell it, for I will use no art.
> (2.2.101–5)

As Polonius himself observes, a foolish figure, which we might describe as a combination of the figures *anadiplosis* (an a/b, b/c sequence) and *antimetabole* (an a/b, b/a sequence), since we have an a/b, b/c, c/b sequence (mad/true, true/pity, pity/true). And it is in part because he speaks in this way that he cuts a comical figure.

We noted earlier, though, that the ancient and Renaissance rhetoricians also observed that orators can employ tropes and figures in order to make people merry and, indeed, to ridicule others and make people laugh at them. In their commentaries on ancient Roman comic playwrights, such as Terence, Renaissance humanists observed how the characters in ancient Roman comedy did this (Herrick). We have seen that Shakespeare's characters, too, call on a wide range of tropes and figures in order to ridicule others in a refined, witty manner or just to have some fun. But there are a few more important things to observe on this count. First, we should enrich our list of these tropes and figures by adding terms used to refer to the kind of wordplay we now associate with punning. Again, I think the ancient rhetoricians improve our ability to describe and understand Shakespeare's language and its effects because they don't dump all wordplay into one category such as punning, but make fine distinctions between types of wordplay, and they assign a special name to each. In one of the classics of twentieth-century Shakespeare criticism, *Shakespeare's Use of the Arts of Language* (1947), Sister Miriam Joseph identifies four of the main types of this wordplay (165–8):

- repeating a word but using it to mean different things, as in Falstaff's repetition of "counterfeit" to mean two different things (*antanaclasis*)
- using a word once to mean two or more different things, as when Mercutio, knowing he has been fatally wounded, says, "ask for me tomorrow, and ye shall find me a grave man" (3.1.85) (*syllepsis*)
- repeating words which are alike but not exactly the same in sound, as when Falstaff speculates what might happen to Hal's credit in the tavern "were it not here apparent that thou art heir apparent" (1.2. 39) (*paronomasia*)
- wittily replying to another person's words, often by way of repeating their words but using them, or words that sound like them, to mean something different from what the first speaker uses them to mean. When, for example, Falstaff tells Hal "do not thou, when thou art king, hang a thief," Hal responds, "No; thou shalt," meaning Falstaff will hang as a thief (1.2.42–43). Or when in *Much Ado* Beatrice responds to the messenger who, speaking of Benedick, says "And [he is] a good soldier too, lady" with "And a good soldier to a lady" (1.1.35–6) (*asteismus*).

We might add a fifth: *double entendre*. This is the use of a word once to mean two or more different things, but where one of those things includes genitalia or some kind of sexual activity, as in Beatrice's use of "Sir Mountato" to mean Benedick and intercourse, or in Antony and Cleopatra's use of "sword" to mean what Antony wields on the battlefield and what he wields in the bedroom (so it is a specific kind of *syllepsis*).

This type of wordplay enters into the very fabric of Shakespeare's comic dialogue across all genres (McDonald). But it is also important to bear in mind that besides raising laughter, it can have a wide range of other effects: it can make us think the characters are real; give us a sense of their minds, sexual identities, and personalities; relieve our own emotional intensities. And because it functions in all of these ways, me might take issue with Samuel Johnson's famous criticism of Shakespeare for having too many puns.

Second, I want to highlight the importance of *simile* and *metaphor* in the comic dialogue of Shakespearean drama, especially where ridicule is involved. In the long wild scene in the middle of *A Midsummer Night's Dream*, for example, the relatively short Hermia thinks the taller Helena is ridiculing her by describing her with a word that is usually used to refer to something that *resembles* her—"puppet."

Hermia replies by using a word that is usually used to refer to something that resembles the taller Helena, "painted maypole." The war of insult by metaphor is on. Wishing to show his love for the taller Helena, Lysander joins in: he ridicules the shorter Hermia by calling her "you dwarf, / You minimus, of hind'ring knot-grass made! / You bead, you acorn" (3.2.339–41).

So, too, do many of the insults exchanged by Hal and Falstaff in *Henry IV, part 1* take the form of *simile* and *metaphor*. At the opening of the great tavern scene, for instance, Falstaff claims to be as melancholy as a cat or a bear, to which Hal adds a hare, or Moorditch (a dirty London drainage ditch). As Falstaff observes, Hal "hast the most unsavoury similes and art indeed the most comparative, rascalli'st, sweet young prince" (1.2.55–6). That's for sure, for Hal then asserts his unflattering comparisons and perceptions of resemblance by way of *metaphor* and calls Falstaff a "wool-sack," "clay-brained guts, thou knotty-pated fool, thou whoreson, obscene, greasy tallow-catch [dripping pan or accumulation of animal fat]," "this bed-presser, this horseback-breaker, this huge hill of flesh," "that trunk of humours, that bolting-hutch [large bin for sifting grain] of beastliness, that swollen parcel of dropsies, that huge bombard [leather wine jug] of sack, that stuffed cloak-bag of guts, that roasted Manningtree ox with the pudding in his belly" (2.4.103–331). But Falstaff can also play this game: he calls Hal "you starveling, you elf-skin, you dried neat's [ox's] tongue, bull's pizzle [penis], you stock-fish…. You tailor's-yard [yard-stick], you sheath, you bowcase, you vile standing-tuck [slender sword]" (2.4.185–8). As Hal observes, these, too, are "base comparisons" (2.4.189). It is in part because all of these expressions are so richly metaphorical and assert resemblances between people and base, unsavory things that they amount to ridicule that is graphic, imaginative, exuberant, and funny.

We want, finally, to observe that besides being a major source of laughter, Shakespeare's highly figurative and tropological language is a source of some other pleasures, which I want to include under the broad category of delight. In so doing, I follow Shakespeare's contemporary, George Puttenham, for he introduces his wonderful catalogue of the tropes and figures in Book 3 of *The Art of English Poesy* as follows:

> So is there yet requisite to the perfection of this art [of poetry] another manner of exornation [ornamentation], which resteth in the fashioning of our maker's language and style to such purpose as it may delight and allure as well the mind as the ear of the hearers with a certain novelty and strange manner of conveyance, disguising it no little from the ordinary and accustomed, nevertheless making it nothing the more unseemly or misbecoming, but rather decenter and more agreeable to any civil ear and understanding.
> (221)

Delight for the ear, and delight for the mind—this is what Puttenham and other Renaissance humanists felt spoken, audible tropological and figurative language could provide to readers and audiences, if it was used in the right way, on the right occasions. In spite of the differences between the Renaissance and modernity, I think this kind of delight is still on offer throughout the plays. Take, for example, Falstaff's melodramatic repetition of verb/proper noun and adjective/proper noun structures (*parallelisms*), and sequences of phrases all beginning with the same word (*anaphora*), as he pleads with Hal not to banish him:

> No, my good lord, banish Peto, banish Bardolph, banish Poins, but for sweet Jack Falstaff, kind Jack Falstaff, true Jack Falstaff, valiant Jack Falstaff, and therefore more valiant, being, as he is old Jack Falstaff, banish not him thy Harry's company, banish not him thy Harry's company: banish plump Jack, and banish all the world.
> (2.4.346–50)

Song

Music and song are major elements of the comedies and romances, and, as we saw in the previous chapter, Shakespeare includes them in part with the aim of providing occasions for his audience to feel sadness, melancholy, and sympathy for some of the characters of these plays. But he also includes them with the aim of giving us more laughs. In some cases, the very act of breaking into song can be a surprising and comical moment. In the wonderful late-night partying scene of *Twelfth Night*, for example, Malvolio intervenes and sternly informs Sir Toby that if he continues to misbehave and wishes to leave Olivia's household, "she is very willing to bid you farewell" (2.3.76). A serious moment, and it looks as though Toby may relent, but no:

SIR TOBY: 'Farewell, dear heart, since I must needs be gone.' *Sings*
(2.3.77)

This can be such a hilarious moment because, just when it looks like Toby might shrink under Malvolio's rebuke, he surprises us by using Malvolio's own word, "farewell," to break into a beautiful song, "Farewell dear love," which appears in Robert Jones' *First Booke of Songes* (1600). In some of the first printed editions of the play, the editors placed the song lyrics in italics to indicate that they *are* song lyrics; our editors do so by placing them in single quotes and adding stage directions in italics. Ignoring Maria's objections, Toby and Feste sing the song to the end, but also wittily revise its words to taunt Malvolio and make for a great comic scene in the play (see, for example, the RSC's fantastic 2012 Globe production of the play, directed by Tim Carroll, with Stephen Fry as Malvolio and Mark Rylance as Olivia).

In other cases, the lyrics of the songs are low or bawdy (but rarely obscene), and they can, along with the music to which they were or could be set, enhance the comical mood and effect of specific scenes, and the plays at large. This is the case with some of the drinking songs in the tragedies, such as "Come thou monarch of the vine" in *Antony and Cleopatra* (2.7.117–22) and "And let me the cannikin clink" in *Othello* (2.3.56–60). True, drunken scenes can fall flat,

94 *Laughter and delight*

but in *The Tempest*, the drunken Stephano can raise a laugh by performing well the "scurvy song" that is written in the lilting *tetrameters* and *trimeters* of *iambic* (unstressed/stressed) and *anapestic* (unstressed/unstressed/stressed) feet that were common in Renaissance ballads: "The **mas**ter, the **swab**ber, the **boat**swain and **I**, / The **gunner and** his **mate**, etc." (2.2.38–41). Caliban's drunken song, "No more dams..." (2.2.137–41), is a fitting conclusion to this wild scene.

Later in this play, after Stephano assures Caliban that he will destroy Prospero, Caliban feels merry and asks Stephano to make him "jocund" by singing a "catch" (which is a round, like "Row, row, row, your boat"). Stephano and Trinculo comply by singing "Flout 'em and scout 'em" (3.2.106–8):

Figure 2.1 "Flout 'em and Cout 'em," from *The Tempest*
Source: *Shakespeare's Songbook* by Ross W. Duffin. Used by permission of W. W. Norton & Company, Inc. Copyright © 2004 by Ross W. Duffin.

This is a simple round, but in order to understand and account for its comic potential we need to observe several things about it and the music that Shakespeare probably had in mind for it:

- the lower, colloquial diction (which means insult them and mock them)
- the rather silly repetition of words that forms the abba sequence which the rhetoricians and Shakespeare would have identified as the figure, *antimetabole*
- the heavier, boisterous *dactylic* meter (**flout** 'em and / **cout** 'em and / **scout** 'em and)
- the 6/4 time signature that suits the dactylic meter and gives the song a boisterous feel
- the way that while Stephano and Trinculo sing the first two lines, Caliban can take the simpler third line, all on one note, "thought is free."

Songs of this kind arise in some of the other plays. In *Twelfth Night*, for example, we get another round that resembles "Flout 'em and Cout 'em" but is sung by Toby, Feste, and Sir Andrew: for the full comic effect, the first two characters could sing "Hold thy peace" while the drunken Agucheek could dumbly chime in with "thou knave" (2.3.48–54). But we get comical song of a different kind in *A Midsummer Night's Dream* when, determined to prove that he is not afraid after he has been transformed into an ass and his friends have fled, Bottom sings, "The Woosel Cock" (3.1.88–96):

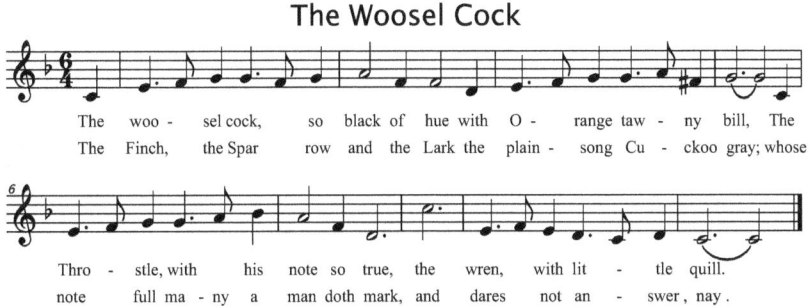

Figure 2.2 "The Woosel Cock," from *A Midsummer Night's Dream*
Source: *Shakespeare's Songbook* by Ross W. Duffin. Used by permission of W. W. Norton & Company, Inc. Copyright © 2004 by Ross W. Duffin.

This song can be so funny because Bottom's performance of it, which cannot be too beautiful, awakens Titania who, under the influence of the love juice, exclaims halfway through the song, "What Angel wakes me from my flow'ry bed?" (3.1.92). But the song then usually gets another laugh because, after suddenly jumping up to a high note, Bottom then descends and finishes with the line, "and dares not answer, nay"—as in neigh, whinny, whinny!

Shakespeare's plays are filled with characters who speak of many other effects the music and song they hear have on them—it makes them merry, makes them sad, eases other passions, arouses other passions, puts them to sleep, wakes them up, makes them remember, makes them think, makes them want to dance. And, indeed, some of the boisterous drinking songs and rounds in the comedies can serve as occasions for the players to invite the audience not so much to laugh as to feel good and join in the merriment and festivity. But Caliban reminds us of another important effect of song when he says, "Be not afeard, the isle is full of noises, / Sounds and sweet airs, that give delight and hurt not" (3.2.118–19). That the musical settings of some songs in *The Tempest* really *should* be sweet and delightful is suggested by Ferdinand's own response to Ariel's singing of "Come unto these yellow sands": he claims that it allayed both the fury of the waters "and my passion / With its sweet air" (1.2.456–7). It

96 Laughter and delight

is likely that Shakespeare's great contemporary, Robert Johnson, also set some of the lyrics of this play to music, including the beautiful song Ariel sings shortly after "Come unto these yellow sands." In "Full fathom five" (1.2.460–7), Ariel informs Ferdinand that, though his father has drowned, he has been changed into something rich and strange and is lamented by the sea nymphs. Performed well to Johnson's lovely setting, this is a sweet but also melancholic air that is a must for performances that are faithful to Caliban's observation that the sounds of the island give delight. Here is the version of it that appears in a seventeenth-century manuscript:

Figure 2.3 "Full Fathom Five," from *The Tempest*. From John Playford's collection of music to *The Tempest* [manuscript] (ca. 1650–67)
Source: Digital Image Collection at the Folger Shakespeare Library.

References

Aristotle. *Poetics*. Trans. Richard Janko. Indianapolis: Hackett, 1987.
Armitage, David, Condren, Conal, and Fitzmaurice, Andrew (eds). *Shakespeare and Early Modern Political Thought*. Cambridge: Cambridge University Press, 2009.
Baldwin, T. W. *William Shakspere's Small Latine and Lesse Greeke*. 2 vols. 1944; Urbana: University of Illinois Press, 1956.
Barber, C. L. *Shakespeare's Festive Comedy*. Princeton: Princeton University Press, 1959.
Bates, Catherine. "Love and courtship." In *The Cambridge Companion to Shakespearean Comedy*. Ed. Alexander Leggatt. Cambridge: Cambridge University Press, 2002. 102–122.

Berry, Edward. *Shakespeare's Comic Rites*. Cambridge: Cambridge University Press, 1984.
Berry, Edward. "Laughing at 'others.'" In *The Cambridge Companion to Shakespearean Comedy*. Ed. Alexander Leggatt. Cambridge: Cambridge University Press, 2002. 123–138.
Bloom, Harold. *Shakespeare and the Invention of the Human*. New York: Riverhead, 1998.
Duffin, Ross. *Shakespeare's Songbook*. New York: Norton, 2004.
Dusinberre, Juliet. *Shakespeare and the Nature of Women*. 1975; London: Macmillan, 1996.
Henze, Catherine. *Robert Armin and Shakespeare's Performed Songs*. New York: Routledge, 2017.
Herrick, Marvin. *Comic Theory in the Sixteenth Century*. Urbana: University of Illinois Press, 1964.
Hope, Jonathan. *Shakespeare and Language*. London: Arden Shakespeare, 2010.
Joseph, Sister Miriam. *Shakespeare's Use of the Arts of Language*. 1947; New York: Hafner Publishing, 1966.
Kott, Jan. *Shakespeare Our Contemporary*. London: Doubleday, 1965.
Mack, Peter. *Reading and Rhetoric in Shakespeare and Montaigne*. New York: Bloomsbury, 2010.
McDonald, Russ. *Shakespeare and the Arts of Language*. Oxford: Oxford University Press, 2001.
Nietzsche, Friedrich. *The Gay Science*. Trans. Walter Kaufmann. New York: Vintage, 1974.
Puttenham, George. *The Art of English Poesy*. Ed. Frank Whigham and Wayne Rebhorn. Ithaca: Cornell University Press, 2007.
Richman, David. *Laughter, Pain, and Wonder*. Newark: University of Delaware, 1990.
Salingar, Leo. *Shakespeare and the Traditions of Comedy*. Cambridge: Cambridge University Press, 1974.
Sidney, Sir Philip. *An Apology for Poetry*. In *Criticism: The Major Texts*. Ed. W. J. Bate. 1952; New York: Harcourt, 1970.
Skinner, Quentin. *Reason and Rhetoric in the Philosophy of Hobbes*. Cambridge: Cambridge University Press, 1996.

3 Wisdom and moral instruction

Plot

When you read or go see a Shakespeare play, do you feel you learn anything about people or how to live? Do you feel edified or instructed in any way? Do you feel that you acquire wisdom about life, or are confirmed in the wisdom you already have? We saw in the Introduction that many men and women over the centuries answer "yes" to these questions—though they provide very different accounts of the nature of this instruction and wisdom. And it is in part because they feel the plays in some sense embody wisdom and provide some kind of moral edification that the plays are of such value and importance to them. This is not to say that you *should* respond in this way to the plays, that there is some kind of moral imperative to find instruction, edification, or wisdom, in them, or that you should throw your hat in with what I'm calling "we" in this book. But even if you don't, you still might want to understand what it is about the plays that accounts for this widespread response and the long-standing positive evaluation of Shakespeare that is grounded in it. And you might be interested in not just understanding its causes, but also discovering ways of experiencing it for yourself. If so, read on.

I think it is important to remember, to begin with, that by the time Shakespeare was writing his plays, *dialogue* of many kinds was strongly associated with teaching and instruction. There were, first of all, ancient Greek dialogues, such as Plato's *Republic* and *Symposium*, which were being published in Greek and Latin during the Renaissance. Notwithstanding his claims to know nothing, Socrates in these dialogues is an authoritative figure who teaches his interlocutors about a range of subjects, and many Renaissance scholars saw these dialogues as expressions of Platonic philosophical doctrines. There were also many works by Cicero which feature ancient Roman statesmen, military commanders, and orators in dialogue with each other, and which Renaissance humanists read as works providing instruction about oratory, ethics, and politics. Renaissance humanists, such as Thomas More and Erasmus, also wrote their own dialogues on religious and ethical matters, some skeptical and some argumentative and didactic. And then there was the dialogue in ancient Greek and Roman drama. As we saw in the Introduction, Sidney and other Renaissance figures strongly associated the dialogue they found in ancient Greek and Roman comedy and tragedy with moral instruction. If they did not quite *define* these two main genres of drama in terms of didactic purpose, they often argued for the value of both genres on grounds that they provided wisdom and moral instruction. Though it may not have been Christian moral instruction, it was still valuable, since it was broadly grounded in ancient Graeco-Roman commitments to justice, courage, wisdom, liberality, seemliness, temperance, and other virtues. Shakespeare and his audiences would also have known of English medieval morality plays. These plays usually take the form of dialogue between a human protagonist and allegorical figures such as Death, Justice, and Knowledge. They, too, were widely understood to provide moral instruction, though here the instruction was grounded in Christian ideas of good, evil, god, grace, faith, and salvation.

In trying to understand what it is about the plays that accounts for the fact that so many have felt that they provide some kind of moral instruction and wisdom, we also need to remember that many of them are based on historical writings. Thus, one of the main sources for Shakespeare's history plays, *King Lear, Macbeth,* and *Cymbeline* was a massive history of England, Scotland, and Ireland: Raphael Holinshed's *Chronicles of England, Scotland, and Ireland* (published in 1577 and 1587). One of his main sources for the Roman plays was a series of biographies of great figures from ancient Greece and Rome: Plutarch's *Lives of the Most Noble Grecians and Romanes* (translated into English by Thomas North and published in 1579). Shakespeare and his audiences expected historical writings such as these to provide instruction of some kind or another. From English medieval and sixteenth-century historical writings they learned that human experience over time was the unfolding of God's plan for mankind, an unfolding that was rich in Christian moral instruction. From ancient Roman historians such as Livy, Tacitus, and Sallust, as well as commentaries on their histories by Renaissance thinkers such as Machiavelli, they derived political wisdom and moral instruction—though some, such as Machiavelli, also lamented that statesmen and military commanders failed to learn the lessons history had to teach. Accounts of ancient Greece and Rome could provide these lessons because, on the one hand, they described individuals of outstanding virtue whose behavior amounted to *examples* for others to emulate. On the other hand, they demonstrated the nature and consequences of inept and immoral conduct and thereby instructed others in how to survive in a dangerous, corrupt world and why they themselves ought not to be inept and corrupt. To top it all off, let us remember that ancient authorities such as Horace taught Shakespeare and his contemporaries to value literature in general because it provided not just pleasure but also wisdom and moral instruction, something, at least, that was useful for living life.

So the fact that Shakespeare was writing dialogue as opposed to narrative with a single authoritative voice does not mean, as some have claimed, that he had no intention of espousing or teaching his audience anything, or that his audiences would not have felt they learned something when they read or saw his plays performed. And the fact that he was creating poetry as opposed to philosophy and (on many occasions) representing historical figures and events does not mean his audiences would not have seen his works as a kind of wisdom literature. Indeed, given the broad traditions and the particular circumstances in which he was writing, I think it is highly likely that Shakespeare was in the game of teaching, affirming some values, and conveying wisdom. But whatever his intentions were, I am more concerned to identify what it is about *the plays* that accounts for why so many readers and audiences have felt that they provide moral instruction, affirm particular values, and convey wisdom on a wide range of subjects.

The plots of the plays account in part for this response. Let us recall Aristotle's claim in the *Poetics* that poetry is more serious and philosophical than history because it deals not with particulars but universals. Universals have a bad name these days, and many Shakespeare critics reject the idea that all humans have important things in common and that Shakespearean drama succeeds in representing that commonality. But before joining these critics, we may want to consider the meaning and premises of documents such as the United Nations "Universal Declaration of Human Rights." We might also want to think about Aristotle's explanation of universals. "A universal," Aristotle explains, "is the sort of thing that a certain kind of person may well say or do in accordance with probability or necessity" (12). If you think that (perhaps because of the ways in which they are raised) certain kinds of people exist in different societies and that people of a certain kind usually act in certain ways, then you might not find Aristotle's idea of a universal so obnoxious. You might also think that, on this idea of a universal, Shakespeare's plays do indeed deal with them. For, however strongly individuated they may be, I think Shakespeare's characters can also fairly be seen as instances of kinds of people: true friends, noble wives, proud soldiers, boastful soldiers, valiant mothers, villains, heroes, heroines, young lovers, tricksters, strict fathers. In *Anatomy of Criticism* (1957), one of the classics of twentieth-century literary criticism, this is how Northrop Frye sees Shakespeare's characters. And we have seen that the characters see themselves, and invite us to see them, not as unique individuals, but as individuals who have important things in common with other humans, if not all humans. We have also seen that a good case can be made for the view that in the tragedies and histories—given the kinds of people they are, and the situations in which they find themselves—these characters say and do things that seem probable, if not necessary. Insofar as this is the case, these plays might be said to show us universals (in Aristotle's sense) and provide a knowledge about what humans are.

But if you share the view that Shakespeare's characters seem true to life, on the basis of what do you do so? Isn't it on the basis of your own ideas of what humans are and how they behave? By the same token, if you do *not* think Shakespeare's characters are true to life, don't you do so on the basis of your own ideas of what humans are and how they behave? If you did not have any such ideas in the first place, you wouldn't be in a position to determine accuracy of representation, and probability of action and event. Thus, some parents with whom I've discussed *King Lear* think that play is wise and true to life not because the action of that play teaches them, as Lear puts it, "how sharper than a serpent's tooth it is / To have a thankless child" (1.4.236–37). These parents *already know* how painful it is to have ungrateful children. They think the play conveys wisdom and offers valuable counsel because it is true to a knowledge they already have, a painful experience they have already undergone, a suffering they know all too well. This is not to say that we never achieve *new* insights into what we are when we watch or read a Shakespeare play. But it is to say that, whether or not we realize it, our own experience and pre-existent ideas of what humans are enable the experience of being struck by the truth and wisdom of Shakespeare's representation of humans. So one reason many people have had the feeling that the plays instruct in some significant way, and convey or embody wisdom, is that their plots are consistent with ideas about human behaviour they already have and the plays are faithful to their own experience.

In connection with the suffering and unhappy endings that feature in Shakespeare's tragedies (and some of the histories), and why they have been taken to be morally instructive, I think it may also be helpful to consider Dryden's view on the matter:

> To instruct delightfully is the general end of all Poetry: Philosophy instructs, but it performs its work by precept: which is not delightfull, or not so delightfull as Example. To purge the passions by Example, is therefore the particular instruction which belongs to Tragedy. Rapin a judicious Critic, has observ'd from Aristotle, that pride and want of commiseration are the most predominant vices in Mankinde: therefore to cure us of these two, the inventors of Tragedy, have chosen to work upon two other passions, which are fear and pity. We are wrought to fear, by their seting before our eyes some terrible example of misfortune, which hapned to persons of the highest quality; for such an action demonstrates to us, that no condition is priviledg'd from the turns of Fortune: this must of necessity cause terror in us, and consequently abate our pride. But when we see that the most virtuous, as well as the greatest, are not exempt from such misfortunes, that consideration moves pity in us: and insensibly works us to be helpful to, and tender over the distress'd, which is the noblest and most God-like of moral virtues.
>
> (231–2)

Dryden here invokes the difference between precept and example, which was commonplace in discussions of literature in Shakespeare's day and which animates commentary on Shakespeare's teaching and wisdom up to the present day. I think, for example, that the idea of teaching by example is a precedent for recent accounts of Shakespeare's wisdom and usefulness in terms of the sensuous embodiment, incarnation, and exemplification of aspects of human experience (Mousley). Defining tragedy in terms of a kind of teaching—teaching by example—Dryden goes on to praise Shakespearean tragedy for doing so. For rather than providing reasons for explicit teachings that one ought to be modest and compassionate (teaching by precept), Shakespeare presents us with actual human beings who are subject to Fortune and who suffer. Note that, for Dryden, these tragic protagonists, though virtuous, are examples not in the sense that they are *ideals*, people who show or exemplify how humans ought to behave. They are examples in the sense that they are concrete individuals who suffer and are subject to Fortune, and who thereby demonstrate that *all* humans, including the virtuous and privileged, suffer and are subject to Fortune.

By *showing* rather than *telling* us that this is the case, Shakespearean tragedy, on Dryden's account, causes us to experience emotion (pity and fear). This emotional experience, in turn, affects our moral sensibilities and causes us to become more humble and kind. If you read the Introduction, you might recall that, in arguing against Samuel Johnson's view that Shakespeare wrote without any moral purpose, Elizabeth Montagu argues in a similar vein. And though (in the passage cited in the Introduction) Hazlitt does not use the term "example," he too emphasizes that it is because Shakespearean tragedy displays the sufferings of individuals such as Othello and thereby causes us to experience sympathy and fear that it can teach and morally edify us. If this is the way it works, not just plot, but all of those other specific aspects of the plays we identified in chapter 1 as sources of the plays' powers to make us feel emotion, are thus also sources of their powers to instruct and morally edify us.

Another feature of the plots of some of the plays that has led many—and might lead us—to feel that in some way they are instructive is that they seem to show that, as result of their own villainy, people lose their power and are destroyed. In *Richard III*, a self-confessed villain succeeds in eliminating his rivals and ascending the throne of England, but that villainy ultimately results in his mental torment, rebellion against him, and his death on the battlefield. His henchman, Buckingham, is also destroyed. In *Macbeth*, an ambitious nobleman manages to gain the throne by killing his king, but that action torments him and sets him on a path of more murder and destruction that ultimately leads to rebellion and his own death on the battlefield. Lady Macbeth, who encourages and conspires with her husband to commit the crime, goes mad and ends up dead. In *Hamlet*, Claudius' political ambition and lust for his sister-in-law, Gertrude, drive him to commit fratricide and marry Gertrude, but these actions unleash a series of events that culminate in the death of his daughter-in-law, his nephew, Gertrude, and himself. In *Othello*, the evil Iago ends up wounded, facing torture and prison, though he does succeed in destroying Othello. And in *Lear*, Edmund's villainy ultimately leads to the death of his father, the mutual destruction of Goneril and Regan, and his own death at the hands of his half-brother. Yes, the plots of these and some of the other plays end with the destruction of people who are in many ways good and outstanding. But these plots also show that there is a strong *causal* connection between villainy and both individual and collective suffering and destruction.

Many have also argued that the plots of the histories and tragedies often show that there is a strong causal connection between not downright villainy but a particular kind of moral condition displayed by the heroes and heroines and both individual and collective suffering and destruction. This view is based in part on the way in which many characters discuss a faculty they often refer to as "reason" or "judgment." In *Hamlet*, for example, the young prince who is so disgusted with his mother for having married her husband's brother so quickly after her husband died, observes, "O heaven! A beast that wants discourse of reason / Would have mourn'd longer" (1.2.150–1)—as though reason is in some important way related to decent behavior, even though beasts without it are capable of a minimal decency. Warning his friend of what the ghost might be or do, Horatio says to Hamlet that it might lead him away and assume "some other, horrible form / Which might deprive your sovereignty of reason / And draw you into madness" (1.4.53–8)—as though sanity is a matter of ensuring reason governs (is sovereign over) or controls other faculties and impulses in our minds and bodies. Later, Hamlet exclaims, "what a piece of work is a man! How noble in reason" (2.2.284); seeing that Hamlet does indeed appear to be mad, Ophelia laments to "see that noble and most sovereign reason / Like sweet bells jangled, out of tune and harsh" (3.1.155–6). Hamlet then berates his mother for indulging her lust for Claudius—shameful behavior that shows how, in her, "reason panders will" (i.e. reason serves or is a go-between for lust) (3.4.86). And chastising himself for not having avenged himself on Claudius, Hamlet observes, "Sure he [God] that made us with such large discourse, / Looking before and after, gave us not / That capability and godlike reason / To fust [grow mouldy] in us unus'd" (4.3.109–12, in quarto edition of play). For Hamlet and other characters in other plays, reason is what many in Christian and Graeco-Roman tradition said it was: a special faculty that humans but not animals have; that God grants to humans; that makes humans noble, even god-like; that enables humans not just to speak, but to speak with eloquence; that can and should be exercised to govern desire and passion and thereby ensure our freedom from those forces to act.

Commenting on the actions they observe, several characters in the plays observe that the failure to exercise properly this faculty of reason results in action that is immoral and destructive. More specifically, it is because strong "passion," "desire," "affection," "blood," or "will" govern or override their "reason" "wit," "brain," and "judgment" that the protagonists and other characters are commonly seen to behave badly and are ultimately destroyed. And one of the names for the virtue that such characters lack is "temperance." Thus in *Richard II*, York observes that the degenerate Richard II will not heed John of Gaunt's wholesome counsel because within the king, "will doth mutiny with wit's regard" (2.1.28). In *Romeo and Juliet*, Friar Laurence chastises Romeo's impulse to stab himself when he says,

> Hold thy desperate hand:
> Art thou a man? Thy form cries out thou art:
> Thy tears are womanish, thy wild acts denote
> The unreasonable fury of a beast.
> Unseemly woman in a seeming man,
> And ill-beseeming beast in seeming both.
> (3.3.111–16)

In *Macbeth*, the noble Macduff responds to Malcolm's strategic confession of his uncontrollable sexual desire by observing,

> boundless intemperance
> In nature is a tyranny: it hath been
> Th'untimely emptying of the happy throne
> And fall of many kings.
>
> (4.3.76–9)

And in *Antony and Cleopatra*, Enobarbus explains to Cleopatra that Antony is at fault for his dishonorable behavior at the battle of Actium because he made "his will / Lord of his reason" and allowed "the itch of his affection" to govern "his captainship" (4.13.4–5). Enobarbus then resolves to leave Antony since his commander's "brain" is now diminished by his furious and futile opposition to Octavius Caesar, and "when valour preys on reason, / It eats the sword it fights with" (3.13.227–33). This is all just further confirmation of Philo's observation at the very beginning of the play, that Antony's heart has renounced all "temper" (1.1.8).

True, in some cases this explanation of misbehavior and misfortune is a ruse. Macbeth, for example, calls on it in order to account for what he wants those around him to think was his rash and impassioned act of killing Duncan's servants. After confessing to the murders in public, he observes that the faculty that allows us to resist passion and pause before we act—reason—was overridden by his passions of fury and love:

> Who can be wise, amazed, temp'rate and furious,
> Loyal and neutral in a moment? No man.
> Th'expedition of my violent love
> Outrun the pauser, reason.
>
> (2.3.112–15)

And in *Othello*, Iago also finds this idea useful when, chastising Rodorigo for wishing to drown himself out of his unrequited "love" for Desdemona, he observes, "if the beam of our lives had not one scale of reason to poise another of sensuality, the blood and baseness of our natures would conduct us to most preposterous conclusions: but we have reason to cool our raging motions, our carnal stings, our unbitted lusts" (1.3.337–41).

But that Iago also takes this idea seriously is clear when he formulates his plan to destroy Othello: he resolves to put the Moor "into a jealousy so strong / That judgement cannot cure" (2.1.284–6). It is a shrewd and ultimately successful strategy, in part because, as Othello himself knows, his passion can indeed get the better of his judgment. Demanding to know who instigated the brawl in Cyprus, Othello exclaims,

> Now, by heaven,
> My blood begins my safer guides to rule,

> And passion—having my best judgement *collied*— [blackened]
> Assays to lead the way.
>
> (2.3.187–90)

Having deceived him, Iago does indeed see that Othello is "eaten up with passion" (3.3.432), and once he is in this state, he moves swiftly to his destruction. It is thus not surprising to find that over the centuries many have felt that the plots of many of the histories and tragedies also demonstrate a causal relationship between, on the one hand, mental states in which passion, desire, or will override reason and, on the other, acts that are wild, beastly, ignoble, common, and destructive.

At the same time, the plots of many of the comedies and romances seem to demonstrate that characters who control passions such as anger and hatred, and who possess and exercise kindness, compassion, forgiveness, and mercy make good things happen. In *As You Like It*, for example, Orlando has good reason to allow a lioness in the forest to attack his brother, Oliver, who mistreated him and conspired to have him killed. But, as Oliver himself observes,

> kindness, nobler ever than revenge,
> And nature, stronger than his just occasion,
> Made him give battle to the lioness,
> Who quickly fell before him.
>
> (4.3.127–30)

Having been the beneficiary of this act of his brother's kindness and natural fraternal care, Oliver undergoes a "conversion," is reconciled with his brother, and along with him gets married at the end of the play. In *A Midsummer Night's Dream*, the four lovers must forgive some very harsh words, betrayals, threats, and rough-housing in order to be reconciled and married in the end. In *Much Ado*, Leonato forgives Claudio and Don Pedro for falsely accusing Hero of infidelity, and he resolves to give his niece (who is really Hero) to Claudio in marriage: "so dies my revenge," he says; "Your over-kindness doth wring tears from me!," cries the contrite and grateful Claudio (5.1.258–60). But Hero herself, and all of the other characters, must also forgive Claudio and Don Pedro (though not the villainous Don John) in order for the happy ending to transpire.

In *The Winter's Tale*, it is in part because Paulina, Hermione, and Polixenes all forgive Leontes for his irrational suspicions and injustices, and have compassion for him, that all can be well in the end. And in *The Tempest*, Prospero has reason and power to avenge himself on his brother Antonio, who usurped his throne, and on Alphonso, who aided and abetted him in this usurpation. But no: Ariel informs Prospero that these men and their supporters who are confined in a grove of trees on the island are "brimful of sorrow and dismay" and that, were he (Ariel) human, his "affections / Would become tender" (5.1.20–1). Prospero replies,

> And mine shall.
> Hast thou, which art but air, a touch, a feeling
> Of their afflictions, and shall not myself,
> One of their kind, that relish all as sharply
> Passion as they, be kindlier moved than thou art?
> Though with their high wrongs I am struck to th'quick,
> Yet with my nobler reason gainst my fury
> Do I take part: the rarer action is
> In virtue than in vengeance.
>
> (5.1.24–32)

Exercising reason to control his fury, containing his impulse to avenge himself upon those who injured him, Prospero resolves to forgive and be kind to them, an action he explicitly associates with nobility, reason, rarity, and virtue. That act is one of the things that enables the happy ending of the play, though Prospero himself does not foresee much joy for himself back in Milan.

True, acts of kindness, mercy, temperance, and forgiveness sometimes have dire consequences: in *Coriolanus*, the direct result of the protagonist's control over his anger and his mercy on Rome is his own destruction. But even here, mercy and temperance have a positive result, in that Coriolanus' family and Rome are spared and Coriolanus does not go down in history as a destroyer of his own people. So the plots of some of the plays also show that there is a strong causal connection between, on the one hand, kindness, compassion, forgiveness, and temperance and, on the other, both individual and collective happiness.

But do we feel that these plot lines teach us anything? Do we think they embody wisdom? Not necessarily, for on the basis of our own experience we might think that, really, crime *does* pay in this world, that bad guys often do well. We might feel that even if they do lead to destruction, great passions are worth it. And we might think that being kind and forgiving those who injure us is unjust and cowardly and that it generally does not have positive results. In that case, we might reasonably think that the plots of the plays mentioned above do not represent reality and that they are idealistic rather than realistic. And we might think that they therefore do not teach us much about our world. Moreover, even if we do think these plots accurately represent the ways of the world, *is* does not imply *ought*: that these plays accurately represented reality would not necessarily mean they teach us that we *ought* to be temperate, just, honest, kind, and forgiving.

Still, I think it is because the plots of some of the histories and tragedies demonstrate a causal relationship between acts of villainy, on the one hand, and misery and destruction on the other that some have taken them to be negative examples or cautionary tales that implicitly urge us to think twice before going down the road of villainy. Because the plots of many of the histories and tragedies demonstrate a causal relationship between intemperate action and destruction, some have taken them to counsel us not to annihilate passion and desire, but to maintain our freedom from them and our command over them through the exercise of our reason and judgment (Gervinus, Campbell). And because the plots of some of the comedies and romances show that there is a causal relationship between acts of kindness/forgiveness and happiness, some have taken them to embody positive examples that implicitly urge us to cultivate these qualities (Hunter).

Another aspect of the plots of the plays that I think has made people feel that they are being taught something of importance is that these plots contain countless scenes in which one character explicitly provides moral instruction or counsel to another. In *Henry IV, part 1*, for example, the hothead Hotspur lets his pride and anger get the better of him, and he insults and offends his ally, Glendower. His uncle and ally, Worcester, then chastises him for being "too wilful-blame" and instructs him: "you must needs learn, lord, to amend this fault," he says, for

> Though sometimes it show greatness, courage, blood—
> And that's the dearest grace it renders you—
> Yet often times it doth present harsh rage,
> Defect of manners, want of government,
> Pride, haughtiness, opinion and disdain,
> The least of which haunting a nobleman
> Loseth men's hearts, and leaves behind a stain
> Upon the beauty of all parts besides,
> Beguiling them of commendation.
> (3.1.177–89)

In *Richard II*, we have the famous scene in which the gardener instructs his servants on how to tend the garden and, by implication, how to govern a country (3.4). In *Romeo and Juliet*, we have Friar Laurence teaching Romeo that, because "violent delights have violent ends," he should "love moderately" (2.5.9–14). And in *The Merchant of Venice*, we have Portia counselling Shylock to be merciful (4.1.199–202).

I know: these characters in Shakespeare's plays are not Shakespeare, and there is little evidence that they speak *for* Shakespeare, or that they convey "the meaning" or "the message" of the plays in which they appear. Moreover, in many scenes of instruction, those who are supposed to learn from the instruction don't: "Well, I am schooled," Hotspur responds to his uncle's counsel, and he then continues in his wilful, hot-headed ways. The servant in the garden at least initially challenges the gardener's instructions on how to garden in light of the way Richard has been governing the kingdom. And as the gardener goes on to acknowledge, Richard has indeed failed to rule in the way that would be consistent with what he is teaching his servants. Romeo does not love moderately. Shylock does not have mercy for Antonio. But as the action of these plays unfolds, we see all of these characters fail and suffer as a result of ignoring the instruction on offer: Hotspur's rebellion fails and he is killed in battle; Richard is deposed and killed; Romeo, along with Juliet, is destroyed; Shylock is humiliated and loses everything.

Even putting aside these outcomes, the teaching and instruction dramatized in these and many other scenes in Shakespearean drama may well strike us as being wise—just on the basis of our own experience and knowledge of our condition. But that the plays also dramatize the failures and suffering of those who do not heed this instruction I think grants a degree of authority to it. I still do not wish to say that these and other counsellors and teachers are Shakespeare's spokesmen, though that is possible. Rather, I want to say just that one of the reasons that so many over the centuries have felt that Shakespeare's plays embody and convey some kind of wisdom is that they contain so many scenes of instruction. That instruction has a degree of authority in the world of the play and beyond because of the person who offers it and the ways in which it is confirmed. And one of the reasons there is such a wide range of views on the content and nature of this wisdom is that in these scenes the characters offer instruction on such a wide variety of subjects.

Character

One way in which character is linked to the audience's experience of learning and gaining wisdom is noted by Gervinus, who observes in connection with the tragedies that "Shakespeare never aims at preaching morals by express and direct precept. He does it for the most part indirectly by the mouth of the least prejudiced, by the spectators rather than by the actors in his plays" (889).

It is easy to see why Gervinus would make such a claim. In *Antony and Cleopatra*, for example, Enobarbus is a minor character who provides a wise, if cynical, running commentary on the main action right up until his own demise in Act 4. He shrewdly notes, for example, that Antony and Octavius Caesar should for the moment put aside their differences and deal with their enemy, Pompey, since there will be plenty of time for Antony and Octavius Caesar to fight each other once they have done so. When Antony chastises him for this cynical remark, Enobarbus tersely responds, "that truth should be silent, I had almost forgot" (2.2.129). As things turn out, he does indeed speak the truth. He continues to do so when, after his marvelous description of Cleopatra on her barge, he says Antony will never leave her—no matter that he has just agreed to marry Octavius Caesar's sister, Octavia. He quite rightly sees that this marriage, which is supposed to make the peace between the two men, "will be the very strangler of their amity," for he knows that Antony "will to his Egyptian dish again" (2.6.139–47). He foresees that Lepidus will be destroyed between the two main adversaries, Octavius Caesar and Antony, who will then "grind the one the other" (3.5.12). His counsel to Antony on the conduct of the war, confirmed by the other military men, is clearly sound, as is his ongoing assessment of Antony as one who makes bad decisions and acts shamefully because his desire, passion, and affection override his reason and judgment. He has good reason to leave Antony, as many do, but after having done so, he observes the ruthlessness of Octavius Caesar and Antony's ongoing magnanimity. Admitting to himself he has "done ill" (4.6.19), he is heartbroken, ashamed, and for all his cynicism and shrewd commentary, he in the end affirms the bounty and nobility of Antony.

True, Enobarbus is just one voice in the play, but he has a certain authority for a wide range of reasons: he has proven himself to be a good soldier; he is sociable and knows how to party with other people; his prophesies come true; though detached, he is still a participant and eye-witness to the events on which he comments; many other characters assert his honesty and wisdom; he admits to himself his error in leaving Antony; he is hard-nosed, yet capable of strong emotion and eloquence; he suffers. Seeing this, we may well take both his specific observations and his many general claims about life for wisdom.

Another candidate for an instructive minor character is Kent in *King Lear*. In the opening scene of the play, he looks on as Lear divides his kingdom between Regan and Goneril and leaves his third daughter Cordelia nothing, for she does not openly and lavishly express her love for her father, as her elder sisters do. Seeing the folly of this move, Kent attempts to be more than a spectator: in the face of the threatening and angry old king, he insists,

> be Kent unmannerly
> When Lear is mad. What wouldst thou do, old man?
> Think'st thou that duty shall have dread to speak
> When power to flattery bows? To plainness honour's bound
> When majesty falls to folly. Reserve thy state,
> And in thy best consideration check
> This hideous rashness. Answer my life my judgement:
> Thy youngest daughter does not love thee least,
> Nor are those empty-hearted whose low sounds
> Reverb no hollowness.
>
> (1.1.140–9)

Kent says and does much in few and plain words. He objects to Lear's division of his kingdom, and he tells him not to do it. He justifies this objection and command by making a specific claim (Lear's act of dividing the kingdom is rash and foolish) and a general claim (those who have a sense of duty and honor are bound to speak out plainly when their ruler is rash and foolish). He implies that Goneril and Regan are merely flattering him and openly asserts that Cordelia does not love him the least. He justifies these claims by making another general claim: those who do not ostentatiously show their love may well love more than those who do.

Lear banishes Kent for speaking out, but before departing and assuming a disguise that will allow him to continue to serve the king, Kent bids farewell in end-stopped, rhymed couplets that make it seem all the more formal, measured, and authoritative:

> Fare thee well, king: sith thus thou wilt appear,
> Freedom lives hence and banishment is here.—
> The gods to their dear shelter take thee, maid,   *to Cordelia*

       That justly think'st, and hast most rightly said.—
       And your large speeches may your deeds approve,   to Goneril and Regan
       That good effects may spring from words of love.

                                                    (1.1.179–86)

As the play proceeds, we see how wise all of this is. As Gloucester observes out on the heath, when the ambition and cruelty of Goneril and Regan have become clear, "His daughters seek his death. Ah, that good Kent! / He said it would be thus, poor banished man!" (3.4.138–9). So Kent is a minor character who observes the action, though he sometimes gets involved, as when he accosts Oswald for disrespecting the king. He serves the old king with courage, intelligence, kindness, and love right up to the bitter end. He speaks out and suffers for it, and other characters and the action itself confirm what he says. He thus has a certain authority, at least within the world of the play. If we do not feel we learn anything from him, we may at least feel that his assessment of his particular circumstances and his more general speculations embody a certain wisdom.

The fool in *Lear* I think also qualifies as a minor character who is essentially a spectator and who embodies, among other things, wisdom. Yes, he is foolish in a way, but one of the paradoxes that runs through all of the plays in which fools appear is that they are also wise, and that they *speak* wisdom, in part because their status as fools gives them a certain licence to do so. We can discern, for example, the hard truths and predictions Lear's fool mixes in and disguises with all of his nonsense, song, riddling, rhyming, story-telling, and metaphor. In the first scene in which he appears, the fool tells Lear he has been full of song,

   e'er since thou mad'st thy daughters thy mothers: for when thou gav'st
   them the rod and put'st down thine own breeches,
   Then they for sudden joy did weep,   *Sings*
   And I for sorrow sung,
   That such a king should play *bo-peep*   [a child's game]
   And go the fool among.
                                                    (1.4.125–30)

After Goneril enters, and rebukes them all, the fool observes,

   The hedge-sparrow fed the cuckoo so long,
   That it's had it head bit off by it young.
   So, out went the candle, and we were left darkling.
                            (1.4.164–6)

A fearsome prophecy, at least if we see the implied similarity between the sparrow and Lear. The fool then asks, "may not an ass know when the cart draws the horse?" before obeying Goneril's command to follow his master. He continues in this vein, avoiding explicit moral judgment and counsel, but strongly implying it—though he also occasionally ventures a more direct and literal mode of expression, as when he says straight out to Lear, "thou shouldst not have been old till thou hadst been wise" (1.5.33). After spending a wild night on the heath with Lear, the fool disappears, but his wisdom perhaps stays with us as we see his analogies borne out and his dark prophecies come true.

Though involved in the action a little more than Lear's fool, the fools in the comedies are also minor characters who act mainly as commentators and spectators (Salinger, Berry). In *As You Like It*, for example, Touchstone recalls that he once was in love, and observes, "we that are true lovers run into strange capers; but as all is mortal in nature, so is all nature in love mortal in folly" (2.4.43–4). This pretty much sums up the play, since, for one thing, it is a rough *antimetabole* (mortal/nature, nature/mortal) that is witty, playful, and a little confusing, as are so many other things in the world of this play. Touchstone's observation is also true to this world, in that the lovers do indeed do strange things, the natural world is mutable, and the lovers are only human in their folly—and mortal in folly perhaps also in the sense that they are fools only for a limited period of time. Notice, too, that the statement is general in nature: Touchstone speaks for "we" and about "all." In response to this playful, figurative, ambiguous generalization, Rosalind quite reasonably responds, "thou speakest wiser than thou art ware of" (2.4.45). In the rest of the play, Touchstone continues to provide a witty, figurative, tropological, playful, sometimes nonsensical, and often cynical commentary on a wide range of subjects: the shepherd's life, the courtly life, poetry, the single life, married life, wit, honesty, quarreling, and wisdom itself: "I do now remember a saying," he tells William. "'The fool doth think he is wise, but the wise man knows himself to be a fool'" (5.1.24–5).

Touchstone's pronouncements on these matters have a certain authority—in relation to both the characters in his world and the audience—because he often speaks from experience, he is eye-witness to the main action, he reiterates "sayings" and proverbs (more on this later), and he is *disinterested* in an important way: he really does not seem to care whether or not he teaches anyone or anyone takes him seriously. True, he pursues and ends up with Audrey, but he has no serious long-term agenda. This cavalier attitude, as opposed to a grave intention to instruct somebody or get something for himself, tends, I think, to enhance his credibility, especially in the eyes of modern audiences that don't like being preached to. Moreover, in the play itself, not just Rosalind but several other characters observe the intelligence and wisdom of this character who operates in the margins of the play. Thus, in the final scene, Touchstone asserts by way of *similes* the generalization that "rich honesty dwells like a miser, sir, in a poor house, as your pearl in your foul oyster" (5.4.50–1). Duke Senior then observes that "he is very swift and sententious" (5.4.52). Just as impressed by him as the duke is, Jaques says, "Is not this a rare fellow, my lord? He's as good at anything and yet a fool." The duke responds by pointing out that, really, Touchstone is no fool: "he uses his folly like a stalking-horse and under the presentation of that he shoots [expresses] his wit" (5.4.78–80).

Similarly, Feste in *Twelfth Night* lives on the margins, *playing* the fool, not really pursuing any agenda but singing songs, picking up a little money on the side, observing the main action of the play, and getting involved at times, mainly just for fun. All the while he provides a commentary on what is happening that is both zany and wise, as the other characters observe. In the opening act he establishes his credentials as a wise man in the usual way—by denying he has wit and intelligence: "Wit, an't be thy will, put me into good fooling! Those wits, that think they have thee, do very oft prove fools, and I that am sure I lack thee, may pass for a wise man. For what says Quinapalus? 'Better a witty fool than a foolish wit'" (1.5.25–8). He then participates in the late-night party with Toby and Agucheek that is so rudely interrupted by Malvolio. In a later exchange with Viola, he produces a *metaphorical* description of sentences that aptly describes much of his own linguistic prowess: "a sentence is but a cheveril [pliable leather] glove to a good wit. How quickly the wrong side may be turned outward!" (3.1.8–9). Viola confirms this observation—"Nay that's certain"—and at the end of this exchange in which Feste gets the better of her, she gives him money and provides a more explicit evaluation of him and his office:

> This fellow is wise enough to play the fool,
> He must observe their mood on whom he jests,
> The quality of persons, and the time,
> And, like the *haggard, check* at every feather   [untrained hawk, swoop]
> That comes before his eye. This is a practice
> As full of labour as a wise man's art,
> For folly that he wisely shows is fit;
> But wise men, *folly-fall'n*, quite taint their wit.   [stooping to foolishness]
> (3.1.43–51)

Indeed, Feste is wise, and he plays the fool well. He is more humane and likeable than Touchstone, but he is still part of the world of error and mistaken identity since he, too, thinks Sebastian is Cesario/Viola (4.1). After having some more fun with Malvolio by pretending to be Sir Topas the curate, Feste then helps him out, and in an exchange with Orsino provides half serious/half comical reasons for his assertion that he is "better [off] for my foes and the worse [off] for my friends" (5.1.9). The conspiracy against Malvolio having been revealed, Feste then aptly sums up the entire play by observing, "thus the whirligig of time brings in his revenges" (5.1.358–9), and singing one last, bitter-sweet song that wisely shows human folly ("When that I was…").

So while I wouldn't want to say that Shakespeare preaches morals by way of minor characters in the plays, I would venture to say that some of these characters do provide a moral commentary on what is happening. For a wide range of reasons this commentary has a certain authority and can therefore come across to both characters in the plays and the audience as being instructive and wise.

Then there are the major characters in the plays. We have already seen that one reason many have felt the histories and tragedies can provide, even if indirectly, moral instruction, edification, and wisdom about human existence is that they show how particular moral failings are causally related to suffering and destruction. And one reason the comedies and romances have been felt to do so is that they show how specific moral traits—such as kindness, honesty, liberality, justice, temperance, and mercy—are causally related to happiness. For the moment, just a couple further general observations on this count.

First, though some, such as the twentieth-century philosopher Wittgenstein, challenged it, one of the longstanding claims about Shakespearean drama is that its main characters seem real, true to life. Life-like characters, more than characters who seem phony or unreal, cause us to feel pity and compassion when they suffer. Given that we have an emotional experience at a Shakespeare play, one that is enabled by characters who suffer and seem real, does it improve us in any way? Some ancient philosophers, such as Plato, had doubts about this. While Plato felt that repeatedly experiencing intense emotion at plays does indeed change us morally, he felt it does so for the worse: that kind of emotional experience tends to make one an emotional, slightly hysterical being who is an unreliable citizen and soldier. But we have seen that many others—Aristotle, Sidney, Dryden, Montagu, and Hazlitt—challenge Plato's position. They claim that our experience of emotion when we read or see a Shakespeare play in some way changes us for the better. If that is so, and if it is in part the life-like quality of Shakespeare's main characters that enable this emotional experience, then the life-like quality of Shakespeare's main characters is one of the things that accounts for the plays' powers to improve our moral sensibilities.

Second, the claim for the verisimilitude of Shakespeare's main characters also informs the long-standing claim that Shakespeare can have a beneficial effect on how we think about and behave with women in particular. Recall that Anna Jameson in the nineteenth century claimed that Shakespeare is a force for good when it comes to attitudes towards and treatment of women in western educational institutions and society at large. Jameson argues that Shakespearean drama can do this because it provides "images and examples" of *real* women (8), because Shakespeare's women are "complete individuals" (10) who are true to "the feminine character" (13) and display "the manner in which the affections would naturally display themselves in women" (26). And in presenting female characters of this kind, Shakespeare represents women who are in virtue, but also "in truth, in variety, in power, equal to his men" (17, 26–7).

I think that Jameson is right in claiming that, like his male characters, Shakespeare's female characters seem real, and that they are in many respects the equal to and in some cases superior to the male characters. In the tragedies, for example, Juliet is superior in pretty much all respects to Romeo; Antony is grand, but Cleopatra surely eclipses him in the end; in *Coriolanus* we can see why Coriolanus' mother, Volumnia, says to her son, "thy valiantness was mine, thou sucked'st it from me" (3.2.150); and Lady Macbeth is the peer of her husband—at least as long as she maintains her sanity. In the comedies and romances, both Hermione and Paulina in *A Winter's Tale* claim a moral superiority to Leontes; though constrained in some ways, the sublime Portia pretty much runs the show in *Merchant of Venice*; in *Twelfth Night*, Viola, Maria, and Olivia pretty much control the action and are superior in many respects to their counterparts Orsino, Toby, Sebastian; Rosalind is by far the dominant figure in *As You Like It* and is wiser and funnier than Orlando; let's call it a tie between Beatrice and Benedick in *Much Ado*. And then there are noble, morally elevated characters such as Desdemona in *Othello*, Cordelia in *Lear*, and Miranda in *The Tempest*. It is because we get these emotionally complex, intelligent, morally elevated, strong, true-to-life female characters who are central to the action of the plays that Jameson and many others feel the plays have the capacity to inform audiences about the nature and capacities of women and implicitly urge them to behave in ways that are consistent with that recognition.

Thought

In chapter 1 we saw that the way in which the protagonists of the histories and tragedies reason and think is one of the things that can incline us to sympathize with them when they suffer. And in chapter 2 we saw that the way in which the characters in all genres reason and think is one of the things that makes us laugh with and sometimes at them. But the characters' *dianoia* also accounts in part for our sense that these plays embody wisdom and convey some kind of moral instruction. This is because the characters often think about themselves in relation to general propositions about the world and human existence, propositions that may well ring true to us simply because they are consistent with our own experience and knowledge of human existence. But many of these propositions may have an additional authority in our eyes because

- the characters are not just idly speculating about life but assert these claims on the basis of their own experience
- the characters often see themselves as evidence or proof of their claims
- we are emotionally engaged with the characters who assert these claims.

Recall, for example, Lear out on the heath during the storm. For all his railing, cursing, and fear of losing his mind, Lear still reasons well about both the general and the particular. Speaking to Kent, who is imploring him to seek shelter, Lear affirms two closely related general claims about human suffering: "where the greater malady is fixed / The lesser is scarce felt," and "when the mind's free, / The body's delicate." The first seems to mean that when we are afflicted with a major pain or injury, we tend not to feel or be conscious of minor ones. The second seems to mean that when we are not mentally preoccupied with some problem, we are more prone to feel physical pain. Lear then asserts a claim about himself: "the tempest in my mind / Doth from my senses take all feeling else / Save what beats there" (3.4.10–16). Suffering so much *mentally* as a result of the ingratitude and cruelty of his daughters, Lear suffers less *physically* in the terrible storm. What is the relationship between this claim about a particular person—himself—and the two general claims that precede it? I think Lear implies that the claim about himself confirms the two general claims. To put it another way, he sees his particular experience as an example or instance that proves that when you are suffering from a major injury, you do not notice minor ones, and that when you are mentally distressed, you become desensitized to physical pain. Though his mental anguish tempers his physical suffering, Lear then imagines how the poor will suffer in the storm, and he commands the rich and powerful ("pomp") to feel what wretches feel so they can act in a way that will make the world more just (3.4.35–9).

Sure, you still might respond critically to this moment: wretches are wretches because they are lazy or because they simply choose to be wretches, which is why the rich and powerful are *not* obliged to share their wealth with them. Still, Lear's new conviction that it is in some basic sense unjust for the rich and powerful not to share their wealth with the poor has a certain authority because it is based on his actually feeling what the poor feel, actually suffering, if only briefly, in the way they suffer. It is because this general claim about distributive justice—and this counsel to the rich and powerful—are arrived at by this kind of person and in this way that they may pull some weight with us as well.

The protagonist in *Coriolanus* is not known for his thinking. Yet, having been banished from Rome, he stands alone in front of his enemy Aufidius' house in the city of Antium, and he pauses to think about friendship and enmity. He thinks that "friends now fast sworn" can "break out / To bitterest enmity" over an apparently trivial matter. And he thinks that, at the same time, "fellest foes" can by "some trick not worth an egg… grow dear friends" and make common cause or even join their children in marriage. These are not just any old claims about life—they are ones that I dare say may strike us as being wise claims about life, ones that are true and that apply to us. I mean, isn't it true that good friends can fall out over an apparently trivial matter? Isn't it true that foes can end up being allies for not the best of reasons? But note that Coriolanus goes on to think that he himself is evidence or confirmation of these claims: "So with me. / My birthplace hate I, and my love's upon / This enemy town" (4.4.14–29). So Coriolanus does not just assert these general claims about friendship and enmity. He explicitly observes that those claims apply to him, that his own experience confirms and bears them out—and he is at least to some extent right!

Similarly, in *Antony and Cleopatra*, after he has disgraced himself at Actium, Antony says to Cleopatra,

> But when we in our viciousness grow hard—
> O, misery on't!—the wise gods seel our eyes,
> In our own filth drop our clear judgments, make us
> Adore our errors, laugh at's while we strut
> To our confusion.
>
> (3.13.135–9)

116 *Wisdom and moral instruction*

On the basis of what does Antony make this general claim about life, this claim about not just him, but "us"? On the basis of his own immediate experience, on the basis of his punishing knowledge of how he himself erred and allowed his infatuation with Cleopatra to influence his military command and judgment, and on the basis of the shame, disgust, and self-hatred he feels as a result of having done so. He is not idly speculating, but driven by his own experience to general and, for him, punishing reflections about life. And he takes his own hard experience as evidence or proof of the general claim he passionately asserts.

Much the same might be said of the many general observations we get from both Lady Macbeth and Macbeth. Plotting to kill the king and make way for her husband to be crowned, Lady Macbeth says to him that the killing "shall to all our nights and days to come / Give solely sovereign sway and masterdom" (1.6.70–1). She goads her husband to commit the deed and participates in the cover-up, but immediately afterwards she finds herself retracting her earlier upbeat prediction:

> Naught's had, all's spent,
> Where our desire is got without content:
> 'Tis safer to be that which we destroy
> Than by destruction dwell in doubtful joy.
> (3.2.6–9)

Beginning to experience first-hand the mental anguish that results from committing "destruction," Lady Macbeth is moved to make a general pronouncement about how "we" feel when "we" do such things: when we get what we want through acts of destruction that undermine our own security and contentedness, we end up with nothing. And that proposition is indeed borne out by the rest of the play, as we see both her and her husband with naught in the end.

But before he ends up with nothing, Macbeth, too, reflects on his experience and ventures some big claims about the meaning of life: having "supped full of horrors" and "made direness familiar to [his] slaughterous thoughts," he says,

> Tomorrow, and tomorrow, and tomorrow,
> Creeps in this petty pace from day to day
> To the last syllable of recorded time:
> And all our yesterdays have lighted fools
> The way to dusty death. Out, out, brief candle.
> Life's but a walking shadow, a poor player
> That struts and frets his hour upon the stage
> And then is heard no more. It is a tale
> Told by an idiot, full of sound and fury,
> Signifying nothing.
> (5.5.19–28)

Is this wisdom? Do you feel that Macbeth provides significant insight into life here? It will depend in part on your own view of what life is. But whatever your view may be, Macbeth's remarks here amount to an evaluation of life in general, the *kind* of claim about life that counts as wisdom. And this claim has a certain authority in relation to those who have been engaging with the play because it is not made by just anybody. It is made by Macbeth, a highly intelligent, emotional, imaginative, ambitious, courageous man who has experienced and undergone so much: he has fought on the battlefield, confronted witches, had visions, experienced tremendous pain, violence, mental anguish, fear, regret, despair. And because he has gone through so much, he may well have engaged our sympathies and fears. Since it is Macbeth's wisdom, it may well become our wisdom unless we have something within us to set against it, something within us upon which we can call to defend ourselves against a fearsome nihilism that is grounded in this individual's massive experience.

Many characters in the histories, comedies, and romances also see themselves and their own lives as evidence or confirmation of general propositions about life that they themselves assert. Recall that early in *Richard III*, Buckingham prays publicly to heaven that God punish him if he ever turns against Queen Elizabeth and her allies. But he does turn against them and helps their enemy, Richard III, to the throne. When he doesn't do everything Richard wants him to do, Richard then turns against him and orders his execution. On the day of his execution, Buckingham remembers his prayer and, in light of all that has passed, infers a general claim about how God deals with wicked men such as himself:

> That high all-seer [God] which I dallied with
> Hath turned my feigned prayer on my head
> And given in earnest what I begged in jest:
> Thus doth he force the swords of wicked men
> To turn their own points in their masters' bosoms.
> (4.5.20–4)

Notice the move from "my" and "I" to "men": on the basis of his own personal experience, Buckingham claims that God has dealt with him in the way he deals with *other* wicked men.

In *Richard II*, the self-pitying, self-indulgent king also has his moments of powerful reflection upon his own punishing experience. For example, finding that much of his support has disappeared upon his return to England from Ireland, and realizing that his enemy Bullingbrook is now in control, he moves to general propositions about kings and death: Death keeps his court "within the hollow crown" that is worn by a king. After scoffing the king who wears this crown, infusing him with vanity, allowing him to "monarchize," and humoring him, Death then at last "with a little pin / Bores through his castle walls, and farewell king!" (3.2.155–65). After he has been deposed and imprisoned, Richard again thinks in general terms. Imagining himself to be many things, he is driven to a punishing conclusion about himself and all men:

                    But whate'er I am,
    Nor I nor any man that but man is
    With nothing shall be pleased, till he be eased
    With being nothing.
                        (5.5.38–41)

On the basis of his punishing experience, which is about to culminate in his own death, Richard speculates that only when one is nothing, or at least not worried about being nothing, can one enjoy being something. As Richard sees it, that goes for everybody.

Notice, too, the general proposition that Richard asserts to support his prophesy that Bullingbrook and Northumberland (who helped Bullingbrook depose Richard and ascend the throne) will turn against each other:

    The love of wicked friends converts to fear;
    That fear to hate, and hate turns one or both
    To worthy danger and deserved death.
                        (5.1.66–8)

Richard here achieves a kind of oracular, authoritative tone by way of two instances of the figure *anadiplosis*: one phrase ends with "fear" and the next begins with "fear"; that phrase ends with "hate," and the next begins with "hate." You may have encountered this figure in *Star Wars*, when wise Yoda says, "fear leads to anger. Anger leads to hate. Hate leads to suffering." I also like the one in the film *Gladiator* (2000), when the evil Emperor Commodus (Joaquin Phoenix) confronts the gladiator Maximus (Russell Crowe) in the Colosseum, and says, "They call for you: The general who became a slave; the slave who became a gladiator; the gladiator who defied an Emperor. Striking story" (the rhetoricians called this series of *anadiploses* a *gradatio*). In the Shakespeare play, Richard calls on this figure to assert with authority a general claim about the emotional transformation and fate of wicked friends. Since he sees Bullingbrook and Northumberland as wicked friends, that claim applies to them. As we see in the *Henry IV* plays, Northumberland—along with his son, Hotspur—does indeed turn against Bullingbrook and embroil England in civil war in which Hotspur is killed. The particulars of history thus bear out Richard's general claim.

At the end of *Much Ado About Nothing*, Benedick infers a general claim about mankind in light of the way he himself ends up engaged to be married after firmly asserting he would never marry: "never flout at me for what I have said against it [marriage], for man is a giddy thing, and this is my conclusion" (5.4.105–6). A rather trite conclusion about what we are, and one that is not grounded in suffering. It is, however, well supported by the behavior of not just Benedick but many other characters in the play. In *Twelfth Night* we have a similar conclusion, but here the general claim comes first and the experience that confirms it comes second: early in the play, Orsino says to Viola/Cesario,

> however we [men] do praise ourselves,
> Our fancies are more giddy and unfirm,
> More longing, wavering, sooner lost and worn,
> Than women's are.
>
> (2.4.33–6)

In the end, Orsino himself, at least, proves this claim to be true, for having professed undying love for Olivia throughout the entire play, he suddenly loses this love and commits himself to Viola/Cesario, who remains true to him from the moment she sees him.

On the basis of our own experience and observation, some of us may deem the characters' speculations and generalizations to be true and wise, and some may not. However reasonable or probable it might be for some characters—given who and where they are—to postulate a just Christian deity presiding over human existence, for example, non-Christians may well not be inclined to take such a postulation on as straight wisdom. And if you are an optimist, you might well object to Macbeth's final verdict: "No! You're wrong! Life is a bowl of cherries!" But I do want to say that in some cases the characters' thoughts have a claim on our attention because these thoughts come to them in the wake of—or are *forced* upon them by—their own intense and punishing experiences. The protagonists' thoughts on life in the histories and tragedies have some of the best credentials such thoughts can have—they are borne of suffering. It is also worth noting that the main characters in the plays generally do not set out to achieve wisdom, are not driven by an ambition to be wise, and do not approach life as an occasion for finding it. Rather, they are characters who by instinct reflect and think about who they are, what is happening to them, other people, human existence, and the world. Instead of just experiencing things and going merrily on their way, they find themselves thinking about those experiences and how they relate to the experiences of other people. So there is something *innocent* about the general claims about life they end up making. These claims are the product not of a deliberate project or ambition of discovering the meaning of life but of their own personal experiences and their own inclination to think about that experience in relation to the experience of other people. Because these claims are often the product not of a moral or political agenda but of raw experience and a natural inclination to reflect upon experience, I think they pull some weight with us.

I also think that the fact that characters respond to what is happening by speculating about the human condition at large and making the *kind* of claim we associate with wisdom encourages us to do the same: the emotion of the characters is a cue to our emotion; the laughter and delight of the characters are cues to our laughter and delight; the speculation and reflection of the characters are cues to our speculation and reflection. Sure, you can refuse to accept and act on these cues. But insofar as you act on them, you may well be moved to do what they are doing: think about human existence and the world. And as a result, you may well feel, as they do, that you achieve or are confirmed in some kind of wisdom, even though it might differ from the wisdom the characters assert.

Another feature of the thinking and reasoning of Shakespeare's characters that accounts for why many readers and audiences have felt the plays qualify as a kind of wisdom literature is that in addition to including many *longer* observations about life, they also include countless *shorter* ones (one or two lines) that would appear to be true. Thus, throughout the seventeenth century many readers regarded Shakespeare's plays—especially the tragedies—as a source of wisdom about a wide range of topics, not so much because of the plots and characters, but because of the many pithy generalizations which they could extract from the plays and which they felt were true and useful (Roberts, Whitney). In the eighteenth century, Samuel Johnson supports his claim that the plays provide some (though not enough) moral instruction by observing that even though "his precepts and axioms drop casually from him," the plays are filled with "practical axioms and domestick wisdom." Just as every line in plays by the ancient Greek tragedean Euripedes "was a precept," so "it may be said of Shakespeare, that from his works may be collected a system of civil and oeconomical prudence" (62, 71).

Elizabeth Montagu adds that the "maxims," "sentences," and "precepts" in the plays amount to a kind of "instruction" because they are uttered in particular, concrete situations by characters with whom we sympathize (20–32). In the nineteenth century, Mary Cowden Clarke published a collection of these one-liners, the title of which says it all: *Shakespeare Proverbs: Or the Wise Saws of our Wisest Poet Collected into a Modern Instance* (1848). These terse statements have less currency and authority for us than they did for those of the past, but if you google "Shakespeare's wisdom," you still get several sites that provide lists of one-liners. So the long-standing association between short generalizations and wisdom survives to some extent in modern western society. And one reason people over the last four hundred years have regarded the plays as a source of wisdom is that they contain so many short generalizations that seem true and applicable to everyday situations.

Many of these axioms and precepts seem to have been invented by Shakespeare, but many were not. Several scholars have shown that many of them are what we call "proverbs" or "sayings," and what Shakespeare would have also called "saws," "adages," "sentences," and "maxims" (Tilley, Dent, Smith). These sayings have a particular force and authority in the plays and beyond, first, because rather than being invented by Shakespeare, they had been passed down through generations of English and western European society and are simply *repeated* by his characters. I think there are three main sources of these sayings:

- English folk wisdom (these ones are usually anonymous)
- ancient Greek and Roman culture (this is the case with the proverbs and adages derived from one of the most popular books of the sixteenth century, one that Shakespeare probably read at grammar school, Erasmus'

Adages. In this work, Erasmus presents thousands of adages and proverbs as embodiments of the wisdom of the ancient world)
- the Bible (not just The Book of Proverbs in the Old Testament, which explicitly presents itself as a collection of wise sayings, but the entire work).

These proverbs, adages, and maxims are continually on the lips of Shakespeare's characters, and they were seen (at least in the Renaissance) to embody the wisdom not just of an individual author (if there was one), but of an entire culture, society, religion, or people—be it English, European, Graeco-Roman, Judaeo-Christian, or western. They were seen as the product of a collective experience and transmission, a product that was no one's private property but owned in common (Crane, Eden). Many of those who recorded and reiterated them over time thus did so in order to pass down what they regarded as collective wisdom and to instruct others in how to live a good life.

Second, it is one thing to hear or read adages, maxims, or proverbs in a collection of proverbs, such as Erasmus' *Adages*, but it is another thing to read or hear them spoken by particular people in particular situations, which is how we hear them in Shakespeare. Thus, what in his society was (and in some quarters still is) regarded as the proverbial wisdom of the ages circulates throughout his plays as we see his characters reiterate hundreds of adages, maxims, axioms, precepts, and proverbs in all kinds of different situations, for all kinds of different purposes. All of the ancient rhetoricians discuss proverbs and maxims as powerful means of persuasion, so it is not surprising to find that, in many cases, Shakespeare's characters cite them to persuade others to believe or do something. This is what, for example, the plebeians in *Coriolanus* do when they cite several "proverbs" (1.1.189) to support their demand for corn. And in *Macbeth*, Lady Macbeth attempts to persuade her hesitant husband to murder the king by likening him to the cowardly cat in the adage, "the cat would eat fish but she will not wet her feet":

> Wouldst thou have that
> Which thou esteem'st the ornament of life,
> And live a coward in thine own esteem,
> Letting 'I dare not' wait upon 'I would,'
> Like the poor cat i'th'adage?
> (1.7.43–7)

In some cases, the characters cite proverbs in their own reasoning with themselves, as when Brutus in *Julius Caesar* observes to himself that "it is the bright day that brings forth the adder" (2.1.14). In some cases they cite them to criticize others, as when the fool in *King Lear* refers to the proverbial description of the snail as a creature that keeps his house on his back: "I can tell why a snail has a house," he says to Lear. "Why, to put's head in, not to give it away to his daughters and leave his horns without a case" (1.5.20–3). In some cases they use them playfully, to taunt or mock others, as when in *Henry IV, part 1*,

Prince Hal says of Falstaff, "Sir John stands to his word, the devil shall have his bargain, for he was never yet a breaker of proverbs: he will give the devil his due" (1.2.79–80). Hamlet does this when he cites half of the proverb, "while the grass grows, the horse starves," in order to suggest to Rosencrantz that he is suffering under the reign of Claudius, but also to mock him: "Ay, but 'while the grass grows'—the proverb is something musty" (3.2.296). And in some cases, the characters cite proverbs to counsel and instruct others. In *Coriolanus*, for example, the protagonist repeats several of the "precepts" his mother taught him with the aim of consoling her and helping her cope with his banishment (4.1.1–11). In *Hamlet*, Polonius cites several of them to counsel his son and daughter. In *Othello* the duke cites several "sentences" to counsel Brabantio, whose daughter has without his permission or knowledge married the Moor (1.3.216–25).

So while Shakespearean drama contains the wisdom of the ages as expressed in proverbs, adages, and maxims, that wisdom is not presented to us by a single authoritative voice, nor is it directly addressed to us. It is embodied by the plays, implanted in concrete situations. This need not prevent us from extracting them from the plays and treating them as discrete pearls of wisdom—as many over the centuries have. But even if we don't, the plays demonstrate how the wisdom of the ages, in the form of proverbs, can be *useful*, how it can be called upon by people to do all kinds of things, such as persuade, ridicule, counsel, reflect, console, and have fun. And, as Elizabeth Montagu observes, because many of them are spoken by life-like characters with whom we sympathize, "their precepts... are an instruction."

Third, some of the maxims, proverbs, and adages in Shakespearean drama have a claim to our attention because the plots of the plays seem to bear out and confirm them. Thus, for example, in *Richard II*, John of Gaunt observes how Richard is governing the country and foretells to his brother York that

> His [the king's] rash fierce blaze of riot cannot last,
> For violent fires soon burn out themselves.
> Small showers last long, but sudden storms are short.
> He tires betimes that spurs too fast betimes.
> With eager feeding food doth choke the feeder.
> Light vanity, insatiate cormorant,
> Consuming means soon preys upon itself.
>
> (2.1.33–9)

Given all of these proverbs and maxims, and given that Richard *resembles* a violent fire, a short shower, a horse rider that spurs too fast, a man who eats too eagerly, and a cormorant (which was believed to eat its young), Richard's rule, Gaunt argues, will not last long. Gaunt is right: Richard's rule does not last long. The play that represents his demise thus bears out Gaunt's maxims and proverbs—at least if we accept Gaunt's perceptions of resemblance.

The tragedies are also filled with adages and proverbs, many of which are borne out by the action of the plays. The action of *Romeo and Juliet*, for example, could reasonably be seen to bear out several of Friar Laurence's proverbial observations: nature is both womb and tomb (2.2.9–10); "virtue itself turns vice, being misapplied, / And vice sometime by action dignified" (2.2.21–2); "women may fall, when there's no strength in men" (2.2.81); "violent delights have violent ends" (2.5.9); "they stumble that run fast" (2.2.97). In *Othello*, Iago explicitly identifies himself as confirmation of an old saying about devils: "Divinity of hell! / When devils will the blackest sins put on, / They do suggest at first with heavenly show, / As I do now" (2.3.314–17). In *King Lear*, the fool's proverbs about putting the cart before the horse, giving away the entire loaf of bread, and the cuckoo killing the sparrow that gave it a home, all have a clear application to the old kind king. If *Coriolanus* shows how one military man (Aufidius) destroys another (Coriolanus), we might think it bears out Aufidius when he reiterates an adage from Erasmus' *Adages* (one that dates back to Aristotle and the ancient Greeks): "one fire drives out one fire: one nail, one nail," (4.7.56)—though there are other ways of understanding this adage and its relationship to the play. And in *Macbeth*, after all of the guests have departed the disastrous banquet at which the ghost of Banquo appears to Macbeth, the frightened protagonist cites what "they say": "It will have blood, they say: blood will have blood" (3.4.142). Like many proverbs, this one is terse, obscure, general, and it is unclear what exactly Macbeth means by asserting it to his wife. But it seems reasonable to think that he means, as we read in Genesis, "whoso sheddeth man's blood, by man shall his blood be shed" (Genesis 9:6). If this is what the proverb means, then the play bears it out: Macbeth sheds man's blood and his blood is shed by man (though one untimely ripped from his mother's womb). That is one reason one might come away from the play thinking, yes, what they say is true: blood will have blood.

This kind of thing also occurs in the comedies and romances. Note, first of all, that proverbs and proverbial language enter into the titles of some of these plays: *All's Well that Ends Well, The Taming of the Shrew, Much Ado About Nothing, Measure for Measure*. Though many now think Shakespeare invented these phrases, he didn't; they all come from old English phrases and proverbs that he picked up by being a linguistically hypersensitive young man in Elizabethan England. And though it would be simplistic to say that these plays simply confirm their titles, both the titles and the plays can be reasonably read in such a way that the plays do correspond in important ways with their proverbial titles—which is perhaps not so surprising! Then we have the proverbs within the plays. The plot of *A Midsummer Night's Dream* might reasonably be seen to confirm the proverb Hermia pronounces early in the play: "the course of true love never did run smooth" (1.1.135). And as Puck himself later promises, as he administers the "remedy" to the sleeping Lysander, the action of this play will bear out another proverb:

> And the country proverb known,
> That every man should take his own,
> In your waking shall be shown.

> Jack shall have Jill,
> Naught shall go ill,
> The man shall have his mare again, and all shall be well.
> (3.2.474–9)

In *As You Like It*, when Phoebe falls for Rosalind, she explicitly observes that her experience proves a saying (which comes from a poem by the dead shepherd, Christopher Marlowe): "Dead Shepherd, now I find thy saw [saying] of might, / 'Who ever loved that loved not at first sight?'" (3.5.80–1). And we might reasonably think that Duke Senior was right when, having been banished to the Forest of Arden, he observes, "sweet are the uses of adversity" (2.1.12). In *Much Ado About Nothing*, we recall that at the opening of the play, in response to Benedick's vehement assertion, "I will live a bachelor," Don Pedro observes, "well, if ever thou dost fall from this faith, thou wilt prove a notable argument." Benedick insists that he will stay true to his commitment, to which Don Pedro responds with a proverb: "'In time the savage bull doth bear the yoke'" (1.1.173). Note that our modern editors place the sentence in quotation marks to indicate that Don Pedro is citing a proverb or saying—he is *reiterating* a saying that had been passed down to his society and that had some currency and authority within it. Our editors also note that this saying was well known in Shakespeare's society, in part because it also occurred in another popular play of the day, Thomas Kyd's *The Spanish Tragedy*. Well, we know that by the end of the play, Benedick has broken his commitment never to marry, he is betrothed to Beatrice, he has proven a notable argument, and he has confirmed the proverb—for the passionate bachelor will now submit to the constraints imposed by marriage. And, indeed, his friend Claudio makes fun of him by reminding him (and us) of this fact: when Don Pedro asks Benedick why he looks unhappy, Claudio explains, "I think he thinks upon the savage bull" (5.4.43). In light of all this, we may well find some wisdom in the proverb that in time the savage bull doth wear the yoke.

Of course, not all of the proverbs and maxims are borne out by the plays in which characters pronounce them. In *Richard II*, for example, Gaunt observes, "O, but they say the tongues of dying men / Enforce attention like deep harmony" (2.1.5–6), and he proceeds to enunciate several more sayings and proverbs to support his claim that Richard might listen to his counsel—but Richard does not listen to him. And the fact that you know your wise proverbs does not necessarily mean *you* are wise. In *Hamlet*, for example, Polonius is a fountain of proverbs as he goes about instructing and counseling those around him, but he is something of a fool who ends up dead, along with his son and daughter. We note, too, that in *Coriolanus*, the protagonist has contempt for the plebeians' "proverbs," and that in *Othello*, Brabantio rebuffs the duke's attempt to console him by way of "sentences." Still, many of the proverbs and adages, even ones that are repeated by fools, are borne out by the plays, which is one further reason they may have a certain authority in the eyes of the audience.

So in addition to accounting in part for our laughter and our sympathy with Shakespeare's characters when they suffer, the thinking and reasoning of Shakespeare's characters also account in part for the impression that the plays embody wisdom and convey some kind of moral instruction. For rather than idly speculating about life, many of these characters assert propositions about human existence and the world on the basis of their own experience, and they often explicitly identify that experience as something that bears out or confirms these propositions. In some cases, they also affirm these general claims to support prophecies that come true. These characters are also continually invoking the wisdom of the ages as it is embodied in proverbs and adages deriving from the Graeco-Roman and Biblical foundations of western culture, and native English tradition and folklore. Rather than directly espousing this wisdom, Shakespeare's plays embody it and dramatize the ways in which it may be mobilized in daily life. We may well think twice before dismissing these sayings as corny one-liners, when we also see that in many cases the plays confirm their truth.

Language

Imagine that, at the end of the play, upon receiving the news that his wife is dead, Macbeth swooned, raved, and wildly cried, "Life is meaningless!" That way of asserting nihilism would be so much less compelling and authoritative than the way in which he does assert it. What is it about his way of asserting nihilism that might incline us to regard it as wisdom, as a general observation about life that has some kind of authority and purchase on us? In order to answer this question, I think we again need to look at the *language*—in particular, the sounds of words, figurative usage, and tropological usage.

On the level of sound, note that we do not have short, sharp, fast witty rhymed couplets, but blank verse with many irregularities (*spondaic* and *trochaic* feet), a mix of *end-stopped* lines and *enjambment*, and several *caesurae*. These features of Macbeth's language bring it closer to everyday speech and allow it to be spoken in a frank, direct, serious tone. But note the high density of particular vowel sounds in the passage (*assonance*): the "o" sounds in "tomorrow," "fools," "out," "shadow," "poor," "hour," "more," "full," "fury." These long "o" sounds slow it down a little, make it longer, heavier, and sonorous. And note the high density of a particular consonant (*consonance*): the "r" in "tomorrow," "creeps," "from," "recorded," "yesterday," "struts," "frets," "hour," "heard," "more," "fury." I detect a quiet, deep growl! And note the repetition of consonants at the beginning of words (*alliteration*) that slightly enhances the striking power and force of the utterance: "petty pace," "day to day," "dusty death," "poor player," "tale told." On the level of figurative usage (unusual sequences of words), we have in the opening line not just a repetition of a single word, "tomorrow" (*ploce*), but also a repetition of a conjunction (*polysyndeton*), in this case the conjunction "and." Both figures, along with the commas, also slow the utterance down, retard forward motion, and thereby give the impression of a measured, deliberate statement that is not driven by uncontrolled passion, but by intense thinking, weariness, grimness, and perhaps a dash of contempt for life. And note the *apostrophe* to "candle." Even if we imagine Macbeth at first responding to Seyton, who has just reported to him the death of Lady Macbeth, he turns from him to address something he imagines, commanding it to go out. Macbeth is alone, speaking only to things in his mind.

All of this is happening within a highly tropological description of many things:

- words which are usually used to refer to the actions of animals or people ("creep") are used to refer to the passing of time
- words which are usually used to refer to language ("syllable") are used to refer to a moment of time (the very last moment of time)
- words which are usually used to refer to things people do ("lighted... the way") are used to refer to what yesterdays do
- words which are usually used to refer to a candle are used to refer to life
- words which are usually used to refer to acting ("player," "struts," "frets," "shadow") are used to refer to living
- words which are usually used to refer to narrating ("tales," "told") are used to refer to life.

It seems that Macbeth perceives *resemblances* between the way time passes and the way animals and people creep, between bits of words and moments of time, between what people do and what past days do, between life and a candle, between living and acting, between living and being an impassioned character in a meaningless story. And this is why he produces a complex *metaphorical* description of time and life—because *metaphor* is the trope where words that are usually used to refer to or mean one thing are used to refer to or mean something that *resembles* that thing. This rich, metaphorical description I think makes Macbeth's assertion of nihilism concrete, graphic, forceful, impressive, and *visionary*. It is thus one more aspect of his language that makes *his* assertion of nihilism come across as an assessment of life that has some degree of authority and command, especially in the eyes of an audience that has been emotionally engaged with him.

It is also worth noting that specific features of the language of the proverbs, adages, and maxims that pervade the plays enhance their standing as wisdom as well. First of all, many of the proverbs and adages we have seen are short: they don't beat around the bush! And the diction is usually simple—mostly monosyllabic words dating back to Old English, and not too many polysyllabic words or words derived from Latin. That sharp and incisive but also homey and frank quality of many proverbs is a function of these basic linguistic features. But being so short and simple, they are also often obscure and ambiguous—this is why at least in some collections of proverbs and adages, interpretations and explanations of them are often provided, as is the case in Erasmus' *Adages*.

But though the *diction* is common, the *usage* is not, for the language of many proverbs and adages is figurative. Thus, if we look at just some of the ones we have considered earlier, we have the following:

- while the grass grows, the horse starves (*antithesis*)
- with eager feeding food doth choke the feeder (*polyptoton*, since "feed," "food," "feeder" are all forms of "food")
- blood will have blood (*ploce*, but also *epanalepsis*, since the same words occur at the beginning and end of the statement)
- one nail drives out one nail (*ploce* and *epanalepsis*)
- better a witty fool than a foolish wit (*antimetabole*)

It is because the usage in proverbs is figurative that they often strike our minds and stay there.

And are the proverbs we have cited really about anything more than cats, adders, snails, sparrows, cuckoos, and bulls? Well, nothing about the linguistic form of the proverbs suggests that they are. But when we look at how they are used and the situations in which they are uttered, it seems clear that these proverbs *are* about more than these animals, or at least that the people who utter them have something more than animals in mind. We could say that what these people are really doing is making a claim about animals and implying an analogy between animals and humans, implicitly asserting that the claim about animals in some way *applies* to humans. But we might also reasonably say that the characters are once again using words that are usually used to refer to one thing to refer to something other than what they are usually used to refer to—they are speaking *tropologically*. And we might reasonably say they are often doing so on the basis of their perception of a *resemblance* between these two things—in this case, between cats, adders, snails, sparrows, cuckoos, and bulls on the one hand, and humans on the other. In that case, the particular trope they are using when they cite these parables is *metaphor*. Though the diction of the parables is thus common, they are often ambiguous, and the usage is figurative and tropological. That is why they are memorable, and why they can seem to embody wisdom.

Song

Song is not often discussed in connection with the wisdom of the plays, but I think it plays a role in making audiences feel that, if the plays do not propound wisdom, they contain it in some way. One reason for this is that song is a significant medium through which the fools and other minor characters in the tragedies and comedies express their wisdom and provide moral instruction to other characters. As Lear observes, his fool is "full of songs" (1.4.124), and this is one of the things that allows him to get away with making so many penetrating observations about both Lear and his scary daughters. Thus, whereas Lear might have the fool whipped for telling him straight out that giving his kingdom to his two daughters was foolish and will leave him with nothing, Lear seems not to mind when the fool insinuates all of this by *singing* a little song about bo-peep, and then another shortly thereafter:

> Mum, mum   *Sings*
> He that keeps nor crust nor crumb,
> Weary of all, shall want some.
>   (1.4.145–7)

Later, when Lear and the fool encounter Kent in the stocks, the fool again makes several shrewd general observations about fathers, children, and the poor—ones that clearly apply to Lear—by way of a simple song:

> Fathers that wear rags   *Sings*
> Do make their children blind,
> But fathers that bear *bags*   [bags of money]
> Shall see their children kind.
> Fortune, that arrant whore,
> Ne'er turns the key to th'poor.
>   (2.2.225–30)

The fool follows this up with "That sir which serves" (2.2.250–7). The lyrics of this song are in a traditional ballad form: quatrains, consisting of rhyming *tetrameters* (lines 1 and 3) and rhyming *trimeters* (lines 2 and 4). These little quatrains might have been set to *Peg a Ramsey* (Duffin: 387), a simple, jaunty, two-chord, up-tempo tune that takes the edge off some hard general truths: those who are supposed to be wise and seek "for gain" will abandon those they serve when the going gets tough; those who are regarded as fools, however, will stay, proving they are not knaves.

Feste in *Twelfth Night* does not need to resort to song in order to protect himself from a choleric king, but he, too, often expresses his general claims about life by way of song. In "O mistress mine" (2.3.26–39), for example, he expresses truths that "every wise man's son doth know." This song may have been set to music that appears in Thomas Morley's *First Booke of Consort Lessons* (1599). In that case, it would be a lovely, plaintive song. A good performance of it should move the audience, as it seems to move both Toby and Andrew. It should suspend the drama for a moment and sweetly express the age-old truths that are relevant to this play and that support the *carpe diem* (seize the day) argument: journeys end in lover's meetings, the future is uncertain, delay brings no pleasure, and youth is fleeting.

Wisdom and moral instruction 129

Figure 3.1 "O mistress mine," from *Twelfth Night*
Source: *Shakespeare's Songbook* by Ross W. Duffin. Used by permission of W. W. Norton & Company, Inc. Copyright © 2004 by Ross W. Duffin.

Finally, in *As You Like It*, we have a minor character, Amiens (though it could be Duke Senior), singing "Blow, blow, thou winter wind" (2.7.178–94), possibly to *Goddesses*, a lovely old and well-known (in Shakespeare's day) melody over a simple bass ground of two minor chords:

Figure 3.2 "Blow, blow, thou winter wind," from *As You Like It*
Source: *Shakespeare's Songbook* by Ross W. Duffin. Used by permission of W. W. Norton & Company, Inc. Copyright © 2004 by Ross W. Duffin.

Note again that the song is an occasion for asserting several *general* observations about human existence: most friendship is feigning; most loving is folly; this life is jolly; the world of the forest, though it does impose some hardships, is less injurious than the civilized world of the court, where there is ingratitude and feigned friendship. And because they are made by way of rhymed *trimeter* lines, set to this music, these assertions are charming, they are made *with feeling*, with sadness, and the song is something of a lament for the way things are. Informed by the suffering and sadness of those banished to the forest, these assertions about the world thus perhaps have more hold upon our ears and minds than they would if we encountered them in a manual for courtiers.

We also note that the song lyrics often contain or are versions of parables and adages, and that, like many of the general claims and proverbs in the dialogue of the plays, they are borne out by the action of the plays. In *King Lear*, for example, Lear keeps neither crest nor crumb, and ends up needing some; as a result of dividing his kingdom, Lear wears rags and enables his children to be blind and cruel; those in the play who pursue gain abandon Lear in the storm, while the fool stays with him, proving he is really not a knave. By the end of *Twelfth Night*, many journeys have indeed ended in lover's meetings, the future is still uncertain, delay brings no pleasure, and youth is fleeting. And we might well say that the experience of Duke Senior and many other characters in *As You Like It* really does bear out Amiens' negative assessment of life at court. It is because the songs are so good, and are related to the plays in this way, that they, too, enter into the causes of the long-standing view that Shakespeare's plays have something significant to say about life.

Over the last four hundred years, many have found moral instruction and wisdom in Shakespeare's plays, but there is an extremely diverse account of the nature and content of that instruction and wisdom. The plays have been said to espouse and affirm the following:

- temperance, moderation, and control over the passions and appetites
- the life of grandiose passion
- a Christian ethos of forgiveness, kindness, mercy
- the Ciceronian virtues of justice, courage, wisdom, honesty, valor
- obedience to political and familial authority (including the Tudor regime)
- disobedience and resistance to unjust authority
- patriarchy
- opposition to patriarchy
- monarchy
- republicanism
- cynicism and skepticism on moral and political matters
- modern values of freedom, authenticity, and individualism
- nihilism
- life, in all its horror and joy.

I think the length and diversity of this list indicate that one of the other main reasons we enjoy the plays, value them, think they are special, and deem them to be "good" is that they provide us with experiences beyond emotion, laughter, and delight. They provide us with the experience of thinking about life, and gaining wisdom about life, or at least the impression of gaining wisdom about life. Even if we don't take on the wisdom or instruction on offer in the plays, we still have the experience of encountering authoritative moral teachings and forceful claims to wisdom, and engaging with them. I suspect that Shakespeare did not thumb his nose at the age-old idea that literature ought to instruct in one way or another and that he did wish to affirm some values in particular. But he did so with discretion, and in the knowledge of the entertainment value of theatre that gives its audience a lot of leeway to determine what wisdom it embodies, and what it espouses.

References

Aristotle. *Poetics*. Trans. Richard Janko. Indianapolis: Hackett, 1987.
Berry, Edward. *Shakespeare's Comic Rites*. Cambridge: Cambridge University Press, 1984.
Campbell, Lily B. 1930; *Shakespeare's Tragic Heroes*. London: Methuen, 1961.
Cowden Clark, Mary. *Shakespeare Proverbs*. London: Chapman and Hall, 1848.
Crane, Mary Thomas. *Framing Authority*. Princeton: Princeton University Press, 1993.
Dent, R. W. *Shakespeare's Proverbial Language*. Berkeley: University of California Press, 1981.
Dryden, John. "The grounds of criticism in tragedy." In *The Works of John Dryden*. Vol. 13. Berkeley: University of California Press, 1984. 229–248.
Duffin, Ross. *Shakespeare's Songbook*. New York: Norton, 2004.
Eden, Kathy. *Friends Hold All Things in Common*. New Haven: Yale University Press, 2001.
Erasmus. *Adages. Collected Works of Erasmus*. Vols 31–36. Toronto: University of Toronto Press, 1982–2006.
Frye, Northrop. *Anatomy of Criticism*. Princeton: Princeton University Press, 1957.
Gervinus, G. G. *Shakespeare Commentaries*. Trans. F. E. Bunnett. 1863; London: Smith, Elder, & Co. 1892.
Henze, Catherine. *Robert Armin and Shakespeare's Performed Songs*. London: Routledge, 2017.
Hunter, R. G. *Shakespeare and the Comedy of Forgiveness*. New York: Columbia University Press, 1965.
Jameson, Anna. *Shakespeare's Heroines: Characteristics of Women Moral, Poetical, and Historical*. 1832; London: Bell, 1916.
Johnson, Samuel. "Preface." In *Johnson on Shakespeare*. Vol. 7 of *The Yale Edition of the Works of Samuel Johnson*. Ed. Arthur Sherbo. New Haven: Yale University Press, 1968. 59–116.
Montagu, Elizabeth. *An Essay on the Writings and Genius of Shakespeare….* 1769; *Bluestocking Feminism*. Vol. 1. Ed. Elizabeth Eger. London: Pickering and Chatto, 1999. 1–113.
Mousley, Andy. *Re-Humanising Shakespeare*. 2007; Edinburgh: Edinburgh University Press, 2015.
Roberts, Sasha. "Reading Shakespeare's tragedies of love…." In *A Companion to Shakespeare's Works, Volume 1*. Ed. Richard Dutton and Jean Howard. London: Blackwell, 2003. 108–133.
Salinger, Leo. *Shakespeare and the Traditions of Comedy*. Cambridge: Cambridge University Press, 1974.
Smith, Charles. *Shakespeare's Proverb Lore*. 1963; Cambridge, MA: Harvard University Press, 1968.
Tilley, Morris Palmer. *A Dictionary of The Proverbs in England in the Sixteenth and Seventeenth Centuries*. Ann Arbor: University of Michigan Press, 1950.
Whitney, Charles. *Early Responses to Renaissance Drama*. Cambridge: Cambridge University Press, 2006.

4 Sublimity

Plot

Witnessing a series of events that, it seems, must end in the destruction of outstanding individuals may well cause us to feel pity, fear, and sadness. Seeing this kind of thing may also be an occasion for us to feel that we learn something about life, that we gain or are confirmed in some kind of wisdom. And if this series of events also includes scenes of ridicule, slapstick, and wordplay, it may provoke laughter. One of Shakespeare's aims in crafting his tragedies as he does is to provide his audiences with an occasion to have all of these experiences, and many feel that his tragedies are special, successful, and great because they do this. Yet some feel that these experiences come a distant second to another kind of experience, and they express disdain for the view that the function of tragedy is merely to make us feel emotion and instruct us.

Let's recall Nietzsche's *The Birth of Tragedy*, which we mentioned in the Introduction. Nietzsche dismisses Aristotle's view that the main function of tragedy is to cause us to experience pity and fear. He also denounces the ancient Greek playwright, Euripedes, for using tragedy to teach morality, for in so doing, Euripedes killed off the genre as established by Aeschylus and Sophocles. For Nietzsche, what really makes tragedy, Shakespearean tragedy included, special is its power to make us feel something that he associates with the sublime. And as we saw in the Introduction, many playgoers have indeed claimed that this is what makes Shakespeare—especially the tragedies—great. There are, though, major differences between accounts of what it is to *feel* sublime. So I am going to use the term "sublime" loosely, to include not just feelings of elevation, exhilaration, ecstasy, joy, transcendence, elation, admiration, and astonishment, but also wonder. On this broad, inclusive definition of "sublimity," I feel obliged to discuss not just the tragedies, but also the histories, comedies, and romances, for while they might not make us feel ecstasy, rapture, or exaltation, they can make us feel wonder.

One reason that Shakespeare's plays make us feel wonder is that, even though they are in many ways true to reality as we know it, they also include some actions and events that are unnatural, supernatural, miraculous, marvellous, wondrous, improbable, or strange. In *As You Like It*, for example, I think our laughter starts giving way to delight and wonder when in the final scene of the play, a supernatural agent, Hymen, the Greek god of marriage, suddenly arrives and ceremoniously delivers Rosalind to her father, Duke Senior, so that he may then join her hand with Orlando's in marriage. Proclaiming that only he can bar confusion and conclude "these most strange events," the god then addresses the four couples who will "join in Hymen's bands." He tells them,

> Whiles a wedlock-hymn we sing,
> Feed yourselves with questioning
> That reason wonder may diminish
> How thus we met, and these things finish.
> (5.4.114–19)

It seems that through questioning and reasoning wonder may be diminished, but at least for the moment the prevailing feeling onstage includes wonder. Even without the characters responding in this way, we the audience may wonder at this epiphany (the appearance of a god). But characters who experience and display their wonder perhaps also encourage and guide us to have this kind of experience as well—we experience a kind of "empathetic wonder" (Cohen: 10–11, 52).

In *A Midsummer Night's Dream*, supernatural agents are on the scene throughout the entire play, and they are behind the wide range of strange, improbable, marvellous actions and events that make up its plot. As Bottom says about his transformation into an ass and his brief amour with the queen of the fairies, Titania, "I am to discourse wonders" (4.2.18). And as Hippolyta observes of the four human lovers' account of their nocturnal adventures, "'tis strange, my Theseus, that these lovers speak of" (5.1.1). So strange that Theseus finds it all hard to believe, but Hippolyta insists that the story "more witnesseth than fancy's images / And grows to something of great constancy; / But howsoever, strange and admirable" (5.1.23). In light of all of these strange events it might well seem that when, in the prologue to his play, he addresses the high-society people who make up his on-stage audience, Quince is also addressing us: "Gentles, perchance you wonder at this show, / But wonder on, till truth make all things plain" (5.1.130–1). Again, it seems that the experience of wonder will pass, but at least for the moment, we along with the mechanicals' audience will follow his orders and wonder on.

Some of the plays which were first categorised as comedies but are now thought of as romances, such as *The Tempest* and *The Winter's Tale*, are also notable for this type of event and overall plot-line, and they attest to Shakespeare's intention to write plays that evoke wonder in the audience. Thus, *The Tempest* opens with a miraculous shipwreck in which no one drowns, and it continues with a series of other strange, apparently unnatural events which are under the control of Prospero: the spirit Ariel's fulfilment of Prospero's many commands; the appearance and disappearance of a banquet; a masque performed by supernatural agents; dog-like spirits chasing the human characters across the island; Prospero's entrancement of Alonso and others; the preservation of the ship. On top of this we have several incidents that, to many of the characters in the play, *seem* miraculous: Gonzalo, Alonso, and the others comment on how strange, unnatural, wondrous it is that Prospero is alive, and that Miranda and Ferdinand are also alive—and in love. Alonso sums things up when he observes, "these are not natural events; they strengthen / From strange to stranger" (5.1.259–60). That is why the prevailing mood at the end of the play is one of amazement and wonder—on the part of many of the characters, and I think, the audience.

In *The Winter's Tale*, we get a report on "the ear-deaf'ning voice o'th'oracle" of Apollo at Delphos (3.1.11) attesting to the innocence of Hermione, but ignored by her jealous husband, king Leontes. That oracular and apparently supernatural voice also prophesies that "the king shall live without an heir, if that which is lost be not found" (3.2.137–8). As Paulina later observes, that Leontes' lost child (Perdita) should be found is "monstrous to our human reason" (5.1.48)—yet Perdita is found, Leontes has an heir, and Apollo's oracle is fulfilled. Bystanders then report that, at the news of Perdita's discovery, "a notable passion of wonder appeared" in Leontes and Camillo, and that "such a deal of wonder is broken out with this hour that ballad-makers cannot be able to express it" (5.2.11–17). But there's more. When Paulina reveals to Leontes what she claims is a remarkably life-like statue of his supposedly deceased wife, Hermione, Leontes in silence displays "wonder" (5.3.25). When Paulina then commands the "statue" to descend from the pedestal and "strike all that look upon with marvel" (5.3.122), it does, with the result that we have an occasion for one of the most wonder-full moments in all of Shakespeare—though "amazement" "joy" and "exultation" are now the words used to describe the feelings of those onstage. We note again that the apparently wondrous event is subject to naturalistic explanation, and that the feelings it elicits are somewhat qualified. For having descended, Hermione reveals that neither magic nor supernatural agency has intervened: she had not in fact died but had "preserved" herself after Paulina had told her about the oracle. Even so, at the many performances of the play I've seen, the audience is hushed and seems astonished as it witnesses this marvellous final scene of the play.

Though we have seen that, generally speaking, there is a strong causal connection between the actions and events that define the plots of the tragedies, we still get some strange, improbable events that seem to cater to the Elizabethan audience's "love of wonder" (Bradley: 55). Examples of this kind of thing are Lear's division of his kingdom on the basis of his daughters' public confessions of love; the strange occurrences in the natural world described by characters in *Julius Caesar* and *Macbeth*; in *Othello*, the destruction of the Turkish fleet in a tempest through which the ships of Desdemona and Othello pass unscathed; in *Antony and Cleopatra*, the "strange" music Antony's men hear before battle; Hamlet's rash act of getting out of bed and reading the king's commission before returning back to Denmark courtesy of a pirate ship that happened to engage with the one he was on.

But in the tragedies and some of the histories, we have another kind of wondrous action. At the beginning of *Macbeth*, for example, Ross observes that after receiving news of Macbeth's performance in battle, the king is overcome with "his wonders and his praises" (1.3.95). What is the nature of this news? Well, it is rather different from the news that a lost daughter is found. In the previous scene, we hear the Captain deliver the news to the king, part of which runs like this:

> For brave Macbeth—well he deserves that name—
> Disdaining Fortune, with his brandished steel
> Which smoked with bloody execution,
> Like valour's minion carved out his passage
> Till he faced *the slave*,   [the rebel, Macdonald]
> Which ne'er shook hands nor bade farewell to him
> Till he *unseamed him from the nave to th'chops* [sliced him from navel to jaw]
> And fixed his head upon our battlements.
>
> (1.2.18–25)

Similarly, in *Coriolanus*, shortly before he returns to Rome, the protagonist's wife Virgilia observes, "in troth, there's wondrous things spoke of him"; Menenius replies, "wondrous: ay, I warrant you, and not without his true purchasing [deserving]" (2.1.99–100). What are these wondrous things that make the Romans flock to see him upon his return from the battle at the city of Corioles? As we know from the opening scenes, they are the protagonist's deeds of valor, which his mother Volumnia grimly describes as follows: "Death, that dark spirit, in's nervy arm doth lie, / Which being advanced, declines; and then men die" (2.1.154–7). In a formal encomium before the senate, the military commander Cominius elaborates:

> Before and in Corioles, let me say
> I cannot speak him home: he stopped the *fliers*,   [those who were fleeing]
> And by his rare example made the coward
> Turn terror into sport: as weeds before
> A vessel under sail, so men obeyed
> And fell below his stem: his sword, death's stamp,
> Where it did mark, it took: from face to foot
> He was a thing of blood, whose every motion
> Was timed with dying cries: alone he entered
> The mortal gate of th'city, which he, painted
> With shunless destiny, aidless came off,
> And with a sudden reinforcement struck
> Corioles like a planet.
>
> (2.2.94–106)

Yes, the *language* Ross, Volumnia, and Cominius use to describe these military men and their deeds in part explains why they seem marvellous—it is filled with *metaphor*, *simile*, and *hyperbole*. But for now, let's just observe that other *actions* of the plays that evoke the wonder of other characters and perhaps the audience are tremendous, almost super-human acts of courage, valor, and military prowess.

We should also note that though in the histories and tragedies the main characters' actions are in the foreground, these plays also represent the actions of large groups of other people. The plots of many of the history plays, for example, include the actions of large numbers of people who side with one particular individual, family, faction, or nation and who wage war against those who side with another particular individual, family, faction, or nation. That is to say, civil war, rebellion, and wars of conquest and invasion are usually major elements of the plots of the histories. Moreover, it is often this kind of conflict that brings the plays to a close. Thus, for example, *Henry IV, part 1* ends with the king's forces defeating the forces of Hotspur and the "rebels"; the final scenes of *Henry V* are enabled by the English victory over the French at the battle of Agincourt; *Richard III* ends with Richmond's forces defeating those of Richard. Note that the fate of the protagonists in these plays very much depends on the outcomes of these larger battles.

The plots of most of the tragedies also include actions and events of this kind: the great tragic protagonists act against a backdrop of large numbers of people who are also acting, and whose actions often determine the fate of the protagonists. *Macbeth*, for example, ends with Macduff killing Macbeth in the context of a broader battle between Macbeth's forces and those of Malcolm, Macduff, and Siward. In the background of *King Lear*, the armies of English dukes and duchesses engage in conflict, the outcome of which sets the scene for the final catastrophe. In *Julius Caesar*, Brutus kills himself as a direct result of his forces being defeated by those of Antony and Octavius Caesar at Philippi. In *Coriolanus*, the ongoing conflict between the Roman and the Volscian armed forces is really central to the main action of the entire play. Antony and Cleopatra act against a backdrop of the armed forces they command fighting the armed forces under the command of Octavius Caesar; in this case, the collective conflict seems even vaster since it proceeds on land and at sea across the entire Mediterranean basin. And even in *Hamlet*, the events at the Danish court proceed against a backdrop of a long-standing conflict between Norway and Denmark.

Thus, while we may well focus on the actions of the tragic protagonists, we are also aware of the ways in which those actions are interrelated with vast, collective actions, and that these actions have consequences for not just the protagonists, but also entire cities, peoples, nations, and empires. Sure, some people may well be saddened, if not sickened, by representations of such events. On-stage representations of such events can be pretty lame, and the plays are far from any simplistic glorification of war. But this kind of action on a grand scale is still one thing that imparts a high seriousness to the plays, and that I think Shakespeare expected would raise feelings of wonder and awe in his audience.

But what aspects of the plots of the plays can account for some of those other feelings which, from Longinus on, have also been associated with the sublime—exhilaration, elevation, ecstasy, exaltation, ennoblement? Perhaps some of the protagonists' particular acts of valor, and descriptions of them, affect us in this way, but I think that for a fuller explanation of these feelings we must turn to other aspects of the action that the plays represent. One of these is the destruction of the protagonist, a destruction that often takes the form of a suicide. You can kill yourself in many different ways for a lot of different reasons. It is the particular way in which the protagonists kill themselves that ennobles their final act and accounts for their powers to elevate us. Take, for example, *Romeo and Juliet*. We have seen that not long after they meet, the lovers assert that they will commit suicide rather than live without each other. When each comes to believe that he/she will have to live without the other, each commits suicide. There is thus a basic sense in which the act is honourable: in so acting, they are true to their word. It turns out that all of the wonderful words they use to describe each other and their feelings for each other are not *just* words—the lovers mean what they say, and they do what they say they will do. But more important are the motives for doing what they say they will do. Of course, their overwhelming true love's passion for each other enters into it, but that is not all. There is also some evidence that Romeo thinks of killing himself as a means of being with Juliet, since he says that, for fear that death will keep Juliet as his paramour, he "will stay with [her], / And never from this palace of dim night / Depart again" (5.3.106–8). But there is also a *demand* on both their parts that they be together, a *refusal* to accept existence on any other terms, an implicit *judgment* that living is not worthwhile if they cannot be together.

We are now supposed to think that the lovers are mistaken in destroying themselves, that they should not have done so, that even if they couldn't be together, they still had the rest of their lives ahead of them and could have found someone else and been happy—they would have gotten over it. And many have said that the terrible outcome of the play implicitly teaches us not to be extreme in our passions as the young lovers are, but to be temperate. In my view this fails to register important aspects of this play, and the feelings it can generate. When you are watching or reading this play, would it not be in some important way disappointing if they *didn't* go through with it? Is there not something exhilarating, however heart-rending, in seeing the impassioned, beautiful young people choose no life over life without each other? Is there not something grand in the way they impose death on themselves out of a judgment not that *life* but that *their lives* are not worth living without each other? I think so, which is why I believe some people, including myself, are not depressed but exhilarated in the end.

Then there are the older, more seasoned, gaudier lovers, Antony and Cleopatra. After his final military defeat off the coast of Alexandria, Antony's rage against Cleopatra abates when he is informed that she has killed herself. He immediately announces that "the long day's task is done" and indicates his intentions as he addresses his lover: "I will o'ertake thee, Cleopatra, and / Weep for my pardon..." (4.14.42–53). Certainly shame enters into Antony's motives for ending his life, but so too does an overwhelming sense that life without Cleopatra is futile. As he goes on to say, "Now all labour / Mars what it does: yea, very force entangles / Itself with strength" (4.14.55–8). But he also sees suicide as a means to be reunited with Cleopatra, not just to ask her pardon, but to live with her in Elysium, the ancient Graeco-Roman paradise reserved for dead heroes, such as Dido and Aeneas (the heroic, tragic lovers of Virgil's epic poem about the founding of Rome, the *Aeneid*):

> Stay for me:
> Where souls do couch on flowers we'll hand in hand   [Elysium]
> And with our *sprightly port* make the ghosts gaze.   [lively bearing]
> Dido and her Aeneas shall want troops,
> And all the haunt be ours.
>
> (4.14.58–62)

We note, too, that Antony imagines this afterlife with his lover as one in which, as they were on earth, they are looked upon as the greatest of lovers—if only by the ghosts of other dead heroes. In his mind, they will maintain their pre-eminence after death.

Antony also thinks of suicide as a means of defeating Octavius Caesar. As he says to his servant Eros whom he asks to do the job, "thou strikest not me, 'tis Caesar thou defeat'st" (4.14.77). This is in part because the suicide would deny Octavius Caesar the pleasure of displaying the defeated Antony in a Roman "triumph" (a kind of Roman victory parade), and spare Antony himself the humiliation and shame of being shown in this way. As he asks Eros,

> Wouldst thou *be windowed* in great Rome and see   [look out from a window]
> Thy master thus with *pleached* arms, bending down   [folded]
> His corrigible neck, his face subdued
> To penetrative shame, whilst the wheeled seat
> Of fortunate Caesar, drawn before him, branded
> His baseness that ensued?
>
> (4.14.83–8)

When Eros kills himself rather than obey his master's command to kill him, Antony again indicates what he wishes to achieve by killing himself when he cries, "I will be / A bridegroom in my death and run into't / As to a lover's bed," and he falls on his sword (4.14.116–18). So the motives of his suicide are complex. He kills himself out of an ongoing grand passion for Cleopatra and shame for having acted dishonourably, but also a conviction and pride in his own elevation and grandeur—in spite of all his failures. He kills himself with the aim of being reunited with Cleopatra in the afterlife, denying Octavius Caesar a triumph over him, maintaining what is left of his own honor, and avoiding being debased in public. True, he makes a mess of it and does not immediately die. But because he does it for these reasons, there is something grand about his final act of self-destruction, with the result that Antony can with good reason say that he "does not basely die" but is a "Roman by a Roman / Valiantly vanquished" (4.15.63–6).

When Antony dies, Cleopatra observes that there is "nothing left remarkable" in the world, and that existence, at least for her, is empty (4.15.76). She continues to believe that, in spite of all their failures, they were extraordinary and "great" (4.15.6), as both of them have asserted throughout the entire play, and she continues to be fiercely proud of their pre-eminence. Since, without Antony, "all's but naught," she resolves "to rush into the secret house of death." She is determined, that is, to kill herself "after the high Roman fashion / And make death proud to take" her and her girls (4.15.90–100). And so she does. For she kills herself not just out of pride and the sense that life is futile without her lover, but also out of an idea of suicide as an exercise of power *over* the things of this world and the forces that govern it, such as Fortune and Caesar:

>   'tis paltry to be Caesar:
> Not being Fortune, he's but Fortune's knave,
> A minister of her will: and it is great
> To do *that thing* that ends all other deeds,   [suicide]
> Which shackles accidents and bolts up change,
> Which sleeps, and never *palates* more the dung,   [tastes]
> The beggar's nurse and Caesar's.
>   (5.2.2–8)

In addition to thinking of suicide in this way, Cleopatra sees it as a means of avoiding the particular humiliations of life under Octavius Caesar. She quite rightly foresees that they include being demeaned at court, but also being displayed in a Roman triumph. As she says to Octavius Caesar's man, Proculeius,

>   I
> Will not wait pinioned at your master's court,
> Nor once be chastised with the sober eye
> Of dull Octavia. Shall they hoist me up
> And show me to the shouting *varletry*   [rabble]
> Of censuring Rome? Rather a ditch in Egypt.
>   (5.2.62–7)

And, like Antony, she sees suicide as a means of being reunited with her lover. Commanding Charmian to fetch her best clothes, she observes, "I am again for Cydnus / To meet Mark Antony," Cydnus being the river on which she first met Antony (5.2.270–1). As she puts on her robes and crown in preparation for her final scene, she says,

>   methinks I hear
> Antony call: I see him rouse himself
> To praise my noble act. I hear him mock
> The luck of Caesar, which the gods give men
> To excuse their after wrath.—Husband, I come!
> Now to that name my courage prove my title!
>   (5.2.319–24)

In Cleopatra's mind, her suicide is thus a noble, courageous, proud act that will achieve a wide range of things:

- it will be a victory over Caesar
- it will demonstrate her power over Fortune
- it will be a final demonstration of her greatness
- it will prevent her humiliation by the Romans
- it will reunite her with the man she still loves
- it will prove she is worthy of being Antony's wife.

That is why it is, as Octavius Caesar himself admits, a "high act," one that might make us feel not so much sadness and compassion, as some kind of elevation.

But even when the protagonists do not take matters into their own hands, their final destruction has given many, myself included, the sensation of elevation, elation, and exhilaration. I think this is in part a result of the ways in which the tragedies and some of the histories intimate that the sequences of causally related actions that culminate in destruction are parts of a larger world, or manifestations of enormous forces and powers. As we saw in chapter 1, many of the characters in the plays speculate about the nature of this world and these forces. Some characters speak and think of *supernatural* agents and powers, such as the pagan gods, heaven, providence, the god of Christianity. Other characters speak and think of *natural* powers, life forces, and principles. This is what the Friar in *Romeo and Juliet* does in his wonderful description of the earth as both womb and tomb; this is what Aufidius does when, in *Coriolanus*, he says the world is a place where one fire drives out one fire, one nail one nail; this is what the doctor in *Macbeth* does when he remarks that in this world, unnatural deeds breed unnatural troubles; this is what Macbeth himself does when he observes that in this world, blood will have blood. Whatever these forces, powers, and principles may be, the characters' ongoing thinking and speaking of them is itself one of the things that suggests that they do indeed exist, and that the final destruction therefore does not just happen to occur, but *must* occur. As Bradley observes in connection with the tragedies, we have a strong sense that, even though the characters are free to act, their tragic experience is merely part of a "vaster life," and that all they do and suffer is subject to some "vaster power," a "supreme power or destiny," a "hidden ultimate power," and "vast universal powers" (139–41, 202). Yes, our sense that the protagonists are subject to these immense forces and powers enters into our experience of pity and fear. But if we share this sense that the events leading to their destruction are part of a vast, powerful, indestructible life or world in which we ourselves participate, we may well also start having those grand, exhilarating feelings which—for Nietzsche, Bradley, and others—are the most precious gift of Shakespearean tragedy.

Character

Some of Shakespeare's characters inspire wonder in other characters and the audience because they are strange, unnatural, marvellous, supernatural, or monstrous. When, for example, we see or read *The Tempest*, we may well wonder, along with many other characters, what exactly Caliban *is*—even after Prospero tells us that he is the son of the witch, Sycorax, and that he is "a freckled whelp, hag-born—not honoured with / A human shape" (1.2.331–2). What exactly *is* Prospero, we ask, as we observe him exercise his powers over not just his slave and other humans but also the natural world, and then renounce "the rough magic" which he claims to have exercised in the past to open graves and raise the dead (5.1.53–5). We know that Iris, Juno, and Ceres are Roman goddesses, but isn't it strange and marvelous that they appear on the island? And while we know Ariel is a delicate "spirit," still we wonder at how he sings and fulfils Prospero's commands after having been pent up by a witch in a pine tree for twelve years! By giving us these and other bestial or supernatural agents, such as the transformed Bottom and the fairies in *A Midsummer Night's Dream*, and Hymen in *As You Like It*, Shakespeare enriches his *dramatis personae* in a way that I think is calculated to provide us with an experience beyond laughter.

While some of the darker supernatural agents in the plays may cause feelings akin to fear in the characters and the audience, they too are qualified to raise feelings of wonder, as the characters themselves sometimes observe. Thus, for example, in his letter to his wife in which he describes his encounter with the weird sisters, Macbeth observes that he "stood rapt in the wonder of it" (1.5.4). And while his cheeks are "blanched with fear" when he sees the ghost of Banquo at the banquet, he also asks, "Can such things be, / And overcome us like a summer's cloud, / Without our special wonder?" (3.4.129–33). Similarly, when in the opening scene of *Hamlet* the ghost of old Hamlet appears, Horatio observes that "it harrows me with fear and wonder" (1.1.50). Relating this "marvel" to Hamlet (1.2.197), he says "it would have much amazed you" (1.2.246); after Hamlet has encountered the ghost, he responds to Horatio's queries with "O, wonderful!" (1.5.127). With Hamlet behaving wildly and the ghost beneath the ground demanding that all swear to secrecy, Horatio quite reasonably observes, "this is wondrous strange" (1.5.182). Commenting on the truth and consistency with which Shakespeare represents these spirits, ghosts, witches, fairies, and sylphs, Schlegel observes, "we are lost in astonishment at the close intimacy he brings us into with the extraordinary, the wonderful, and the unheard-of" (363).

Other characters inspire wonder and awe because, though human, they are royalty, or are exceptionally beautiful and handsome, or are *described* as being exceptionally beautiful and handsome. Since, for the Renaissance audience, kings and queens were figures of great prestige, authority, power, and sanctity, Shakespeare's on-stage kings and queens would have struck many at the time with wonder (Cohen: 15). Though, in our age of democratic republics, royalty has less prestige and is indeed repellent to some, the British royals still fascinate people in many parts of the world, and I think representations of them on stage can still do so as well. But as King Henry IV observes in *Henry IV, part 1*, even real kings and princes had to manage their majesty properly in order to command wonder from their subjects (Cheney: 181–2). In his great meeting with his wayward son, Prince Hal, the king observes that no one wondered at King Richard II because he "grew a companion to the common streets" and was "daily swallowed by men's eyes" (3.2.68–70). But before he, King Henry IV, became king, he was different:

> By being seldom seen, I could not stir
> But like a comet I was wondered at,
> ...
> Thus did I keep my person fresh and new;
> My presence, like a robe pontifical,
> Ne'er seen but wondered at: and so my state,
> Seldom but sumptuous, showed like a feast
> And won by rareness such solemnity.
> (3.1.46–59)

King Henry IV thinks that his son, Prince Hal, does not understand this, and that he has lost the people's admiration by fraternizing with lowlifes like Falstaff in pubic. But he is mistaken. For Hal has informed us earlier that he has really been pursuing a similar strategy of concealment all along:

> Yet herein will I imitate the sun,
> Who doth permit the base contagious clouds
> To smother up his beauty from the world,
> That when he please again to be himself,
> Being wanted, he may be more wondered at,
> By breaking through the foul and ugly mists
> Of vapours that did seem to strangle him.
> (1.2.134–40)

True, being privy to these designs for commanding wonder and thereby legitimizing claims to political power, we are perhaps less awe-struck than the subjects of the king and the prince. But when Hal does indeed break through the clouds and prove himself a formidable soldier, an effective military commander, and ultimately a successful, even heroic King Henry V, we may find it difficult to escape his strategy.

We saw earlier that many of the characters in the histories and tragedies remark upon the exceptional physical beauty of the protagonists, and that this beauty, as embodied by the players on stage, is one thing about them that may intensify our compassion for them when they suffer and die. If this kind of beauty itself does not also evoke feelings of astonishment and wonder, I think other characters' *descriptions* of it can. This, at least, was the effect Vernon's celebrated description of Prince Hal mounting his horse in *Henry IV, part 1* (4.1.102–15) had on the great eighteenth-century theorist of the sublime, Edmund Burke (Cheney: 179–80). And this is surely the case with Enobarbus' famous description of Cleopatra on her barge on the river Cydnus (2.2.223–51). This description establishes Cleopatra as a "rare Egyptian" as Agrippa remarks (2.2.252), a majestic human figure whose exceptional beauty is really beyond description and comprehension, and who is therefore qualified to evoke wonder in both the other characters and the audience. So, too, does Cleopatra's description of Antony (which we will consider in more detail later) make him out to be a rare, magnificent, wondrous figure. As Cleopatra goes on to observe after describing him in such grandiose terms, nature lacks material to compete with what he was, or what she imagines him to have been. Even the skeptical Dolabella to whom she is speaking concedes, "your loss is as yourself, great" (5.2.122). The lovers are indeed great, and these descriptions of them make them even greater, which is why they may well evoke wonder in us.

In *On Sublimity*, Longinus claims that Homer's epic poem about the Trojan war, the *Iliad*, is much more sublime than the epic he wrote later in his life, the *Odyssey* (which is about Odysseus' return from the Trojan war to his family and home in Ithaca). One reason he gives for this evaluation is that the *Iliad* has more "realism" and "abundance of imagery taken from the life." Indeed, when he wrote the *Odyssey*, Homer was an old man who was "lost in the realm of the fabulous and incredible" and who failed to reach true sublimity because he told a story in which "the mythical element... predominates over the realistic" (153). So Longinus thinks that truly sublime works like the *Iliad* can evoke wonder in us, and he affirms *hyperbolic* (exaggerated) descriptions of characters and events as a way of doing this. Nevertheless, he still thinks that in order to provide us with this experience, poets and playwrights must present characters who are still recognisable as humans, who are still in some sense accurate, credible representations of people and how people behave in particular situations. If this is so, then another thing about Shakespeare's great protagonists that qualifies them to make us feel awe and wonder is that, however colossal they may be, they still seem real.

When it comes to the causes of those other feelings of transcendence, elevation, exaltation, ennoblement, and ecstasy, we need to turn to other aspects of Shakespeare's characters. Longinus also observes that

> in ordinary life, nothing is truly great which it is great to despise; wealth, honour, reputation, absolute power—anything in short which has a lot of external trappings—can never seem supremely good to the wise man

because it is no small good to despise them. People who could have these advantages if they chose but disdain them out of magnanimity are admired much more than those who actually possess them.

(148)

If this is so, then one of the things about some of Shakespeare's characters, especially the protagonists of the tragedies, that makes us admire them is that they display contempt for many of those things it is great to despise, and that this contempt enters into the causes of their destruction. Hamlet, for example, has immense potential to obtain and indeed to enjoy the things of this world, and he is aware that, having married his mother, Claudius has "popp'd in between the election and my hopes" (5.2.70)—that Claudius has prevented *him* from becoming king on the death of his father. And we note his concern with political affairs when with his dying breath Hamlet supports the election of Fortinbras to the throne of Denmark. But he can hardly be said to be ambitious, and he often makes a point of displaying his disdain for external trappings as he attempts to set things right in his family and his country. In *Lear*, the old king does not display disdain for his political power and material wealth, but neither does he cling to them: in his old age he divests himself of them in order "to shake all cares and business from our age," but also to prevent strife in his kingdom (1.1.30–36). In *Julius Caesar*, the noble Brutus loves the name of honour, but he displays disdain for money and material wealth: even when his republican forces need money to wage the war against Antony, he chastises his ally Cassius for raising money by questionable means, and he refuses to do anything dishonorable in order to get the money he needs to pay his troops (4.2). Throughout the play, he asserts his commitment to "the general good" (1.2.91), and it is clear that that commitment, and not any ambition to get more wealth or political power for himself, is driving him. As Antony observes at the end of the play, while the other conspirators acted out of envy of Caesar's power and prestige, Brutus acted out of care for "the common good to all" (5.5.77).

In *Coriolanus*, the protagonist despises his plebeian soldiers who, even before the battle is over, gather spoils and booty. When the day has been won—in large part as a result of his own efforts—he turns down the offer of a tenth of all the treasure taken in battle and accepts only his "common part" (1.9.44). As Cominius later observes, "our spoils he kicked at, / And looked upon things precious as they were / The common muck of the world" (2.2.117–19). While he places great importance upon his own honor, Coriolanus repeatedly discourages those around him from praising his great deeds, and he walks out when Cominius praises him before the senate. The tribunes' claim that he values and seeks absolute power is, moreover, slander: though he stands for the highest political office in the early Roman republic (consul), he does so at the bidding of his mother and the patricians, and he displays no intention whatsoever to transform the limited powers of consul into the absolute power of a king—indeed, he had recently participated in the successful military effort to oust the king and establish a republican constitution. Moreover, just when he is on the verge of becoming consul, he ruins his chances by openly expressing his hatred of the plebeians and their political representatives, the tribunes. As Menenius observes, "his nature is too noble for the world: / He would not flatter Neptune for his trident, / Or Jove for's power to thunder" (3.1.300–2).

The last thing on the minds of Romeo and Juliet are wealth, political power, or winning the feud in which their families are engaged. Their behavior over the course of the entire play bespeaks their disdain for such external trappings, but Romeo explicitly voices his contempt for wealth when, paying the impoverished apothecary for poison, he says to him, "there's thy gold, worse poison to men's souls, / Doing more murder in this loathsome world, / Than these poor compounds that thou mayst not sell" (5.1.83–85). The lovers in *Antony and Cleopatra* are different because they do place value on kingdoms, provinces, political power, military victory, fame, and wealth, and we see them strive to get and retain these things. Yet throughout the play they, too, often display a disdain for these things when they interfere with their enjoyment of each other. In the wonderful opening scene of the play, for example, Antony angrily dismisses the messengers from Rome for interrupting his conversation with Cleopatra, and exclaims,

> Let Rome in Tiber melt, and the wide arch,
> Of the ranged empire fall: here is my space.
> Kingdoms are clay: our dungy earth alike
> Feeds beast as man. The nobleness of life
> Is to do *thus*.   [he embraces Cleopatra]
>   (1.1.35–9)

After he has dishonored himself at the battle of Actium, he says to his attendants, "My treasure's in the harbor: take it" (3.11.12). We then observe his magnanimous act of sending Enobarbus' treasure, along with additional gifts, to him after he has left him. As the end approaches, Cleopatra, too, expresses her disdain for such things: "all strange and terrible events are welcome, / But comforts we despise," she says (4.15.4–5). After expressing her opinion that it is paltry to be Caesar, and her contempt for the "dung" of the world, she protests to the Roman, who has come to deceive her, "sir, I will eat no meat, I'll not drink, sir" (5.2.59). Indeed, the lovers' final acts confirm the disdain they have for the things of this world once they can no longer enjoy each other in it.

So while they do have some ambitions and desires, and while they do not renounce this world, Shakespeare's tragic protagonists often display disregard and even disdain for "external trappings" and the things of this world: they are *above* such concerns and ambitions, and are committed to things that many would see as higher, grander things, such as justice, civil liberty, good government, a political society, an outstanding person, a grand passion, themselves. Perhaps Macbeth, with his ambition for secure political power, is an exception here, but by the end even he seems to have become strangely indifferent to and even contemptuous of the things of this world. It is in part because these characters are like this that many others around them describe them as being *noble*, a word that recurs throughout the tragedies, especially the big three Roman tragedies. This nobility, moreover, is one of the *causes* of their destruction: it is in part because they do not look out for themselves and do not make their first priority getting the things of this world, such as wealth and political power, that they do not get those things and are in fact destroyed by those who *do* make getting those things their first priority—men such as Antony in *Julius Caesar* or Octavius Caesar in *Antony and Cleopatra*. Their destruction is thus proof of their nobility. It is proof of the human capacity—our capacity—for being higher, for being noble, for rising above the common concerns of life in the name of something great. How do you respond to such a proof? The great eighteenth-century poet, Goethe, claimed that we can really only respect a man if he does not always look out for himself. If this is so, then Shakespeare's heroes and heroines who do not look out for themselves may cause us to admire and respect them. But I think these characters may do more than this: because their destruction is a proof of their nobility, I, at least, affirm it, and I come out of the theatre feeling exhilarated, inspired to be noble like them, come what may.

Another thing about these characters that I think helps to account for the exaltation and exhilaration we may feel in the end is what, as a result of their extraordinary suffering, they *become* by the final act. In some cases the protagonists end up being *resigned* to the disaster they sense is imminent. In the final scene of *Hamlet*, after he has agreed to compete against Laertes, for example, Hamlet tells Horatio, "how ill all's here about my heart" (5.2.143–4). Dismissing his friend Horatio's counsel to pull out, Hamlet competes, since he feels that "There's a special providence in the fall of a sparrow" (5.2.150–1). Rather than entering the competition with a definite will or plan to kill anyone, much less himself, he does so in a mood of resignation to whatever may happen. Similarly, we saw earlier that in *Coriolanus*, after his mother, Volumnia, has persuaded him not to destroy Rome, he says,

> O my mother, mother, O!
> You have won a happy victory to Rome.
> But for your son, believe it, O believe it,
> Most dangerously you have with him prevailed,
> If not most mortal to him. But let it come.
> (5.3.197–202)

It is not as if Coriolanus has thrown in the towel, since he does try to swing a deal with the Volscians. But he, too, feels his destruction is likely, and he is resigned to it. Here we might recall Schopenhauer, whose great discussion of sublimity we mentioned in the Introduction. At least for him, the kind of resignation displayed by Hamlet and Coriolanus signals the hero's elevation above the will to live and thrive in this world, and its effect is to raise in us a similar frame of mind—this is the "exalted pleasure" that only great tragedy, such as that of Shakespeare, provides.

But in other tragedies I think we have a different variety of exaltation, in part because something different happens in the end: the doomed protagonists *think* less and *will* more. Look at *Romeo and Juliet*. We saw in chapter 1 that, as the play proceeds, both of the lovers assert a *will* to die if they cannot be together. In the final scenes, that will is not surrendered but prevails. Immediately upon receiving news of Juliet's death from Balthasar, Romeo says,

> Is it even so? Then I deny you, stars!—
> Thou know'st my lodging, get me ink and paper,
> And hire post-horses: I will hence tonight.
> (5.1.24–6)

At this moment in his life, Romeo does not think, speculate, lament, indulge in his emotions, complain, or go to the Friar. He becomes willful: he commands Balthasar, and asserts what he himself will do. He then orders Balthasar to leave, do what he has told him to do, and hire the horses; as for him, "Well, Juliet, I will lie with thee tonight," he asserts (5.1.36). Remembering an apothecary he saw in Mantua, he immediately goes to him, gets the poison, goes to the tomb, and continues to command both his page and Paris, before killing him. True, he pauses for one last look and kiss, but he then follows through on his resolution and drinks the poison. Having on many earlier occasions asserted *her* resolution to die if she cannot be with Romeo, Juliet awakens to find Romeo dead, and, without further thought or ado, she stabs herself. In these final scenes, the time for counsel, reasoning, whining, thinking is over; it is time for willing, commanding, and acting alone.

I think something similar to this happens in some of the other tragedies—on the protagonists' own account. In *Antony and Cleopatra*, for example, as Antony lies dying in her arms, she says, "my resolution and my hands I'll trust"; immediately following Antony's death, she tells her girls, "we have no friend / But resolution and the briefest end" (4.15.57; 102–3). Repeatedly asserting what she will and will not do, and issuing many commands to her girls, she then asserts, "my resolution's placed" (5.2.282), and she acts on it. Cleopatra, in short, becomes resolute, *willful*, and this enables her to perform her noble deed. Similarly, in *Macbeth*, after he visits the witches to get more information, the protagonist receives news that Macduff is fled to England. Rather than agonize in thought over eliminating him, as he did in connection with the killing of Duncan, he forms a new resolution: "from this moment / The very firstlings of my heart shall be / The firstlings of my hand. And even now, / To crown my thoughts with acts, be it thought and done" (4.1.159–61). It is not that he is resolved to stop thinking, but that he will not indulge in thinking and imagining as he did in the past. He is resolved to act as soon as he thinks, and so he does: he immediately orders Macduff's entire family be put to death, and it is. In the final scenes of the play, we see him gruffly telling everyone around him what to do, and asserting his will: "I'll fight till from my bones my flesh be hacked" (5.3.34). True, he can't quite shut down his wonderful mind, and we get his profound brief thoughts on human existence and even some weakening of his resolution; nevertheless, he asserts, "At least we'll die with harness on our back," and he does (5.5.55).

So as they approach the end, the major characters in some of the tragedies become less inclined to think, they become more inclined to will, they command others, and they act on their resolutions. I think this makes them come across as serious people who are no longer just talking, deliberating, or fooling around and who now mean business. Because their wills and resolutions become so powerful, their final acts seem necessary, and there is a kind of rush to the final catastrophe. This intensity of will, high seriousness, and authority to command, all enhance the grandeur of these characters and qualify them to give us that special experience of being swept away.

This talk of height and rising above I think leads us to another closely related aspect of these characters, one which I think is fruitfully understood in connection with *transfiguration* and *transcendence*. If you raise yourself above the human, you may find that you *transcend* the human—that you shed or lose your humanity—and become something else: a thing, a god, a beast, fire, air, or nothingness. And this is indeed how some of the characters in the plays describe the protagonists. In *Coriolanus*, for example, we see these possibilities for the noble protagonist adumbrated early in the play when others describe him not as a person or a human but as a *thing*: on the battlefield at Corioles, he was, Cominius says, "a thing of blood" (2.2.107). The tribune, Brutus, resents that the people talk of the man as though whatever "god" leads him "were slily crept into his human powers" (2.1.181–3); Brutus later openly chastises Coriolanus for acting as though he were a god: "You speak o'th'people as if you were a god / To punish, not a man of their infirmity" (3.1.99–100). After the Romans have banished him and Coriolanus offers his services to his former enemies, the Volscians, their leader Aufidius welcomes him and calls him "thou noble thing" (4.5.13). He later observes that he "fights dragon-like" (4.7.25), a description Menenius confirms when he claims that Coriolanus "is grown from man to dragon: he has wings: he's more than a creeping thing" (5.4.8–9). Cominius again comments on how Coriolanus has become a thing, a god, or at least a human of a higher order: "He is their god: he leads them like a thing / Made by some other deity than nature, / That shapes man better" (4.6.10911). After he has gone to Coriolanus and failed to persuade him to relent, Cominius identifies another possibility for those who transcend humanity when he observes that Coriolanus forbade all names: "He was a kind of nothing, titleless, / Till he had forged himself a name o'th'fire / Of burning Rome. (5.1.14–16). Indeed, "he does sit in gold, his eye / Red as 'twould burn Rome" (4.1.73–5).

As for Coriolanus himself, well he would actually *like* to be a god, or at least some kind of self-begotten creature beyond the natural world of family and kinship. For when his immediate family comes to persuade him to relent, he exclaims,

> But out, affection!
> All bond and privilege of nature break:
> ...
>   I'll never
> Be such a *gosling* to obey instinct, but stand, [young goose/fool]
> As if a man were author of himself
> And knew no other kin.
>
>   (5.3.25–38)

True, at least in this play, the noble man who rises above humanity and the muck of the world in some ways ultimately cannot sustain his transcendence: moved to compassion by his mother's persuasion, he relents. For devotees of individuals who have made themselves into gods, things, dragons, fire, or nothingness, this may be rather disappointing! Still, having momentarily left nature and humanity behind, Coriolanus can provide us with the thrill of seeing how we can be transfigured and refined into something else before we are destroyed.

Another example of a protagonist who seems to be moving in an upward direction beyond humanity is Cleopatra. We have this impression in part because of the way she displays her disdain for things of this world after Antony has died. This impression is strengthened when she then states her intention to do "what's brave, what's noble... after the high Roman fashion" (4.15.98–9). And as she herself observes as she prepares herself for this final act, "I have nothing / Of woman in me: now from head to foot / I am marble-constant: now the fleeting moon / No planet is of mine" (5.2.282). After she receives the poisonous asps from the rural fellow, she elaborates upon this transformation: "I have immortal longings in me... / I am fire and air: my other elements / I give to baser life" (5.2.317). True, like Antony, she imagines the afterlife as a state in which they will both continue to be themselves and resume their love affair. But like the gods they will be immortal, and they will be higher, more refined versions of themselves. She, at least, will be made of fire and air, and she will have shed the other, baser elements of water and earth that entered into her earthly constitution. As if to confirm some features of this transfiguration of her Egyptian queen, Charmian addresses her, "O eastern star!" (5.2.346). No wonder that she is "an identity that has long left readers and theatregoers exalted" (Cheney: 192).

It might seem that, in becoming something nonhuman, these characters ultimately fail as representations humanity and so cannot finally be sublime. But perhaps not, for in transcending the human and undergoing these transformations, these characters might be seen to fulfill a particular, somewhat frightening capacity that we humans have—the capacity to negate, deny, or shed our humanity and to become inhuman.

Thought

In *On Sublimity*, Longinus claims that the most important source of sublimity is the power to conceive great thoughts, that "sublimity is the echo of a noble mind," and that "real sublimity contains much food for reflection" (148–9). Authors, characters, and texts that have these qualities are the ones that make us *feel* sublime—they sweep us away, overwhelm us, and make us feel exalted, noble, ecstatic, or astonished. If this is so, then another thing that accounts for the powers of Shakespearean drama to provide us with these experiences is that, as we have already seen to some extent, the characters have wonderful minds that they exercise in ways that provide us with much food for thought. But let's consider a few further examples of thought that meet this Longinian criterion of sublimity.

Discussion of sublime works of literature rarely turns to comedy, but Shakespeare likes to mix his genres in order to give his audience a rich and diverse experience, and one of the ways he does this is by having characters in his comedies think and argue in serious and elevated ways. In the comedies we have seen that even the comic *dianoia* has a serious, even wise, side to it, but we also find some characters occasionally thinking and reasoning in ways that are not funny at all. To my mind, some of these moments are rather grand, and they stand out from the prevailing mood of festivity, delight, and laughter. In the final scene of *A Midsummer Night's Dream*, for example, we have Theseus' marvelous discourse on poets, lovers, and madmen (5.1.2–22). And in *As You Like It*, we have Duke Senior's wonderful, wide-ranging speech on the difference between the court and the forest: he thinks of how life in the forest is sweeter than life at court, which he identifies with peril, dishonesty, flattery, and even sin. And he thinks of how the physical pain one experiences in the forest can help one realise what one is, how, in general, "sweet are the uses of adversity," and how in the green world of the forest there is "good in everything" (2.1.1–17). Shortly after this we have Jaques' famous sobering thoughts on the seven ages through which all men pass (2.7.142–69).

And then we have Portia's celebrated attempt to persuade Shylock to have mercy on Antonio in *The Merchant of Venice*:

> The quality of mercy is not *strained*,   [compelled]
> It droppeth as the gentle rain from heaven
> Upon the place beneath. It is twice blest:
> It blesseth him that gives and him that takes.
> 'Tis mightiest in the mightiest, it becomes
> The thronèd monarch better than his crown.
> His sceptre shows the force of temporal power,
> The attribute to awe and majesty,
> Wherein doth sit the dread and fear of kings.
> But mercy is above this sceptred sway,
> It is enthronèd in the hearts of kings,
> It is an attribute to God himself;
> And earthly power doth then show likest God's
> When mercy seasons justice: therefore, Jew,
> Though justice be thy plea, consider this,
> That in the course of justice, none of us

Should see salvation. We do pray for mercy,
And that same prayer doth teach us all to render
The deeds of mercy.

(4.1.184–202)

Sure, the situation demands that Portia make some kind of attempt to persuade Shylock to relent, but why does Shakespeare include such a long, serious speech in what is supposed to be a comedy? To make you laugh? I don't think so. To teach you to be merciful to others? Perhaps. To provide you with the pleasures afforded by elevated, noble thought and argument? Yes, I think so. For here we have argument and reasoning from big ideas about God, monarchy, prayer, the relationship between justice and mercy, and the reasons that both ought to be exercised by all earthly powers. Note that Portia also argues from her conception of the human condition at large, from her idea of a situation in which "we" all find ourselves. For after observing that mercy benefits both the giver and receiver, and that God himself exercises it, she claims that "none of us" would achieve salvation if God was not merciful—she seems to be working on a Christian premise that all humans are sinful and that strict justice without mercy would therefore mean that no human would achieve salvation. Just as we hope God will be merciful to us and grant us salvation, so we ourselves should be merciful to our fellow human beings. Even if we don't buy into these ideas, I would say that this is elevated reasoning and argument that reflect Portia's noble mind and that do indeed provide matter for reflection.

In *Richard II*, we have John of Gaunt's famous impassioned speech devoted to prophesying the fall of Richard, praising England, and lamenting the way Richard has been governing it—what might be called the patriotic sublime (2.1.31–68). But since this one is so well known, let's turn to another example of what I think qualifies as high argument. It comes in the great scene later in the play when King Richard II surrenders the crown to Bullingbrook, who will become King Henry IV. In this scene, often referred to as the "deposition scene," Bullingbrook finally comes clean and indicates he does indeed intend to take the crown from King Richard II: "In God's name I'll ascend the regal throne" (4.1.107). The Bishop of Carlisle then cries, "Marry, heaven forbid!" and presents an impassioned argument against these proceedings:

What subject can give sentence on his king?
And who sits here that is not Richard's subject?
Thieves are not judged but they are by to hear,
Although apparent guilt be seen in them.
And shall the figure of God's majesty,
His captain, steward, deputy-elect,
Anointed, crowned, planted many years,
Be judged by subject and inferior breath,
And he himself not present? O, forbid it, God,
That in a Christian climate souls refined

> Should show so heinous, black, obscene a deed.
> I speak to subjects, and a subject speaks,
> Stirred up by heaven, thus boldly for his king.
> My lord of Hereford here [Bullingbrook], whom you call king,
> Is a foul traitor to proud Hereford's king.
>
> (4.1.115–29)

In the cutthroat world of the history plays, characters often argue out of their commitment to a faction or their own desires and ambitions. Here, I think we have a higher kind of protest and argument because Carlisle is not out mainly for himself or any faction. His argument is sincere, and it is based mainly on principles of justice and political ideas grounded in his Christian faith, ideas that were widely accepted at the time in England and beyond. At least in Christian countries, he argues, God appoints kings to their office. This is one reason that subjects in Christian countries are not entitled to judge or depose their kings, and especially not in their absence. Those who presume to do so are violating God's will and are traitors. It follows that Bullingbrook is contravening God's will and is a traitor. And it follows that the acts of judging King Richard II, accepting (or forcing) his surrender of the crown, and giving it to Bullingbrook are unjust and wrong. Carlisle continues in this high argumentative vein when he then assumes a prophetic stance and argues from consequences which he graphically envisions: "if you crown him, let me prophesy / The blood of English shall manure the ground, / And future ages groan for his foul act...." So the reasoning and argumentation here are also grounded in prophecy, vision, and the bishop's genuine concern for the welfare of his country—not to mention his courage in challenging the Bullingbrook faction which, by this time, has the upper hand. In light of all of these reasons and visions he concludes by imploring his countrymen to "prevent it, resist it, and let it not be so" (4.1.130–43). For his pains he is charged with treason and arrested. Yet at the end of the play, Bullingbrook—now King Henry IV—spares his life, on grounds that he has seen "high sparks of honour" in him (5.6.29). Those high sparks are on display in this great argument, which can make for a moment of high drama in the play.

At the end of *Julius Caesar*, Brutus' adversary Antony calls him "the noblest Roman of them all" (5.5.73). This seems right because Brutus is continually taking the high moral road, thinking noble thoughts, presenting elevated arguments, and acting accordingly. As Nietzsche puts it, he is "the most awesome quintessence of a lofty morality" (150). Early in the play, for example, Cassius proposes that all of those who want to participate in the conspiracy to murder Caesar swear to it. "No, not an oath," Brutus says, and he proceeds to give a lengthy speech in which he provides his reasons for his objection (2.1.124–45). His thinking is high-minded because he argues against taking an oath with his fellow conspirators on grounds that oaths are *beneath* them. Brutus argues that if you are low, bad, cowardly, and sick, or if you doubt your compeers, or if your cause is bad, you and your compeers might need to take an oath, for taking an oath is the only thing that will keep you true to your cause. If, however, you are a Roman and your cause is just, you don't need an oath to stay true to your cause. That is because Romans are noble, virtuous, honest people who will be true to a just cause, simply by virtue of saying they are committed to it. Brutus and his conspirators are Romans, and their cause is just. It follows that they don't need an oath to ensure that they will do it, or that they will maintain secrecy. Indeed, those who think such men require an oath "stain" and debase their enterprise. The argument is thus an echo of Brutus' rare and noble mind, since it is an argument against the *common* way of securing conspiracies amongst ignoble people, and one that is grounded in Brutus' elevated ideas about himself, his fellow Romans, and the enterprise of assassinating Caesar. It is worth noting, too, that the conspirators are persuaded, and they rise to the standard Brutus sets for them: they don't take an oath, they don't divulge the conspiracy, and they kill Caesar.

In some cases, the grand and noble thoughts of the characters are not in the service of argument or persuasion, but are simply part of intellectual activity stimulated by particular experiences and powerful feelings. In *The Tempest*, for example, Prospero pauses to reflect following the disappearance of the spirits he has summoned to perform a celebratory masque for Ferdinand and his daughter, Miranda. Having commanded the spirits to disappear, Prospero says to Ferdinand, his future son-in-law,

> Our revels now are ended. These our actors,
> As I foretold you, were all spirits and
> Are melted into air, into thin air,
> And, like the baseless fabric of this vision,
> The cloud-capped towers, the gorgeous palaces,
> The solemn temples, the great globe itself,
> Yea, all which it inherit, shall dissolve,
> And, like this insubstantial pageant faded,
> Leave not a rack behind. We are such stuff
> As dreams are made on: and our little life
> Is rounded with a sleep.
> (4.1.161–71)

The thought here has a grandeur in part because of the way Prospero moves from the particular to the general. Beginning by speaking of the particular vision he has just created and then made to vanish, he asserts that the entire world resembles it: like the vision, the entire world will vanish without a trace (the assertion is made in the form of a *simile*). The thinking here is grand also because it includes ideas about the ultimate fate of this world. Sometime in the distant future, it seems, the entire world will dissolve, just like the vision he has just created. Prospero is thus thinking about grand, vast things: the entire world, all that is in it, the entire future, the end of the world, total annihilation, nothingness. Notice, too, that like many of Shakespeare's thoughtful protagonists, Prospero speaks in the first person plural: the "we" and "our" might include just Prospero and Ferdinand, but it can also include everyone, including the audience. And if we take him to be speaking of everyone, then his thinking also includes speculations about the substance of all humans, and their fate: all humans are made of dream-stuff, and all our little, insignificant lives end with nothing more than sleep.

Another example of thought that is in a sense *above* persuasion is the heroine's thought in *Romeo and Juliet*. We feel that Juliet's passion is majestic, but this is in part because of the grand ideas and conceptions that enter into her description of it and herself. We have seen her, for example, invoke (by *simile*) the boundlessness of the sea to describe her bounty, the depth of the sea to describe her love, and infinity to describe what she gives to Romeo and receives from him (2.1.184–7). And the great soliloquy she delivers as she awaits news of Romeo (3.2.1–31) brings home to us not just the intensity of her sexual desire for him but also the elevation of her person, in part because of the grand ideas she continues to invoke. Thinking of her situation on a cosmic scale, she imagines the sun as Phoebus, the Greek god of the sun, driving his horse-drawn chariot to the west, and she commands those "fiery-footed steeds" to go faster, so night and Romeo will arrive sooner. She moves to an *apostrophe* to "love-performing night" and then asserts a claim about *all* lovers: "Lovers can see to do their amorous rites / By their own beauties, or if love be blind, / It best agrees with night." Note how, continuing to address and command the night, she also invokes a *paradox* (a statement that seems self-contradictory but also true in some sense): she asks night to teach her how "to lose a winning match, / Played for a pair of stainless maidenhoods." And note how she resorts to abstract concepts to describe and legitimize the sexual encounter with Romeo she is anticipating: their "true love acted" will be "simple modesty." She then returns to thoughts of the cosmos when she imagines her death as an occasion for night to cut up Romeo into stars and scatter him across "the face of heaven." The result of this will be of a similar magnitude: "all the world will be in love with night / And pay no worship to the garish sun." So Juliet's thoughts are taken up with vast, boundless, grand, infinite, mysterious things, such as night, the sun, the stars, the sky, the gods, all lovers, death, and all the world. They also include abstract moral concepts and ideas that seem beyond comprehension. Exercising her intellect in this way and calling on these grand thoughts and ideas to express her impatience and passion, she displays a nobility of mind that sweeps us up and away.

In addition to noting such specific instances of elevated thought and argument, I want also to register the way in which Shakespeare's main characters exercise and display—*on an ongoing basis*—brilliant minds and extraordinary powers of thought, cognition, and argumentation. I think all of the main characters do this to some extent or other, but two outstanding examples are Hamlet and Falstaff. For Hamlet is relentless in the way he brings his powerful intellect, argumentative finesse, awareness, and biting wit to bear on his situation and everyone who comes near him—indeed, he seems to be a victim of his own intellect. At least up until he achieves a kind of peace and resignation just before the end, he seems unable to turn off his mind and relax. We have seen that Falstaff, too, is a supremely accomplished thinker and debater, though in a more serio-comic, playful mode, as he banters with his mates in the bar, enjoys life, and deals with an endless series of pickles, games, and dangerous situations. From the slightest remarks to extended speeches and meditations, the words of these characters intimate such incredible intellectual, linguistic, and cognitive powers that they may well manifest, as Bloom claims, "the most comprehensive consciousnesses in all of literature" (4). For Bloom, it is in part this ongoing display of intellectual power, hyper-consciousness, and capacity to argue upside down and sideways that go to make these characters sublime. This is what empowers them to provide us with the exhilarations of feeling our minds expand, and knowing what we humans can be.

Finally, we are concentrating on what it is about the plays and not their author that accounts for their powers to make us feel sublime. But while we are on the topic of thought, mind, and consciousness, I think we should also note that one of the other things that may make us wonder and experience awe when we read the plays or see them performed is the awareness that behind the wonderful minds of the characters is the mind of a single person, Shakespeare. Isn't it amazing and awe-inspiring that one person could produce all of these plays that include complex characters of such tremendous cognitive and linguistic power?

Language

The power of Shakespeare's strange and marvelous characters to make us wonder and admire is enhanced by the words they use. In *A Midsummer Night's Dream*, for example, Puck and all of the fairies seem so magical and wondrous in part because their words are arranged in unusual ways. Many of the lines in which these words are placed are

- relatively short
- *end-stopped* (no *enjambment*)
- rhymed
- unusual metrically.

When, for example, Oberon, king of the fairies is administering the love juice to Titania, he says,

> **What** thou / **see'st** when / **thou** dost / **wake**,
> **Do** it / **for** thy / **true**-love / **take**,
> **Love** and / **languish** / **for** his / **sake**.
> (2.2.27–9)

Here we have a charming little triplet, three lines that rhyme. I think we can also say they are end-stopped lines because even though there is no period at the end of each line, each line forms a complete phrase or clause and ends with a comma or period that calls for a pause. The lines also lend themselves to a reading in which the words and syllables in bold are stressed more than the others. In that case, we have very regular *trochaic tetrameter* lines: four trochaic feet (stressed/unstressed) per line, with the last trochaic foot missing the final unstressed syllable. I think these basic features of Oberon's language make it seem incantatory, enchanting, strange, and they dispose us to wonder at the mystical powers of the juice and the supernatural agent that is administering it. Notice, too, that this little utterance is figurative—that is to say, the order of words is unusual. For it is unusual for us to put the verb at the end of a command, as Oberon does. If we still used the now obsolete pronoun "thou," we would probably say, "take what thou see'st as thy true love when thou dost wake," or perhaps, "when thou dost wake, take what thou see'st as thy true love." Since there is a basic reversal of common order, we have a little *hyperbaton*, another small feature of Oberon's language that makes the spell he is casting a little strange and enchanting.

Strange and enchanting, but not majestic and grand, and so not qualified to cause in us those other feelings that we are taking the sublime experience to include: nobility, elevation, pride, dignity, exaltation, ecstasy. But that language does indeed have the capacity to be high and lofty and, so, to cause in us these other feelings is suggested by another character in this play, one who usually speaks in prose. When the mechanicals are planning their play, Bottom says his inclination is to play the part of a tyrant, or "Ercles," by which he means Hercules, the ancient Greek hero. He then provides what he takes to be evidence that he would be up to it:

> The raging rocks
> And shivering shocks
> Shall break the locks,
> Of prison gates.
> And Phibbus' car
> Shall shine from far
> And make and mar
> The foolish Fates.
>   (1.2.21–8)

"This was lofty," Bottom says (1.2.29). Though we might not share his evaluation of his performance, Bottom does help us see that for Shakespeare and his contemporaries, speeches and language itself could be high and "lofty." But what could make them so?

Not rhymed, very regular *iambic dimeter* lines (two iambic feet per line), like Bottom's. This kind of line can be enchanting, fearsome (as in some of the witches' lines in *Macbeth*), or comical (as it is in Bottom's case), but it lacks many of the features that enable Shakespeare's language to achieve the grandeur and majesty that evoke awe and exaltation in the audience. Those features include some that we have observed previously in connection with other effects.

Let's take Cleopatra's description of Antony, which we mentioned earlier in this chapter, as an example:

> His face was as the heavens, and therein stuck
> A sun and moon which kept their course and lighted
> The little o'th'earth.
> ...
> His legs bestrid the ocean: his reared arm
> *Crested* the world: his voice was propertied   [crowned]
> As all the tunèd spheres, and that to friends:
> But when he meant to *quail* and shake the orb,   [overpower, terrify]
> He was as rattling thunder. For his bounty,
> There was no winter in't: an autumn it was
> That grew the more by reaping. His delights
> Were dolphin-like: they showed his back above
> The element they lived in. In his *livery*   [uniform of a noble's servants]
> Walked crowns and crownets; realms and islands were
> As plates dropped from his pocket.
>
> (5.2.96–110)

Note, first of all, that the prevailing meter is *iambic*, but that there are many irregularities, as in lines beginning with stressed syllables, such as "**Crested** the..." and "**Walked crowns**...." So while it moves forward with an iambic rhythm, it does not have the sing-song feel of Bottom's lines and nursery rhymes that usually have very regular meters. Second, we have a mix of *end-stopped* lines and *enjambment*: only five of the fourteen lines are *end-stopped*. The frequent *enjambment* I think is one of the little things that gives a sense of force and surging energy to the speech. True, the many *caesurae* (pauses in mid-line) stop the utterance, and prevent it from having the sweep and expansiveness it might achieve without them. But along with the *enjambment* they prevent it from sounding like an artificial list of lines, and to my ear give it a rugged, frank quality. And the lines are unrhymed, which brings it a little closer to real speech. Blank verse with many metrical irregularities, frequent *enjambment*, and *caesurae*—this is the work-horse of Shakespeare's dramatic dialogue, and in this case it is in the service of Cleopatra's elevated speech in praise of Antony. I'm not saying that this verse form is always lofty, but that it lends itself to elevation more than other verse forms, and that Shakespeare avails himself of this potential on this and many other occasions.

In his great treatise, Longinus provides a wonderful, detailed account of how particular figures and tropes can be a source of sublimity. Indeed, his treatise is one of the great ancient catalogues of the tropes and figures, one you might wish to consult for definitions and further commentary on this crucial dimension of Shakespeare's language and western literary language at large. Note that one of the things that makes Cleopatra's speech so lavish, forceful, and grand but also coherent and unified is that the entire speech is really structured as a single figure: *anaphora* (a series of phrases or clauses that all begin with the same word or words). For the speech consists of a series of statements all beginning with the same word or words: "his face... his legs... his reared arm... his voice... for his bounty... his delights... in his livery...." Rather than moving forward, the utterance thus stays in one place, as a fountain does, and like a fountain it overflows, not with water but with an abundance of praise. But note that this praise, though impassioned and excessive in some ways, is not hysterical. It is controlled and dignified, in part because Cleopatra also arranges her words into repetitions of basic grammatical structures called *parallelisms*: "His legs bestrid the ocean" (subject/verb/direct object), "his reared arm / Crested the world" (subject/verb/direct object). We get another little *parallelism* in the line near the end with a repetition of a noun/conjunction/noun structure in "crowns and crownets" and "realms and islands." This figure subtly creates a sense of control and order and contributes to the elevated tone. Finally, I think the rugged, forceful, direct tone is further enhanced by *asyndeton* (a list of words or phrases that are not joined by conjunctions). Imagine how it would sound if she had structured her speech as a *polysyndeton*, and joined all of her phrases and clauses with conjunctions, as in, "his legs bestrid the ocean, **and** his arm crested the world, **and** his voice...." I think it would come across as a longer, slower, sadder, rather prosaic list. The tone is more elevated, forceful, dignified because Cleopatra asserts one claim, pauses, then asserts another without any conjunction.

The breath-taking quality of the speech is also a function of its being highly tropological: words which are usually used to mean or refer to one thing are used to mean or refer to another thing. First, we have several *similes* that elevate the tone, not just because they are similes, but because they are *similes* that assert resemblances between Antony and vast, grand, beautiful, vital things:

- Antony's face was as the heavens
- Antony's voice to friends was as the sound of the planets (which was thought to be harmonious and musical), but to enemies it was as thunder
- Antony's delights lifted him above the world as dolphins jump above the sea
- Antony distributed realms and islands as he allowed coins to drop from his pockets.

Several *metaphors* further assert Cleopatra's perception of resemblances of this kind. For she uses words that usually refer to an act of crowning or placing one's crest on top of something—"to crest"—in order to refer (it seems) to acts that resemble it—Antony's act of conquering and ruling the world. And she uses words that are usually used to refer to the season of plenty and harvest, "autumn," to refer to something that resembles it: Antony's "bounty" (generosity).

Notice here, as well, Cleopatra's further description of this generosity: the more it was reaped, the more it grew. How could that be? That seems like a self-contradictory statement. But by challenging our reason in this way, Cleopatra seems to be claiming that Antony's generosity was *so* grand that it was beyond our comprehension, beyond our capacity to reason, and she thereby represents it as something marvelous that she admires. If this is so, then we have another *paradox*, a trope that also features in Enobarbus' description of Cleopatra. And let's note in passing that the Renaissance provides us with another name for this trope. In *The Art of English Poesy* (1589), Shakespeare's contemporary, George Puttenham, writes that "many times our poet is carried by some occasion to report of a thing that is marvelous, and then he will seem not to speak it simply but with some sign of admiration." Puttenham observes that the ancient Latin term for this is *paradoxon*, a term that derives from ancient Greek *para* (beside, beyond) and *doxa* (belief or opinion). But he thinks a better name for it, at least in English, is "the Wonderer" (311).

I think Cleopatra's language displays another trope: *metonymy*. For she uses the words "crowns and crownets"—which are usually used to refer to precious, ornamented head-gear—in order to refer to kings and princes who wear such things. Kings and princes, she is saying, wore the "livery" (uniform) of his servants and so, by implication, served him. Crowns do not resemble kings and princes, but they are often close in space or time to them (when kings and princes wear them). So words that are usually used to mean one thing are being used to mean something that is close in space or time to that thing. That is why Cleopatra's expression here is not a *metaphor* but a *metonymy*. But perhaps most important of all is Cleopatra's *hyperbolical* language: she uses words which are usually used to refer to huge, vast, grand things in order to refer to things which, we must think, are smaller than those things. Many of the metaphorical descriptions of Antony are also hyperbolical, but we get further instances of this trope when she says that Antony's legs straddled the ocean, that he sometimes at least intended to shake the entire "orb" (the earth), and that kings and princes were among his servants.

Some aspects of the diction also contribute to the elevated tone. First, we have a few relatively long, polysyllabic words that derive in one way or another from Latin: trisyllabic words such as "propertied," "element," and possibly "livery," and bisyllabic words such as "ocean," "bounty," and "autumn." At least to the ear of Renaissance Englishmen, such Latinate terms had a certain prestige. And note that the grammatical form of some words is rather strange: "propertied," as well as "crested," were unusual past participles in Shakespeare's day. We also have a rather unusual trisyllabic compound, "dolphin-like." "To quail," as a transitive verb meaning to frighten or intimidate someone, is strange to us and is extremely rare in the plays. Note also that many of the words have an unusual aural quality: we have long "o" sounds running through the whole speech (a kind of *assonance*) which is one more thing that makes it sound orotund, resonant, lofty. But we also need to observe that though some words are unusual, and though they are arranged in blank verse that is highly figurative and tropological, the speech still has a wonderful quality of directness and frankness, and I think it is relatively easy to understand. This is because the end-stopped lines and *caesurae* break it down into short, simple phrases and clauses which we can take in one at a time, and also because most of the words are fairly common monosyllabic words that derive from Old English. This simplicity of diction I think tempers the ornate quality of the speech and saves it from the dangers that Longinus and the ancient rhetoricians identified for anyone who was attempting the high, lofty style: falling into *bombast* and *turgidity*. That is to say, the ancient authorities all observed that if you push your language too hard, it can sound phony, inflated, padded—in short, ridiculous. In my view, the relatively short phrases and simple diction protect the speech from this danger and qualify it as a grand expression of Cleopatra's passion and admiration that elevates her, Antony, and us.

While we're on the topic of diction, and looking at *Antony and Cleopatra*, we might also notice Octavius Caesar's language when he informs his sister, Octavia, what Antony is really up to: though Octavia thinks her new husband Antony is in Athens, he is in fact back in Egypt with Cleopatra, and both of them are now

>   levying
> The kings o'th'earth for war. He hath assembled
> Bocchus, the King of Libya, Archelaus,
> Of Cappadocia, Philadelphos, King
> Of Paphlagonia, the Thracian king, Adallas,
> King Malchus of Arabia, King of Pont,
> Herod of Jewry, Mithridates, King
> Of Comagene, Polemon and Amyntas,
> The Kings of Mede and Lycaonia,
> With a more larger list of sceptres.
>
>   (3.6.76–85)

Since all Octavius wants to do is to inform his sister that Antony and Cleopatra are levying all the kings from the eastern Roman empire against him, he really does not need to go into such detail. But this is what he does by way of a single, long sentence that is a list of proper names, and that takes the form of an *asyndeton*. Again, I think this makes it harder, more forceful and direct, than it would be if there were conjunctions such as "and" in between each item in the list. Also, many of the names are polysyllabic, and they would have sounded, at least to English Renaissance ears, as names of marvelous and exotic lands—like Egypt of the pyramids, crocodiles, and the Nile. Moreover, catalogues of proper names of kings and princes from distant lands who are preparing for war is a convention of ancient western epic poems, such as Homer's *Iliad* and Virgil's *Aeneid*. Employing diction that was associated with the high and serious style of epic, Octavius Caesar thus elevates his own language and further enhances the grandeur and expansiveness of the world of this play.

Longinus sometimes seems to rank persuasion below the feelings of ecstasy and elevation he associates with the sublime, but he still provides many passages from ancient persuasive orations, especially those of Demosthenes and Cicero, as examples of sublimity. Had he known of Shakespeare's plays, I think he might also have cited Brutus' great speech to the plebeians (the populace) of Rome in *Julius Caesar*. I think this speech is more dignified, noble, and elevating than Antony's well-known speech that follows it ("Friends, Romans, countrymen..."). Since Brutus is giving "public reasons" for the assassination of Caesar, and attempting to persuade the Roman populace that the assassination was just, we might account for its sublimity by focusing on the reasoning the speech presents. But I'd like to focus on specific aspects of Brutus' language in order to account for its sublimity:

BRUTUS: Romans, countrymen, and lovers! hear me for my cause, and be silent, that you may hear. Believe me for mine honour, and have respect to mine honour, that you may believe. Censure me in your wisdom, and awake your senses, that you may the better judge. If there be any in this assembly, any dear friend of Caesar's, to him I say, that Brutus' love to Caesar was no less than his. If then that friend demand why Brutus rose against Caesar, this is my answer: not that I loved Caesar less, but that I loved Rome more. Had you rather Caesar were living, and die all slaves, than that Caesar were dead, to live all free men? As Caesar loved me, I weep for him; as he was fortunate, I rejoice at it; as he was valiant, I honour him: but, as he was ambitious, I slew him. There is tears, for his love: joy, for his fortune: honour, for his valour: and death, for his ambition. Who is here so base, that would be a bondman? If any, speak, for him have I offended. Who is here so rude, that would not be a Roman? If any, speak, for him have I offended. Who is here so vile, that will not love his country? If any, speak; for him have I offended. I pause for a reply.
ALL: None, Brutus, none.
BRUTUS: Then none have I offended.

(3.2.14–30)

This is lofty! It is so austere, direct, forceful, dignified, noble—it makes me feel elevated and dignified when I read it out loud in class, and the class is usually hushed by the end of it. What is it about the language that can account for this? So many things, but first, it is in prose, not blank verse. True, this brings it *down* in a way, since it makes it closer to common usage than blank verse is: the sequence of stressed and unstressed syllable is irregular, and the utterance does not break down into lines of the same length as blank verse sometimes does. But I think this is one of the little things that accounts for our sense that Brutus is speaking seriously, honestly, directly to his audience. Note, too, that the speech is close to common speech in that the diction is fairly common and it is not very tropological. True, Brutus uses "rose against" instead of "murder," which might be seen as a *euphemism* that softens the deed. And perhaps there is some *hyperbole* when he says that the citizens of Rome would have "all" been slaves had Caesar been allowed to pursue power, but that they are "all" freemen now that he is dead. But Brutus stays away from *simile, metaphor, metonymy,* and *irony*. This is in part why the speech seems hard and austere rather than flowery.

The force of the utterance derives in part from the way Brutus directly commands and interrogates his audience throughout. But I think the main reason the speech comes across as forceful, elevated, and dignified is that it is highly figurative: there is a wide range of unusual orders and grammatical structures. I'll try to highlight the main ones (and remind you of the definitions) in the following:

asyndeton (lists of words, phrases, clauses, lines that are not jointed by conjunctions): throughout the whole passage

anaphora (the repetition of a word or word at the beginning of a series of phrases, clauses, lines):

> *As* Caesar loved me, I weep for him;
> *as* he was fortunate, I rejoice at it;
> *as* he was valiant, I honour him:
> but *as* he was ambitious, I slew him.

epistrophe (the repetition of a word or words at the end of a series of phrases, clauses, lines, sentences):

> Who is here so ... that would be.... *If any, speak, for him have I offended.*
> Who is here so... that would be.... *If any, speak, for him have I offended.*
> Who is here so... that would be.... *If any, speak, for him have I offended.*

parallelism (the repetition of a grammatical structure):

> hear me... that you may hear
> believe me... that you may believe
> censure me... that you may the better judge

> As Caesar loved me, I weep for him;
> as he was fortunate, I rejoice at it;
> as he was valiant, I honour him:
> but as he was ambitious, I slew him.

There is
tears,	for his love:
joy,	for his fortune:
honour,	for his valour:
and death	for his ambition

antithesis (a special type of *parallelism*, one where the meaning of one term is the opposite of the meaning of another term):

> not that I loved Caesar *less*
> but that I loved Rome *more*

Sublimity   163

| Had you rather | Caesar were *living*, and die all *slaves*, |
| Than that | Caesar were *dead*, to live all *free men*? |

Note that some of these examples display more than one figure. Speaking in this highly figurative way, Brutus organizes his words into discrete patterns, orders, and structures and thereby makes the *argument* seem more orderly, measured, and rational. In addition, I think he implicitly represents himself as a *man* who, while feeling several emotions, is yet rational and just: as the speech is ordered, controlled, measured, and balanced, so is the man. And the manifold repetition of words, phrases, and structures enhances the force of the utterance. Combining a wide range of figures as he does, Brutus produces an argument of tremendous dignity, austerity, authority, and power, one that not only convinces the plebeians of the justice of the assassination but also goes further than Brutus would have liked: they call for Brutus to live, for a triumph in his honor, for a statue with his ancestors and—what could only have made Brutus shake his head in dismay—for him to be Caesar! But, in the face of such sublime oratory, who can blame them if they don't really understand what Brutus is saying and just want to celebrate him—at least for the moment? True, we might sit back and coolly analyze the scene. But if in performance Brutus addresses us as though we are the plebeians, we too might find his high and mighty eloquence irresistible.

Shakespeare does not reserve sublimity of the austere, dignified kind for his Roman men. Consider, for example, Hermione's great formal speeches in her defence in *The Winter's Tale* (3.2), or Desdemona's speech on her first appearance in *Othello*. At the beginning of this play, Desdemona is summoned to appear before the nobility of her city and challenged by her father, Brabantio, to renounce her husband Othello and obey him, her father. She replies,

> My noble father,
> I do perceive here a divided duty.
> To you I am bound for life and education:
> My life and education both do *learn* me   [teach]
> How to respect you. You are the lord of duty,
> I am hitherto your daughter. But here's my husband,
> And so much duty as my mother showed
> To you, preferring you before her father,
> So much I challenge that I may profess
> Due to the Moor my lord.
>   (1.3.196–205)

To my mind, this too is lofty, and it is lofty for some of the same reasons Brutus' speech is. Desdemona begins by directly addressing her audience (in this case her father) and she continues to address him throughout. She keeps the diction simple. Though speaking in blank verse and not prose, her phrasing is close to common speech as a result of a combination of *enjambment, end-*

stopped lines, and *caesurae*. The variations in the iambic meter also help to make it seem real, frank, and sincere. She stays away from tropes, but utilizes figures, one of which is *anadiplosis*, for she repeats words with which she ends one phrase at the beginning of the next phrase, as in "life and education: / My life and education," and "How to respect you. You...." Impeding motion forwards, slowing it down, emphasizing the meaning of the repeated words, this figure makes a significant contribution to the overall tone of high seriousness, control, sincerity, and dignity. As does the *anaphora* with which she concludes: "so much.... so much...." I think this figure here works to represent her as a rational, noble *person* who is in control of her emotions. It also enhances the reasonableness of her argument for ranking duty to husband above duty to father and for disobeying her father. Using language in this way on her very first appearance in the play, the gentle Desdemona thus establishes a high, solemn style that commands our admiration, even if it fails to move her father.

Song

Generally speaking, I don't think the music and song Shakespeare had in mind for his plays is of the grand, sweeping, magnificent kind that might overwhelm and sweep us away, as can, for example, Beethoven's symphonies, Wagner's operas, or Bach's passions and masses. But I believe that the music and song in some plays can and should enhance our wonder. Indeed, the marvelous, enchanting, wondrous worlds of plays such as *A Midsummer Night's Dream* and *The Tempest* can be greatly enhanced by them (Cohen: 14), especially if the lyrics are sung to the music that Shakespeare had in mind or that was composed by his contemporaries for those lyrics. Some of the characters themselves observe that this is so. In *The Tempest*, for example, when he hears Ariel singing "Full fathom five," Ferdinand wonders, "Where should this music be? I'th'air or th'earth? / It sounds no more: and sure it waits upon / Some god o'th'island" (1.2.451–3). Later, when the goddesses perform the wedding masque and sing "Honour, riches, marriage-blessing," Ferdinand remarks, "This is a most majestic vision, and / Harmonious charmingly" (4.1.127–8). Moreover, I think some of the stage directions in the early printed editions of the plays suggest that the music ought to create an atmosphere and mood of wonder and enchantment. For Ariel puts Gonzalo and others asleep by "*playing solemn music*" (2.1.171), and when, in Act 3, Prospero conjures a banquet for Alonso and company, the stage direction is not just *music* but "*solemn and strange music*"—which Gonzalo calls "marvellous sweet music" (3.3.20). It is again "*solemn music*" that charms but also comforts Alonso and company in the final scene (5.1.62). True, in some cases the audience knows it is Ariel who is singing and playing the music while the characters do not, and this in part accounts for the characters' wonder. And we have seen that some of the songs are merry rounds and scurvy songs sung by the lower characters. Even so, much of the song and music throughout this play is of the sweet and solemn kind, it seems to exercise magical powers over many of the characters, and it is produced by Prospero's supernatural powers and his spirit, Ariel.

We have already had a look at the lovely "Full fathom five," in which Ariel sings sweetly of Ferdinand's father's sea-change "into something rich and strange," so let us consider Ariel's final song, "Where the bee sucks," as an example of another song that I think enhances the marvelous world of the island (5.1.93–9). Shakespeare's contemporary, Robert Johnson, may well have composed the music to which the lyrics are set in several seventeenth-century manuscripts (Duffin: 455; Henze: 156). Ariel sings this as he helps Prospero dress for the final scene and anticipates his freedom.

Such an enchanting little song, in part because Ariel describes how he does, or will, lie in a flower where the bees suck, fly on the back of a bat, or live under a blossom—how wondrous! The strange, enchanting quality of the song is further enhanced by the rhyme and, in the first five lines, the fairly regular *trochaic tetrameter* lines we have seen before: "**Where** the **bee** sucks, **there** suck I: / In a **cow**slip's **bell** I **lie**," etc. But note that in the final two lines of the song, the meter changes to *dactylic tetrameter*: "**Mer**rily, **mer**rily shall I live now, / **Un**der the **blos**som that **hangs** on the **bough**." Here we have a stressed/unstressed/unstressed sequence repeated four times in each line (with the last foot in each line missing the two final unstressed syllables). And note what Johnson does out of sensitivity to this metrical change: though he stays in a major key, he changes the time signature from 2/2 to 6/4. This makes it sound more like a waltz and, at least in most

Figure 4.1 "Where the bee sucks," from *The Tempest*. From John Playford's collection of music to *The Tempest* [manuscript] (ca. 1650–67)
Source: Digital Image Collection at the Folger Shakespeare Library.

performances of it I know, it becomes lighter and faster. Like many other aspects of this play, this song is intended to "give delight" as Caliban says the sounds of the island do (3.2.119), but it also enables us to enter into the characters' experience of wonder and enchantment.

References

Bloom, Harold. *Shakespeare: the Invention of the Human.* New York: Riverhead, 1998.

Bradley, A. C. *Shakespearean Tragedy*, 1904; London: Macmillan, 1971.

Cheney, Patrick. *English Authorship and the Early Modern Sublime.* Cambridge: Cambridge University Press, 2018.

Cohen, Max. *Wonder in Shakespeare.* New York: Palgrave Macmillan, 2012.

Duffin, Ross. *Shakespeare's Songbook.* New York: Norton, 2004.

Henze, Catherine A. *Robert Armin and Shakespeare's Performed Songs.* New York: Routledge, 2017.

Longinus. *On Sublimity.* Trans. D. A. Russell. In *Classical Literary Criticism.* Ed. D. A. Russell and Michael Winterbottom. 1972; Oxford: Oxford University Press, 1989. 143–187.

Nietzsche, Friedrich. *The Gay Science.* Trans. Walter Kaufmann. New York: Vintage, 1974.

Puttenham, George. *The Art of English Poesy.* Ed. Frank Whigham and Wayne A. Rebhorn. Ithaca: Cornell University Press, 2007.

Schlegel, Augustus William. *Lectures on Dramatic Art and Literature.* Trans. John Black. London: George Bell & Sons, 1879.

Conclusion

Another way of stating one of the main observations of this book is to say that one of the things that makes Shakespearean drama special is that it is entertaining. What does it mean for something to be entertaining? It means serving as an occasion for an audience to experience certain pleasures. What pleasures? The pleasures of emotional experience; laughter and delight; seeing accurate representations of what we are; hearing music, song, and language; learning, gaining wisdom, and being confirmed in our own wisdom; thinking about life; feeling wonder; feeling exalted, ecstatic, and ennobled. On this definition of "entertaining," Shakespeare's plays qualify as entertaining drama, since over the last four centuries many people have claimed to have had, and I believe *have* had, these pleasures as a result of reading or seeing performances of them. And since I think Shakespeare intended to write plays that were entertaining in this sense, I would also claim that he succeeded in doing one of the main things he intended to do.

I have been content merely to claim that the power of Shakespeare's plays to cause us to have these experiences makes them "special" and "successful." But I hope to have suggested along the way how you might make judgments about the quality of the plays. Judgments of quality depend in part on criteria of judgment. For Aristotle and many others, one criterion for judging of the quality of any given tragedy is whether it causes the audience to have intense emotional experiences. If we adopt this criterion, then Shakespearean tragedy would qualify as good tragedy, since over the centuries it seems to have met this criterion. But if another criterion for judging the quality of any given tragedy is that it does *not also* cause the audience to laugh, then the quality of Shakespearean tragedy would be compromised. This is because, as we have seen, Shakespeare mixes genres, and in his tragedies he includes comic scenes that have caused readers and audiences to laugh. Similarly, if a criterion for judging the quality of comedy is that it causes the audience to laugh, then Shakespearean comedy would qualify as good comedy since over the centuries it seems to have met this criterion. But if another criterion of judging the quality of any given comedy is that it does *not also* cause the audience to feel wonder, delight, and some degree of melancholy and compassion, then the quality of Shakespearean comedy would be compromised, since he mixes genres and includes scenes in his comedies that have caused readers and audiences to have these other experiences.

You might object that to make what is special and good about Shakespeare's plays depend on their effect on audiences is to make it all "subjective." Since different people feel different things, some people might think they are good, others might think they are bad, and there is no objective standard for arbitrating between these conflicting judgments. I think objecting in this way is like objecting to those who base their evaluation of a drug on how it affects patients. Different people can respond to a given drug in different ways. But given that a drug has a purpose, and given that that purpose is to affect patients in a certain way, it is still reasonable to asses the success and quality of that drug at least in part on how it affects patients. Similarly, given that Shakespeare's plays have a purpose, and given that at least one of their purposes is to affect the audience in a certain way, it is reasonable to assess the success and quality of those plays at least in part on how they affect audiences. True, different people respond in different ways to the plays. But over the long term there is a consistency of response that warrants the claim that Shakespeare's plays often fulfill their purpose, which is to provide a particular kind of entertainment. If we take fulfillment of purpose as a criterion of goodness, then his plays are good, even allowing for the existence of some audiences that do not find them entertaining. And by the way, in *An Apology for Poetry*, Sidney observes that literature is like "a medicine of cherries" (92); many others in Shakespeare's day drew the analogy between literature and drugs (Pollard).

The focus has been on what it is about the plays that accounts for their power to entertain us. And I have argued that it is specific aspects of plot, character, thought, language, song, and spectacle that do this. In making this argument, I hope to have at least provided you with some useful information about the plays and some insights into why they are as they are, why Shakespeare made them that way. I hope as well to have suggested the value of the special technical vocabulary in which Shakespeare himself was schooled. Learning and using this vocabulary, which derives from ancient Greece and Rome, improves our ability not just to describe Shakespeare's spectacular script but also to understand it and deliver it in performance.

In making this argument in this way, I want to discourage the idea that the plays are great no matter what and that their effect upon audiences—including you—is irrelevant to their success and value. The aim is to get away from thinking of the plays as monuments that are great in and of themselves, puzzles to be solved, or merely evidence of the nature of western society. I want to think of them as things that have a purpose: to entertain us. By thinking and discussing them in this way, I hope to dispose you to share those experiences which Shakespearean drama has provided readers and audiences over the last four centuries. That is to say, the book aims to help you discover ways of experiencing pity, compassion, sympathy, fear, horror, laughter, joy, delight, enlightenment, thought, wonder, ennoblement, and exhilaration when you read and see performances of the plays.

Knowing that Shakespeare intended to entertain us, knowing how he attempted to fulfill this intention, and knowing that he often fulfilled that intention over the last four hundred years may dispose us to share in that entertainment experience. But we still might not, for that experience depends on not just the plays but also what we are. We noted along the way that, in order to have some of the experiences afforded by Shakespeare's plays to audiences in the past, we have to put in a bit of work, since Shakespeare's English differs from ours. We might, in addition, have to read widely in order to appreciate his ongoing allusions to other texts. But we may differ in more significant ways from those who, in the past, have found entertainment value in Shakespeare. Sociologists inform us that our capacity to experience some emotions is diminished by the pornography and painkillers that are widespread in western society. They inform us, too, that aspects of the digital age have diminished our attention span and our capacity to comprehend the written and spoken word. If this is the case, then we and those who come after us may become incapable of having the experiences Shakespeare wanted his audiences to have, and the plays would lose some of the entertainment value they have had up until now. Yes, they still might be important and valuable to us for other reasons. We might have experiences other than those Shakespeare wanted us to have, but which we still value. And we might value the plays as sources of information about Elizabethan society and western society and culture at large. But they would not have the entertainment value they had for audiences in the past.

Even if they don't, I hope at least that this book will help you understand what it is about the plays that has caused audiences, including many modern audiences, to have these experiences. And I hope that it makes clear why your engagement with the plays, whatever it may be, is relevant to their success and the value they can have for us now.

References

Pollard, Tanya. *Drugs and Theater in Early Modern England*. Oxford: Oxford University Press, 2005.
Sidney, Sir Philip. *An Apology for Poetry*. In *Criticism: The Major Texts*. Ed. W. J.Bate. 1952; New York: Harcourt, 1970.

Index

ambition: of characters 27, 28, 40, 44, 102, 110, 119, 143–6, 152, 161
anger: of characters 37, 38, 39, 49, 50, 51, 105–7, 118
Aristophanes 4, 6, 7, 75, 78
Aristotle: on *catharsis* 3; on character 25, 41; on *ergon* (function) 3–4, 6, 12, 31, 113, 132, 167; on language 47, 49, 123; on plot 29, 59, 100; on spectacle 59; on *dianoia* (thought) 41–2, 78; on universals 6, 100

Barber, C. L. 6, 74
Bate, Jonathan 21
beauty: of characters 58–9, 77, 85, 143
Berry, Edward 6, 74, 76, 77, 111
Bible 121
blank verse *see* sounds
Bloom, Harold 11–12, 14–15, 58, 77, 155
Bradley, A. C. 3, 14, 15, 134, 140–1
Burke, Edmund 13, 143

catharsis see Aristotle
Cicero 33–4, 36, 47, 83, 98, 130, 160
characters: as cause of emotion 33–41; as cause of instruction 108–114; as cause of laughter and delight 74–77; as cause of sublimity 141–9; *see also* realism
Cheney, Patrick 13, 142, 143, 149
Christianity 10, 11, 12, 35, 37, 80, 99, 103, 119, 121, 130, 140, 151–2; *see also* Bible
comedy: ancient Graeco-Roman 4, 6–7, 16, 74–5, 90, 98–9; *see also* Aristophanes; Shakespearean 4–6, 17–20, 56–7, 62–96, 105–7, 111–14, 117–19, 123–4, 128–30, 133, 150–1, 167
Cowden Clarke, Mary 10, 120

danger: to the audience 31; to the tragic protagonists 30–31, 36, 40–41, 69, 99, 146; of bombast 160
deception 30, 34, 66, 68
delight: of audience 5–7, 15, 17, 32, 52, 56, 70–5, 77–8, 85–8, 92–6, 101, 119, 132, 165, 167–8
de Staël, Madame 2, 57, 58
dialogue 52, 53, 66, 91, 98–9, 157
dianoia see Aristotle; thought
Dryden, John 13, 101–2, 113
Duffin, Ross 54–6, 128, 165

emotion: of audience 1–6, 9, 12, 15–17, 24–60, 77–8, 102, 113–14, 119, 126, 132, 167–9; of characters 38–9, 77, 109, 114, 117, 119, 147, 163–4; *see also* pity; fear
Erasmus 98, 120–1, 123, 127
ergon see Aristotle; function
Erne, Lukas 16, 58
example: teaching by 7, 10, 28, 99, 101–7, 113, 115, 135

Falstaff 5, 11, 14, 15, 35, 62–4, 74, 75, 78–81, 89–93, 121–2, 154–5
fear: of audience 1, 3, 7, 14, 16–17, 19, 20, 31–3, 40–1, 45, 53, 59–60, 101–2, 132–3, 141, 156, 168–9; of characters 28, 34, 38–9, 50–2, 59–60, 81, 95, 114, 117, 118, 137
figures 47, 88–90, 92–3, 157, 163; anadiplosis 80, 90, 118, 163–4; anaphora 50, 52, 89, 93, 158, 162, 164; antimetabole 52, 90, 94, 111, 127; antithesis 53, 127, 162; aposiopesis 50; apostrophe 51–2, 126, 154; asteismus 66, 91; asyndeton 158, 160, 162; epanalepsis 127; epistrophe 50, 89, 162; epizeuxis 89; gradatio 82, 118;

hyperbaton 51, 156; *parallelism* 52, 89, 90, 93, 158, 162; *paronomasia* 91; *periphrasis* 90; *ploce* 125, 127; *polyptoton* 127; *polysyndeton* 125, 158
fools 36, 37, 74, 76, 81–4, 110–12, 121, 123, 127–8, 130
forgiveness 5, 37, 71–2 105–7, 130
Frye, Northrop 25, 100
function (*ergon*): of Shakespearean tragedy 3–4, 16, 40, 56, 132; of Shakespearean comedy 4–5, 56; *see also* Aristotle, Horace, Longinus, Puttenham, Sidney

generalizations 67, 109–11, 114–25; *see also* Aristotle; proverbs
genre: Shakespeare's mixing of 4, 56–7, 63–5, 150–1, 167; *see also* comedy; history play; romance play; tragedy
Gervinus, G. G. 10, 107, 108
Goethe, Johann Wolfgang von 146

Hazlitt, William 3, 4, 5, 9, 58, 75, 102, 113
Hegel, G. W. F. 5, 6, 31, 33, 75–6
history play 1, 3, 4, 15–17, 24–5, 31, 35, 58, 62–3, 78–9, 85, 89, 99, 100–8, 113–14, 117–19, 136, 140, 143, 152
Holinshed, Raphael 99
Homer 49, 143, 160
Horace 7, 13, 99

ingratitude: of characters 56, 101, 115, 129
instruction: audience's experience of 6–12, 17–19, 98–131, 133; scenes of 107–8; *see also* example; thought
in utramque partem 11, 83
isolation: of tragic protagonists 27–9, 49, 52

Jameson, Anna 3, 5, 9–10, 11, 113–14
Johnson, Robert 96, 165
Johnson, Samuel 2, 4, 5, 8, 13, 25, 41, 91, 102, 120
Jones, Robert 93
Joseph, Sister Miriam 47, 83, 91
joy *see* delight
justice: of characters 34–6, 39, 77, 99, 105, 113, 115, 130, 145, 150–2; of the world order 25, 31–3, 43

Lamb, Charles 57, 58
language: as cause of emotion 46–53; as cause of instruction 125–7; as cause of laughter and delight 86–93; as cause of sublimity 155–64; Shakespeare's English 86, 169; *see also* figures; proverbs; sounds; topics; tropes
laughter: of audience 2, 4–6, 56, 62–8, 70, 73, 75, 76, 78–95, 119, 125, 132, 167; of characters 5, 17, 70, 75, 119
Livy 26, 99
Longinus 12, 13, 136, 160; on character 143–4; on thought 149–50; on language 51, 157, 160
love: Antony and Cleopatra's 30, 36–9, 50, 137–40, 145; in comedies 17–19, 57, 65–8, 70, 71, 73, 76, 85–6, 89, 105, 111, 119, 123–4, 150, 155–6; Romeo and Juliet's 16, 20, 26, 30, 36–8, 48–9, 64, 107, 137, 145, 154; in other tragedies 8, 26, 27, 35, 37, 54–5, 104, 109–10, 161

Machiavelli, Niccolò 41, 99
maxims *see* proverbs
Meredith, George 4, 5
mimicry 63–4, 68, 80
Montagu, Elizabeth 9, 11, 102, 113, 120, 122
Morley, Thomas 128
music *see* songs

Nashe, Thomas 2
Nietzsche, Friedrich 10–11, 13–14, 74, 132, 141, 152
nobility: audience's feeling of 13, 137, 143–6, 150–1, 156, 167–8; of characters 19, 33, 35, 38, 42, 65, 77, 103, 105–6, 108, 114, 140, 144–50, 152–4, 161, 164

parody 89
persuasion 12, 30, 36, 44–5, 47, 121–2, 146, 148–9, 150–4, 160–3
pity: of audience 1–4, 9, 14, 16–17, 24–62, 101–2, 113, 132, 141, 168–9
Plato 98, 113
plot: as cause of emotion 24–33; as cause of instruction 98–108; as cause of laughter and delight 62–74; as cause of sublimity 132–41; *see also* probability
Plutarch 99
probability 6, 30, 68, 100; *see also* realism
proverbs 8–9, 111, 120–7, 130
Puttenham, George 7, 8–9, 92, 159

Quintilian 47

reading (Shakespeare's script) 2, 8, 15–16, 20, 46, 48, 53–4, 57–8, 60, 86–8, 99,

121, 137, 155–6, 161, 169; *see also* Erne; sounds
realism 6–10, 41, 44–5, 81, 100–1, 113–14, 132; *see also* instruction
reason: faculty of 10, 31, 41–2, 102–8, 133–4, 158–9; *see also* thought
revenge: of characters 17, 26, 34, 37, 50, 55, 70, 73, 103, 105–6, 112; *see also* forgiveness
rhetoric 5, 47, 52–53, 66, 83, 88; *see also* figures; *in utramque partem*; persuasion; topics; tropes
ridicule 64–6, 68, 72, 75, 79, 89–92, 122, 132
romance plays 4, 17, 19–20, 62, 68–74, 77, 85, 93, 105, 107, 113–14, 123, 132–4

sacrifice 25–6
Schiller, Friedrich 58
Schlegel, A. W. 2, 3, 60, 141
Schopenhauer, Arthur 13, 146
Seneca 7, 46, 59; *see also* tragedy
Shakespeare: aims of 8–12, 15–21, 27, 53–4, 56–8, 60, 62–4, 68, 74, 77, 87, 93, 99–100, 102, 107–8, 112, 120, 130–3, 136, 150–1, 164, 167–9; education of 5, 7, 13, 16, 26, 27, 41, 47, 59, 81, 83, 86, 88, 91, 98–9, 101, 120–3, 155, 168; works of: *Antony and Cleopatra* 16–17, 19, 26, 27, 28, 29–30, 34, 35, 36, 37, 38–9, 50, 63–5, 91, 93, 104, 108–9, 113, 115–16, 134, 136–40, 143, 145, 146, 147, 149, 157–60; *Coriolanus* 17, 25, 26, 27, 28–9, 30, 34, 35–8, 40–1, 51, 59, 64, 84–5, 106, 113, 115–16, 121–4, 135–6, 140, 144, 146, 148–9; *Hamlet* 11, 14, 17–20, 25–7, 32, 34, 35, 37–8, 39, 40, 42–3, 55–6, 58, 59–60, 64, 90, 102–3, 122, 124, 134, 136, 141, 144, 146, 154–5; *Henry IV, part 1* 5, 35, 62–4, 78–81, 89–90, 92, 107, 118, 121–2, 136, 142–3, 151–2; *Henry V* 136, 142; *Julius Caesar* 19, 25–7, 32, 34, 35, 36, 41, 42, 43–4, 51, 59, 60, 121, 134, 136, 144, 146, 152, 161–3; *King Lear* 2, 14, 16, 25, 26, 28, 29, 32–40, 44–5, 49–50, 52, 59, 99, 101–2, 109–11, 114–15, 121, 123, 127–8, 130, 134, 136, 144; *Macbeth* 2, 14, 24, 28, 29, 32–3, 34, 36, 37, 38, 39, 42, 43, 46, 50, 52, 53, 59, 60, 99, 102, 104, 113, 116–17, 119, 121, 123, 125–6, 134–6, 140–1, 145, 147, 156; *The Merchant of Venice* 107, 114, 150–1; *A Midsummer Night's Dream* 17, 18, 20, 62, 64, 65, 67–74, 87–9, 91–2, 95, 105, 123–4, 133, 141, 150, 155–6, 164; *Much Ado About Nothing* 5, 20, 56, 62, 64, 65, 68, 70, 71, 73–7, 85–7, 91, 105, 114, 118, 123–4; *Othello* 9, 14, 25, 26, 27, 30, 33, 34, 36–40, 42, 51, 54, 59, 75, 93, 102, 104–5, 114, 122–4, 134, 163–4; *Richard II* 16, 24, 35, 103, 107, 117–18, 122, 124, 142, 151–2; *Richard III* 24–5, 31, 39, 59, 75, 102, 117, 136; *Romeo and Juliet* 3, 16, 19, 24, 25, 27–9, 32, 34–5, 37–40, 46, 48–9, 51, 58–9, 64, 103, 107, 113, 122–3, 137, 140, 145, 147, 154; *The Tempest* 3, 17, 19, 63, 70, 71, 77, 83–4, 94–6, 105–6, 114, 133–4, 141, 153–4, 164–5; *Twelfth Night* 17, 20, 56–7, 62, 65–74, 76, 77, 81, 93, 95, 112, 114, 118–19, 128–30; *The Winter's Tale* 19, 70, 77, 105, 114, 133–4, 163
Shakespeare in Love 15
Sidney, Sir Philip 5, 7, 73, 98, 113, 168
Skinner, Quentin 5, 47, 66, 83
slapstick 62–3, 68, 132
songs: as cause of emotion 53–7; as cause of instruction 127–30; as cause of laughter and delight 93–6; as cause of sublimity 164–5; "Blow, blow, thou winter wind" 129; "Bonny sweet Robin" 56 ; "Come away, come away, death" 57; "Flout 'em and Cout 'em" 94; "Full Fathom Five" 96; "O mistress mine" 129; "Where the bee sucks" 165; "Willow, willow" 54; "The Woosel Cock" 95
sounds: *alliteration* 87, 125; *assonance* 125, 159; blank verse 7, 46–7, 53, 125, 157, 159, 161, 163; *caesura* 46, 88, 125, 157, 159, 163; *consonance* 125; end-stopped lines 46, 53, 88, 109, 125, 155, 157, 159; *enjambment* 46, 53, 88, 125, 155, 157, 163; meter 46, 53, 87, 89, 94, 128–9, 156–7, 163, 165; rhyme 46, 53, 87, 89, 109, 125, 129, 155, 156, 157, 165
spectacle: as cause of emotion 57–60; as cause of wonder 20
sublimity: audience's feeling of 12–15, 19–20, 132–65
suffering: in comedies 57, 67, 69, 75; in tragedies 3, 9, 18, 24–5, 29, 39–40, 45, 59, 78, 101, 102, 108, 113, 114–15, 118–19, 122, 129, 146
suicide 28, 29–30, 59, 137–40
supernatural 31, 59–60, 72, 73, 77, 133–4, 140, 141, 156, 164

temperance: of characters 36, 99, 103–7, 113, 130; *see also* reason
thought (*dianoia*): as cause of emotion 41–6; as cause of instruction 114–25; as cause of laughter and delight 78–86; as cause of sublimity 149–55; *see also* Aristotle
topics (of argument) 83
Tractatus Coislinianus 4
tragedy: ancient Graeco-Roman 3, 7–8, 10–11, 13–14, 16, 25, 27, 59, 98–9, 120, 133; Shakespearean 1–4, 6–15, 21, 24–60, 78, 99, 101–2, 132–64
tropes 47, 88, 90, 92, 158; *antanaclasis* 81, 91; *antonomasia* 66; *double entendre* 66, 89, 91; *hyperbole* 49, 64, 89–90, 135, 161; *irony* 49, 161; *malapropism* 87; *meiosis* 64; *metaphor* 48, 64, 66, 89, 91–2, 110, 112, 126, 127, 135, 159, 161; *metonymy* 159, 161; *paradox* 110, 154, 159; *personification* 89; *rhetorical question* 66, 90; *syllepsis* 91
ugliness: of characters 74
universals *see* Aristotle

virtue: of characters 10, 28, 33–7, 74, 77, 103–6, 113, 123, 143–6; Christian ideas of 35, 37, 99–101; Cicero on 33–6, 99, 130; Longinus on 143–4; *see also* forgiveness; temperance; revenge

will: of characters 9, 10, 13, 29–30, 67, 76, 88, 103–5, 146–8
wisdom *see* instruction
wonder: of audience 12–15, 20, 132, 133–6, 141–3, 155, 156, 159, 164–5, 167–8; of characters 17, 19–20, 59, 133–6, 141–3, 164–5